The Mindfulness-Informed Ed

MW00772667

The Mindfulness-Informed Educator moves a growing body of evidence related to the efficacy of mindfulness- and acceptance-based approaches to the context of higher education, suggesting ways to foster psychological flexibility within and outside of the classroom. In this book, professionals across education and psychotherapy will find best practices for teaching, treating, researching, and serving their communities in ways that are sensitive to context, consistent with their values, and mindful of the diverse array of mental-health and behavioral difficulties experienced by college and university students. Chapters incorporate the most cutting-edge research across disciplines and span educational levels and contexts within higher education, provide strategies for strengthening mindfulness- and acceptance-based pedagogy and program development, and provide user-friendly supplemental materials such as transcripts and sample assignments.

Jennifer Block-Lerner, PhD, is an associate professor in the department of advanced studies in psychology at Kean University.

LeeAnn Cardaciotto, PhD, is an associate professor in the department of psychology at La Salle University.

The Mindfulness-Informed Educator

Building Acceptance and Psychological Flexibility in Higher Education

Edited by Jennifer Block-Lerner and LeeAnn Cardaciotto

Routledge
Taylor & Francis Group

NEW YORK AND LONDON

First published 2016
by Routledge
711 Third Avenue, New York, NY 10017

and by Routledge
2 Park Square, Milton Park, Abingdon, Oxon, OX14 4RN

Routledge is an imprint of the Taylor & Francis Group, an informa business

Library of Congress Cataloging in Publication Data
Names: Block-Lerner, Jennifer, author. | Cardaciotto, LeeAnn, author.
Title: The mindfulness-informed educator : building acceptance and
    psychological flexibility in higher education / Jennifer Block-Lerner,
    LeeAnn Cardaciotto.
Description: New York, NY : Routledge, 2016. | Includes bibliographical
    references and index.
Identifiers: LCCN 2015034103| ISBN 9781138012967 (hardback : alk. paper) |
    ISBN 9781138012974 (pbk. : alk. paper) | ISBN 9781315795584 (ebook)
Subjects: LCSH: College teaching—Psychological aspects. | College students—
    Psychology. | College teachers—Psychology. | Commitment (Psychology) |
    Educational psychology.
Classification: LCC LB2331 .B545 2016 | DDC 378.1/25—dc23
LC record available at http://lccn.loc.gov/2015034103

ISBN: 978-1-138-01296-7 (hbk)
ISBN: 978-1-138-01297-4 (pbk)
ISBN: 978-1-315-79558-4 (ebk)

Typeset in Minion
by Swales & Willis Ltd, Exeter, Devon, UK

To Jason, Benjamin, and David; and to Bobby–

The biggest rocks in our jars

Contents

Contributors and Affiliations

Christina Barrasso-Catanzaro	Kean University
Anthony Biglan	Oregon Research Institute
Jennifer Block-Lerner	Kean University
Martin Brock	University of Derby
LeeAnn Cardaciotto	La Salle University
Susan Daflos	University of Nevada, Reno
Sara B. Danitz	Suffolk University
Elizabeth H. Eustis	University of Massachusetts Boston
Sandra Georgescu	The Chicago School of Professional Psychology
Michael B. Gross	Kean University
Steven Hammonds	University of Nevada, Reno
Elisa Hanna	Private practice in Austin, Texas
Steven C. Hayes	University of Nevada, Reno
Sarah Hayes-Skelton	University of Massachusetts Boston
Laura G. Hill	Washington State University
Nic Hooper	University of the West of England
Karolina M. Kowarz	Kean University
Derek Kosty	Oregon Research Institute
Agnes K. Lenda	Kean University
Michael E. Levin	Utah State University
Jason Lillis	Brown University Medical School
Robert Locklear	University of Nevada, Reno
Douglas M. Long	Brown University Medical School
Chelsea MacLane	Private practice in Portland, Oregon
Donald R. Marks	Kean University

Louise McHugh	University College Dublin
R. Ashlyne Mullen	Kean University
Susan M. Orsillo	Suffolk University
Jacqueline Pistorello	University of Nevada, Reno
Lizabeth Roemer	University of Massachusetts Boston
Emily K. Sandoz	University of Louisiana Lafayette
John Seeley	Oregon Research Institute
Kendahl M. Shortway	Kean University
Sarah Krill Williston	University of Massachusetts Boston
Andrew T. Wolanin	Kean University
Roger Vilardaga	University of Washington
Jennifer L. Villatte	University of Washington

Acknowledgments

This edited volume is a reflection of a lot of hard work—challenging methodological decisions, time with students at all developmental levels, the development and refinement of protocols, thoughtful consideration and contextualization of results, and carefully crafted sentences that convey both promise and caution.

It is also a celebration and an honoring. A celebration of practices that at their essence are about turning toward, living fully within the moments of our lives, whatever they hold. Further, this volume is about choosing life directions (what matters most to a given individual in any moment) and taking steps in those directions, however small or slowly at times.

And finally and most saliently in these final weeks, as we (the two of us, along with all of the contributors to this volume) worked together more closely than ever before to bring this product to fruition, it is a celebration of partnership, of mentoring, and of collaborative possibility (perhaps even of "prosociality," to give a taste of what is to come in the conclusion chapter). A celebration of friendship, of teamwork, and of gratitude for all of the people and experiences that brought us to this moment in time.

It is in this spirit that we first thank our editor at Routledge, Anna Moore. We are deeply grateful to Anna for her flexibility, steadfast kindness, and belief in our ability to see this project through. Our lovely interactions with her fostered our capacity to navigate this journey (at least on most days!) consistently with our values. And, we are honored to have had the opportunity to work with and learn from such incredible contributors, who truly embody what they write, teach, and study. They helped make the possibility of promoting well-being and resilience in a context with which we are deeply connected even more tangible.

We offer a deep bow of gratitude for so many reasons to Sue Orsillo and Liz Roemer. Sue especially for that fateful dinner in National Harbor that convinced us that an edited book along these lines was both feasible and important; Liz for wholeheartedly supporting us in all our endeavors. They both have taught us so much, as individuals and especially as a collaborative unit, about how to be whole people who engage in teaching, supervising, other forms of mentoring, and everything else that comprises our professional positions (aptly referred to as "one life" by Kelly Wilson). We have also come to appreciate, joyfully, that collaborative relationships go beyond two-person partnerships. In this vein, we are delighted to have gotten to know Sarah Hayes-Skelton, and eagerly look forward to continued

Sunday morning breakfasts at ABCT and whatever shared projects may spring forth from our friendship. Additionally, we would like to express our thankfulness to our colleagues at Kean and La Salle universities who teach and inspire us daily and to Wendy Alfaro for her painstaking editorial assistance.

And last, and in many ways most importantly, we together thank our students—those who we currently teach, advise, and mentor; those who are long-gone and off doing incredible things; and those who have yet to walk on campus. They are at the core of and the reason for this incredible project, and are our tremendous teachers.

Jennifer Block-Lerner and LeeAnn Cardaciotto

I must first thank LeeAnn—my true companion on this wild journey. From the day of your interview at La Salle to two practically chance meetings in Coral Springs, FL and Churchville, PA this summer—the universe has truly aligned to foster our friendship and partnership. You continually amaze me—with your capacities to think critically and see the big picture, to share feedback kindly, to find humor in the madness, and to listen with deep heartfulness. I feel beyond fortunate to have shared this experience and to have grown up together through some of the early stages of faculty life. Through a fun series of happenstances, I recently learned the etymology of the word companion—it literally means "one who breaks bread with another." Especially given that our two serendipitous meetings this summer took place at Panera, I am more than happy to continue to trust the process itself, my friend.

I also hold immense gratitude to and for . . . The classmates and friends who have been fellow travelers in the chapters of my career—at the University at Albany, Boston VAMC, Skidmore, La Salle, and Kean. I want to particularly thank Don Marks for being a phenomenal colleague and partner in much of this (adventurous!) work. Julie Hartley, whose letters continually ground and inspire. Liz Pratt, who offers "reassurance" at so many pivotal moments. Deb Rhatigan-Moore, whose life and death taught more than words can express. Merry Auerbach Walker, for first showing me that doing school work is much more fun when with a good friend. And, the Philly teachers' sangha and ACT-NYCE crew for their warmth and embodying of these practices.

The mentors who have seen and taken time to nurture potential in me. Especially Elga Wulfert, who lit the flame of my passion for clinical psychology in an abnormal psychology course way back when and who has guided me at so many forks in the road; Sue Orsillo, who made it clear that one could do meaning-ful work *and* be the kind of mom that I hoped to be someday; Mary Ann Foley, for giving me the opportunity to fall in love with teaching at Skidmore and exem-plifying kindness and balance; and Frank Gardner, for building two incredible doctoral programs and helping me carve out significant roles within them.

My mom and dad—without a doubt the wind beneath my wings and source of quiet strength. My sisters—Dori, for inspiring me with her capacity to put words to experience in poetic and powerful ways and for being a profound source of support as we share the journey; Sarah, for allowing me some of my first experi-ences of nurturing and continuously showing me how to dance in the rain. My grandparents for their fierce love, devotion to family, and persistence in the face of challenge; and for helping to keep us on track by always asking about the book. The wider circle of our family—the Blocks, Lerners, Glickmans, Walds, Epsteins, and Pearls—I am very grateful for all of their support and love. Jacob, Emma, Katie, and Olivia—for brightening my path with their smiles and laughter.

And, most of all, for the three "boys" who encircle me with love every day and who were patient and understanding as I worked, tirelessly at times, to bring this project to completion. To David, for his incomparable sweetness, for welcoming me into the present, over and over, and for asking what "companion" means at exactly the right moment. To Benjamin, from and with whom I learn so much on a daily basis. I thank Ben especially for the before-bedtime laughs and mind-blowing conversations, as well as for keeping me company as I worked (I am grateful to our beloved Rocky for this too). And to Jason, my true partner and teammate in every sense of these words. I thank him deeply for holding my hand through it all.

Jennifer Block-Lerner

I truly feel blessed to have been part of this project, which was the brainchild of my colleague, co-editor, and dearest friend, Jennifer Block-Lerner. I thank her for the immeasurable ways she supports me and continually points me toward my values. Her way of working—and of being—writing from a place of truth, making space for everything that shows up—inspire me. And I am ever so amazed and apprecia-tive of our rhythm, how we seamlessly pick up the slack when the other is bogged down (and secretly hoping to find that golden shovel), all the while giving remind-ers to breathe and take one step at a time. My gratitude for our collaboration and deep friendship is endless. I thank my loving husband Bobby for his unwavering support of and belief in me, for recognizing the importance of this project, and for his willingness to experience the sacrifices that come along with it. He, along with friends and family (including my parents, who I thank for their constant support of my work) are continuous reminders of the "big rocks" and what really matter. I also have tremendous gratitude for the many mentors I have had the privilege of learning from over time and within different contexts. Specifically, I thank James Herbert for introducing me to mindfulness and ACT, and more largely, for guid-ing me toward experiences that have shaped my career; Adele Hayes for drawing my attention to the importance of process and for modeling "laser-sharp" think-ing; Stephen Leff for welcoming me onto his team that illustrated the value of community and yielded so many lasting memories; and for the many others who have planted seeds that would grow into important lessons (when asked how to begin solving a proof, my high school geometry teacher would tell us "by pushing the pencil"—an early lesson on committed action when feeling stuck). I feel espe-cially fortunate to have the support and encouragement of so many colleagues and friends at 20th and Olney; they are the reason that La Salle has become my aca-demic home. Last, I am deeply appreciative for the opportunity to work with such incredible students—past, present, and future—who serve as an anchor amidst numerous daily tasks that pull at my attention. They generously welcome me on their professional journeys, and are at the heart of mine.

LeeAnn Cardaciotto

Part I
Setting the Scene

1   Making the Case

Mindfulness- and Acceptance-Based Interventions in Higher Education

Jennifer Block-Lerner and LeeAnn Cardaciotto

Need I say it? The curricula offered by our institutions of higher education have largely neglected this central, if profoundly difficult task of learning to love, which is also the task of learning to live in true peace and harmony with others and with nature.

(Zajonc in Palmer & Zajonc, 2010, p. xi)

Introduction

In the day-to-day of tasks related to teaching, scholarship, service and all the other hats that educators wear; to accreditation, retention, and budgets that administrators' days revolve around; to the suicide, sexual violence, and hazing that counseling center, residential life, and other student support staff find themselves battling, how many professionals within higher education connect with what Zajonc (in Palmer & Zajonc, 2010) considers this "central, if profoundly difficult task" (p. xi), helping students learn to love? To, even if not *feeling* peaceful and harmonious in every moment, realize their interconnectedness with one another? Yet research suggests that these students, at institutions of higher education of all shapes and sizes, desperately need all of those who serve them—faculty, staff, administration—to connect with this purpose, and maybe even to embody it.

Indeed, colleges and universities, as multifaceted entities with the potential to engage in evidence-based practice at many levels, have significant potential to serve as what Biglan, Flay, Embry, and Sandler (2012) deem "nurturing environments." Biglan et al. describe these as environments that foster successful development and prevent (and/or ameliorate) the development of behavioral/psychological problems. While this work has emphasized influencing the trajectory of children and adolescents, Biglan and colleagues have spoken to related possibilities for higher education (Biglan, Hayes, & Pistorello, 2008). Also addressing this enormous potential, Eisenberg, Golberstein, and Hunt (2009) speak to "the many ways in which college settings can reach young people," and go on to state "college represents the only time in many people's lives when a single setting encompasses their main activities, social networks, and a range of supportive services and organizations" (p. 1). Further, as large institutions and microcosms of broader communities, colleges and universities provide fertile ground for study-ing processes of engagement and transformation (DiGiuseppe, 2014).

Given that students are at the core of higher education activities, this chapter will "set the scene" to provide a rationale as to why increased attention needs to be paid to intervention and prevention for this population. Specifically, this chapter provides an overview of behavioral health difficulties college students often struggle with; discusses help-seeking in these students; presents innovative services that have been developed to target the behavioral difficulties and what is known about help-seeking; speaks to the theoretical rationale for and promise of mindfulness- and acceptance-based approaches in this context; and provides a roadmap of the parts of the book to come.

College Student Mental Health

Psychological Disorders and Symptomatology

Years spent in college are brimming with opportunity and challenge. Students often live away from their families for the first time, have much more control over their schedules than they have had previously, get to set and work toward career goals, find new and/or nurture existing hobbies and passions, and develop formative and intimate relationships with peers and supportive and guiding con-nections with new mentors. However, they are also often engaging in part-time if not full-time employment (American College Health Association, 2009), balanc-ing family responsibilities, engaging in high-risk health behaviors, and navigating often fragmented systems within the institution. Further, students in institutions of higher education face many of the same challenges that all members of the population in developed countries are facing, including the barrage of media on difficult (and often out of the viewer's direct control) situations all over the world and pressures and pulls to be "on" at all hours of the day via increasingly sophis-ticated technology (e.g., Rosen, Carrier, & Cheever, 2013).

Indeed, college students facing these opportunities and challenges are vulnera-ble to a host of mental health difficulties, including depression, anxiety, substance use, and disordered eating, which often result in subsequent impairments in aca-demic and social functioning (e.g., American College Health Association, 2009; Eagan et al., 2014). Blanco et al.'s (2008) widely-cited study comparing college students and their non-college-attending peers found that approximately half of college students met DSM-IV criteria for one or more mental disorders in the previous year (comparable to young adults not attending college). A recent large-scale study found somewhat lower, but still substantial percentages: Approximately 17% of college students screened positively for depression, 4% for panic disorder, 7% for generalized anxiety disorder, 6% for serious suicidal ideation, and 15% for nonsuicidal self-injury, with many experiencing co-occur-ring mental health difficulties (32% of students total screened positively for one or more mental health problems; Eisenberg, Hunt, & Speer, 2013). Variations across demographic groups as well as campuses were described (most notably that all other ethnic groups relative to white students had a higher likelihood of screening positively for depression), and those who reported struggling or having struggled financially were particularly at risk for depression, anxiety, and suicidal ideation (Eisenberg et al., 2013). Buchanan (2012) summarizes the results of many studies that speak to implications of depression for college students, including decreased grade point average (GPA) and academic productivity, increased levels of smoking and alcohol consumption, and self-injurious behavior and suicidality.

In addition to research that speaks to diagnosed or potentially diagnosable mental health conditions, other studies address psychological issues more generally that may play a role in the college experience. For example, the American College Health Association (ACHA; 2009) found that 33.9% of its over 80,000 student participants reported that stress affected their academic performance. Sleep difficulties were similarly named as contributors to academic performance for 25.6% of participants, alcohol use for 7.8% and the following falling somewhere in between in terms of the percentage of students endorsing the impediment to academic success: depression and anxiety, relationship difficulties, death of a friend or family member, and concern for a troubled friend or family member. Further, 43% reported feeling so depressed it was difficult to function on at least one occasion over the past academic year, and 9% seriously considered attempting suicide at least once in the past school year (ACHA, 2009).

Changes in Symptomatology Over Time

Directors of counseling centers, those who oversee the individuals treating many students with mental health concerns, tend to believe that there has been an increase in the number of students with severe psychological problems (Barr, Rando, Krylowicz, & Winfield, 2010; Gallagher, 2005; Watkins, Hunt, & Eisenberg, 2011). For example, Barr et al. (2010) found that 71% of the 385 counseling center directors who responded to their survey believed that the number of students with psychological problems had increased in the past year. This belief is supported by a birth cohort study of over 63,000 college students that found a large generational increase in psychopathology over the long time span between 1938 and 2007 (Twenge et al., 2010). Hunt and Eisenberg (2010), however, acknowledge and address the complexities of this topic, drawing on epidemiological data related to the prevalence of mental health problems as well as help-seeking in the general population across the lifespan. These authors conclude that the overall prevalence of mental health disorders has likely remained stable or possibly increased by a small amount. It is probable, however, that the increased use of mental health services among children and adolescents has allowed a broader range of young adults to enter college than was the case in previous years, supporting counseling center staff's experience of increased severity within their caseloads (Hunt & Eisenberg, 2010). Interestingly, in a study that involved review of archival data of a random sample of students seeking treatment at a large college counseling center across seven years, Jenks Kettmann and colleagues (2007), simultaneously considering client self-report and clinician ratings, found that diagnosis severity ratings did not meaningfully increase over time. However, the *complexity* of student issues (i.e., presence of multiple disorders) did increase. This increasing complexity (if borne out by studies with more attention to external validity; Jenks Kettman et al.'s data were from one university), coupled with increased use of mental health services in younger populations discussed above (Hunt & Eisenberg, 2010) and the substantial needs of diverse millennial students (Watkins et al., 2011) likely all contribute to the overall impression of increasing severity among professionals working in this area. At the very least, data converge to indicate that the numbers are not moving in the directions of better health for today's college students.

Substance Use

Substance use and abuse, mentioned above as a student-reported impediment to academic performance, is of particular concern for individuals on college and university campuses. Johnston, O'Malley, Bachman, and Schulenberg (2011) indicate that 65.8% of full-time college students reported engaging in some alcohol use in the past 30 days. While this may not necessarily be problematic or illegal, 42.4% report being drunk within that same timeframe, suggesting increased vulnerability to alcohol-related problems including risky sexual behavior (e.g., Turchik, Garske, Probst, & Irvin, 2010). Further, 36% of full-time college students report using any illicit drug (including marijuana) in the last year; 20.7% within the last 30 days (Johnston et al., 2011). Kolek (2009) studied recreational use of prescription drugs in a generally representative college sample, and found that 12.8% of students endorsed having engaged in such use within the last year, with 23.7% of those reporting using their own prescription for such use. Finally, according to the most recent ACHA-National College Health Assessment, discussed in ACHA (2012), 18.3% of students identify as tobacco smokers (have smoked at least once in the last 30 days).

To some degree, substance use is a normative behavior for individuals in the age groups of individuals who form the majority of those who attend college (e.g., 18–24 years). Authors of the large-scale rigorously conducted ongoing study Monitoring the Future (Johnston et al., 2011) specifically compared substance use rates in college students with those of their non-college-attending peers. While rates of illicit drug use tended to be higher in young adults not attending college, college students specifically report higher levels of many indicators of alcohol use (i.e., lifetime, annual, and last-30-days use, as well as occasions of heavy drinking or five or more drinks in a row in the previous two weeks; Johnston et al., 2011). These high levels of substance use may be problematic for many reasons, especially those related to impact on academic and other elements of success during one's college years.

Implications of Mental Health and Substance-Related Issues for Students' Success

Psychological difficulties as well as substance use and abuse can be strongly related to students' success in college. In a longitudinal study with a random sample of students, Eisenberg, Golberstein, et al. (2009) found depression to be a significant predictor of lower GPA and a higher probability of dropping out, especially among those students who also screened positively for anxiety disorders. Symptoms of eating disorders were also correlated with lower GPAs. Ruthig, Marrone, Hladkyj, and Robinson-Epp (2011) also employed longitudinal methods and found that binge drinking negatively predicted academic performance for females, and tobacco use predicted the same for males. Additionally, Arria and colleagues (2013) found that both mental health issues and substance use were associated with lower levels of persistence in college, albeit at different times in the college experience. Studying "discontinuity" (a gap in enrollment of one or more semesters) specifically, Arria et al. reported that higher scores on a measure of depression predicted discontinuity within the first two years of college, while alcohol and cannabis use predicted late discontinuity (i.e., in the second two years of college). Finally, Hartley (2013) found that mental health and resilience variables, both as main effects and an interaction between them, predicted the amount of credits completed over time (but not GPA, which may be attributable to the unreliability of measuring this via self-report).

Taken together, these findings are concerning for all involved in higher education in terms of apprehension for students' own well-being; consideration of how these issues shape classroom, cohort, and program-related experiences; and implications for the financial health of the institution (Eisenberg, Golberstein, et al., 2009). This is especially so, given increased attention to and pressure on colleges and universities related to 4- and 6-year graduation rates (e.g., Carr, 2015)[1] and the implications for students of earning versus not earning a college degree in terms of employment and salary rates (Pew Research Center, 2014).

Campus-Based Resources for College Students

Considering this picture of substantial mental health and substance-related issues facing students attending colleges and universities, as well as the impact of these on functioning, understanding the resources available to these students, as well as their use of them, is extremely important. College counseling centers, as the designated place for students struggling with behavioral difficulties to go, offer an obvious starting place. While the numbers vary a great deal based on type and size of institution, a relatively recent survey reports an average ratio of paid staff members to students of 1:1738.4 (Barr et al., 2010). Even based on low estimates of students struggling with psychological difficulties and/or substance-related concerns, these numbers suggest very high caseloads and/or long waiting lists for students in need. Brunner, Wallace, Reymann, Sellers, and McCabe (2014) summarize literature that suggests that approximately 60% of counseling center professional staff time is devoted to direct service, and they (along with Schwartz, 2013) speak to the many ways that counseling center professionals aim to help their student bodies, both directly and indirectly (e.g., outreach, consultation with faculty and staff, workshop leading) in their remaining work hours. It is important to ensure that the time of these staff members is put to good use, and many researchers indicate that the evidence base for interventions of all sorts on campuses is sparse (Eisenberg, Hunt, & Speer, 2012; Hunt & Eisenberg, 2010), to be discussed further below, making it difficult to make informed decisions about the use of limited resources.

Help-Seeking in College Students

One important consideration in the picture of students' mental health is counseling center staff availability. Another is students' willingness to access the services that are available to them. In a large survey representing 26 institutions, Eisenberg, Hunt, Speer, and Zivin (2011) found that 35.6% of students who screened positive for at least one mental health problem received some sort of mental health care (including both psychotherapy and psychotropic medication) in the previous year, and 21.8% of these students were receiving such care at the time of the survey. Minority groups, including Asians, Blacks, and Hispanics, were less likely to receive mental health services than Whites. Of the students (with or without a "need" as per the mental health screens) who did seek services, approximately one-third reported having had one to three visits. Why are levels of formal help-seeking on college campuses so low? It is to a review of the main issues (and barriers in particular) related to college students' help-seeking that we now turn.

Barriers to Help-Seeking in College Students

Given the established high prevalence of psychological difficulties and, at least according to some studies, the increased severity (e.g., Barr et al., 2010) and/or complexity (i.e., Kettmann et al., 2007) of psychopathological conditions in students attending colleges and universities, many researchers have attempted to address the important topic of help-seeking in these students. Stigma associated with mental health conditions and treatment might seem to be a powerful barrier. Indeed, the public tends to portray those who experience mental illness in a negative light (Vogel, Wade, & Hackler, 2007), and it is reasonable to believe that this portrayal might impact college students' view of themselves and/or their likelihood to seek help. However, more recent research related to stigma indicates that the picture is more complicated than originally believed. Important distinctions between different types of stigma have been made (Corrigan, 2004; Eisenberg, Downs, Golberstein, & Zivin, 2009). For example, personal stigma refers to any given person's stereotypes and prejudices, while perceived public stigma refers to one's perception of others' collective stereotypes and prejudices. Self-stigma is a phenomenon that occurs when one identifies him or herself with the stigmatized group (Corrigan, 2004). Focus of work in this area was initially on perceived public stigma, and an important longitudinal study conducted by Golberstein, Eisenberg, and Gollust (2009) indicated that this form of stigma was not significantly related to help-seeking behavior. Further, while these authors' dichotomization of continuous measures limits the conclusions that may be drawn, Eisenberg, Speer, and Hunt (2012) recently found that the majority of college students with untreated psychological problems reported low levels of personal stigma too and positive beliefs about treatment effectiveness.

Reflecting these conflicting findings, Eisenberg, Hunt et al. (2012) indicate that traditionally-recognized barriers such as stigma only explain a portion of help-seeking behavior. While Tucker et al.'s (2013) recent work further disentangling self-stigma into mental illness and help-seeking components suggests promise in understanding as well as targeting these processes, research on help-seeking more generally suggests that there are other important barriers to consider.

Eisenberg et al. (2011) asked students directly about the reasons they received no mental health services or fewer than they might need. The most commonly endorsed reasons by those with likely mental health problems were students preferring to deal with issues on their own (54.9%), believing that stress is normal in college/graduate school (47.3%), not having enough time (43.4%), feeling that they get a lot of support from other sources (33.2%), and financial concerns (33.2%).

Eisenberg, Hunt, et al. (2012), in a review of issues related to help-seeking for mental health on college campuses, state that when considering the totality of the empirical picture, "[a] salient theme becomes evident: novel intervention approaches are needed to supplement traditional approaches that focus on attitudes and knowledge about mental illness" (p. 222). These authors indicate that many of the interventions that have been used on campuses to try to increase help-seeking, the main ones being stigma reduction and education about mental illness and treatment, identifying students in distress (screening) and steering them toward appropriate services (linkage), and gatekeeper training, have been implemented creatively and with some promise (especially screening/triaging-based systems). However, Eisenberg and colleagues conclude that the implementation of these programs generally has sped ahead of research (at least, of published research; p. 228) supporting their ultimate outcomes (i.e., use of services by students). Hunt and Eisenberg (2010) speak to the state of this sparse literature and the fact that, because of this sparseness, only preliminary conclusions may be drawn about how colleges and universities should proceed. Because of the many avenues through which to intervene with students, strategies "based on a holistic, public health approach" (pp. 7–8) seem especially important. These types of approaches "view mental health as a foundation for (student) well-being and success" (p. 8).

Efforts at Prevention and Intervention

Prevention Programs, Including Those Aiming to Foster Resilience

Indeed, many campuses have taken on the task of attempting to prevent mental health difficulties and/or promote positive mental health. Some have done so through the framework of attempting to understand and/or build *resilience*. This term has been defined as "the ability to adjust to stressful circumstances and persevere in the face of adversity" (DeRosier, Frank, Schwartz, & Leary, 2013, p. 538). Campbell-Sills, Cohan, and Stein (2006) indicate that resilience is viewed as a multidimensional construct, involving both dispositional varia-bles (e.g., temperament, personality) and specific skills (e.g., problem-solving) that foster people's capacity to cope well in the face of adverse or traumatic experiences.

DeRosier and colleagues (2013) assessed resilience and its relation to the experience of stress in 644 first-year college students from seven universities. They found that approximately half of the students reported "possessing" one or more of the resilience factors assessed by their measure (i.e., indicating that the factor was "very true about me"), including positive cognitions (57%), life skills (50%), positive self-care behaviors (45%), and positive social connections (41%). Not surprisingly, greater cumulative stress was correlated with lower resilience, and in hierarchical regression analyses, resilience factors significantly contrib-uted to the prediction of three indices of well-being (DeRosier et al., 2013). In their earlier study with college students, Campbell-Sills et al. (2006) found that resilience was negatively correlated with neuroticism and positively correlated with extraversion, conscientiousness, and task-oriented (i.e., active, problem-solving style) coping. Further supporting the value of the resilience construct, Hartley (2013) found that within the context of a moderating model, resilience alone and the interaction of resilience and mental health predicted time to credit completion. Hartley's study was with help-seeking college students (recruited from campus mental health offices), and suggests that intrapersonal resilience (vs. interpersonal resilience as assessed by a social support measure) is particu-larly important for those students dealing with the highest levels of adversity and distress.

So, how might resilience, or this process of responding adaptively in the face of adversity, be fostered? Indeed, Rogers (2013) indicates that "a portion of resilience is innate and biologically determined, but life experience and other environmental factors seem to play an equally strong role" (p. 546). Researchers have pointed to the extensive attention devoted to the promotion of resilience/ mental health and prevention of difficulties in children, and have begun to study similar broadly implemented interventions in college students (Conley, Travers, & Bryant, 2013). Conley et al. compared a psychosocial wellness seminar with an alternative first-year seminar that addressed global citizenship. Participants in the intervention group exhibited higher levels of perceived improvements in psychosocial adjustment and stress management relative to those in the control condition. Importantly, two measures of engagement in the intervention, class attendance and student-rated skills practice, significantly contributed to the pre-diction of psychosocial adjustment (after adjusting for baseline levels) and stress management outcomes.

The seminar employed by Conley and colleagues (2013) was multifaceted in nature. Their psychosocial wellness seminar aimed to foster development of skills in stress management, problem-solving, cognitive restructuring, mindful-ness, social communication, and life enrichment. It is possible that some of the material within the seminar was not readily compatible with other material. For example, assumptions underlying cognitive restructuring and mindfulness-based approaches (i.e., that the content of thoughts can and should be changed in cognitive restructuring; that the aim is to increase awareness and acceptance of one's thoughts and other elements of emotional experiences in mindfulness) may contradict one another at times (e.g., Arch and Ayers, 2013). This is not to say that these tools cannot be utilized together in a coherent way (e.g., Segal, Williams, & Teasdale, 2012), and conversations about compatibility are continuing to evolve as the approaches themselves do (e.g., Abramowitz & Arch, 2014). However, it is feasible that the impact of this type of intervention could be strengthened by a coherent framework that guides the choice and implementation of specific elements.

Mindfulness- and Acceptance-Based Approaches for College Students

Approaches that specifically aim to develop skills in mindfulness (i.e., nonjudgmental present-moment awareness; Kabat-Zinn, 1994) may offer this more coherent framework, within which many associated practices can be integrated, and they may be particularly well suited for the college population, both in prevention and intervention frameworks. Rogers (2013) discusses the opportunities and challenges of "emerging adulthood" (Arnett, 2004), an extended period of development from late teens through the twenties that many in modern Western cultures experience that is centered around personal growth and identity development. Rogers' discussion of the value of mindfulness-based practices for the development of resilience specifically highlights a neuroanatomical pathway between the prefrontal cortex and the amygdala, emphasizing the building of positive emotions. While other mechanisms of these approaches have been presented and are increasingly being evaluated (Keng, Smoski, Robins, Ekblad, & Brantley, 2012; Paul, Stanton, Greeson, Smoski, & Wang, 2013), their capacity to build skills that help individuals handle stressful life events has been strongly supported across many studies in both clinical and non-clinical populations (Keng, Smoski, & Robins, 2011; Khoury et al., 2013).

Shapiro, Brown, and Astin (2008) discuss the benefits of meditation (concentrative and mindfulness) with implications for various elements of college students' experiences. Specifically, these authors review studies supporting the value of meditation practice for facilitating achievement of traditional educational goals; for supporting student mental health under the stress of academic challenges; and for enhancing education of students as "whole people." Many of the studies reviewed in Shapiro et al.'s paper targeting undergraduate and graduate-level students employed mindfulness-based interventions including mindfulness-based stress reduction (MBSR; Kabat-Zinn, 1990). MBSR is an 8-week program that aims to help people bring friendly and curious attention or awareness to various elements of their present-moment experience (e.g., breathing, bodily sensations; experiences of hearing, seeing, and tasting), through formal practices including mindful eating, sitting and walking meditations, body scans, and hatha yoga as well as informal practices (e.g., bringing one's full attention to the present-moment while walking to class, brushing one's teeth, or sitting at red lights).

Researchers have continued to examine the value of MBSR and other mindfulness-based approaches with college students in particular, some targeting specific health behaviors of concern (e.g., Bowen & Marlatt, 2009; Mermelstein & Garske, 2015) and others addressing stress and anxiety levels (e.g., Gallego, Aguillar-Parra, Cangas, Langer, & Mañas, 2014). Regehr, Glancy, and Pitts (2013) recently conducted a meta-analysis of various interventions aimed at reducing stress in university students. Regehr et al. combined cognitive, behavioral, and mindfulness-based interventions into one category for most analyses, and concluded that this group of approaches reduced anxiety. Mindfulness-based interventions specifically resulted in a standardized difference in means relative to control groups of -0.73 (confidence interval of -1.00 to -0.45) for anxiety. While reducing anxiety is not necessarily the goal of mindfulness-based approaches, Regehr and colleagues' pooled results suggest that these interventions do have this impact on many college and university students. Given the link, albeit correlational, between such symptomatology and academic outcomes including GPA (e.g., Silva, Dorso, Azhar, & Renk, 2007–2008), these findings suggest promise for students' academic functioning.

Most of the studies that employed mindfulness-based interventions reviewed to this point utilized MBSR and other standardized interventions developed for adult populations (first in the context of chronic pain and other medical conditions; Kabat-Zinn, 1990). Rogers and Maytan (2012), however, have developed a mindfulness-based approach specifically for the population of college students and other emerging adults. Greeson, Juberg, Maytan, James, and Rogers (2014) highlight the essence of this time: "Because the primary emphasis in emerging adulthood is on identity exploration, this life stage is associated with frequent changes and uncertainty in all life spheres" (p. 223). Greeson and colleagues suggest that mindfulness meditation may be a particularly powerful tool for navigating these frequent changes and overarching sense of uncertainty, helping students hold with kindness a wide range of thoughts and emotions about various evolving parts of their lives. They also indicate that emerging adults may not be willing to engage in training programs built for older adults due to factors including time constraints and skepticism about possible benefits.

Through their long-standing work with college students in the context of Duke University's Counseling and Psychological Services, along with deep consideration of this developmental stage, Rogers and Maytan (2012) developed an innovative program known as *Koru*. Rogers and Maytan describe the word choice thus: "*Koru* is the Maori word for the spiral shape of the unfurling fern frond. It symbolizes new, developing life as well as balance, harmony, and stability and thus . . . what we believe to be most important for our emerging adults" (p. 9).

Greeson and colleagues (2014) describe key differences between *Koru* and mindfulness-based programs developed for adults more generally. For example, they indicate that *Koru* introduces particular mind-body skills (e.g., abdominal breathing, guided imagery, insight meditation practice) that provide participants with tools to rapidly reduce distress, which the developers posit will build motivation for continued practice. They also speak to the relative brevity of the intervention. Standard MBSR entails eight 2.5-hour sessions plus a full-day retreat, along with approximately 45 minutes of daily or nearly daily home practice; *Koru* consists of four 75-minute sessions (attendance at all four is required) and 10-minute daily practice sessions. Finally, the language and metaphors of *Koru* have been specifically designed to be relatable to emerging adults, and the program is taught by counseling center staff in small-group sessions to allow for invaluable peer interactions.

Greeson et al. (2014) recently conducted a randomized clinical trial comparing *Koru* to a wait-list control condition. Results suggest that *Koru* helps reduce levels of perceived stress and sleep problems and increase levels of mindfulness and self-compassion. Further, the intervention group exhibited many significant correlations between changes in mindfulness, self-compassion (overall and several components) and other outcome measures. While a preliminary study with notable limitations, including limited diversity of the sample and reliance on self-report measures, Greeson and colleagues' findings suggest promise for *Koru* and other mindfulness-based interventions specifically designed for college students and other emerging adults.

Other related approaches also have valued flexibility and meeting college students where they are. Further, these do not typically aim to "rapidly reduce distress," as is one of the elements of *Koru* (Rogers & Maytan, 2012), but instead to help individuals relate differently to that distress, for example by targeting experiential avoidance (EA). EA refers to an unwillingness to experience particular private events (e.g., thoughts, feelings, bodily sensations) and behavior aimed toward changing the form or frequency of occurrence of these events (Hayes, Wilson, Gifford, Follette, & Strosahl, 1996). While the notion that "avoiding negative affect influences psychopathology is as old as the various schools of clinical psychology" (Chawla & Ostafin, 2007, p. 871), EA has received increased attention in recent years. Indeed, recent studies have indicated that EA may underlie diverse forms of psychological suffering and problematic behaviors including the overuse of substances (e.g., Bardeen, 2015; Kingston, Clarke, & Remington, 2010), issues particularly relevant to college students.

Acceptance-based behavioral approaches, including acceptance and commitment therapy (ACT; Hayes, Strosahl, & Wilson, 1999, 2012), directly target this and aim to build what have been collectively called psychological flexibility (PF) skills (Hayes, Luoma, Bond, Masuda, & Lillis, 2006). In the ACT model, interrelated PF processes involve both mindfulness and acceptance processes and commitment and behavior change processes (Hayes et al., 2006). Contact with the present-moment and self-as-context (i.e., connection with a sense of self as a perspective or locus from which the world is experienced, as opposed to one's concepts about the self, such as "I am smart," or "I come from a broken family") form the foundation for both. Additionally, acceptance and cognitive defusion (i.e., stepping back and seeing thoughts as passing mental events) are considered core mindfulness and acceptance skills, and values and committed action round out the commitment and behavior change processes. Overall, PF is defined as "the ability to fully contact the present-moment and the thoughts and feelings it contains without needless defense, and, depending upon what the situation affords, persisting in or changing behavior in the pursuit of goals and values" (Bond et al., 2011, p, 678). A recent meta-analysis suggests that ACT-based interventions are at least comparable to established psychological interventions for clinically relevant mental and physical health problems (A-Tjak et al., 2015).

PF skills may be particularly helpful for students (of all ages, not just those in the emerging adult category) struggling with the challenges and demands of college life. Juggling many roles and pulls, academic demands, financial concerns and such, along with social comparison processes, can lead students to often "live inside their heads," further feeding the struggles. Putting PF skills into play may allow students instead to fully experience the moments of their lives (scary, painful, joyful, boring, exciting, etc.) and take action in the directions of what they most care about. Further, those who serve these students, including their faculty members, advisors, supervisors, coaches, and administrators might benefit from developing similar skills as they navigate the challenges of their positions and the ever-evolving state of higher education. In other words, to echo the opening quote, these practices, engaged over and over, may foster a deep "learning to love," (Zajonc in Palmer & Zajonc, 2010, p. xi).

Aims and Spirit of This Volume

Momentum, based on empirical evidence and strong communities that value openness and collaboration[2] in the development, implementation, and rigorous evaluation of mindfulness- and acceptance-based approaches within higher education, is building. Still, this work is in its infancy, with uncontrolled designs or less stringent controls and reliance on self-report measures characterizing much of the research. Thus, it is with a great deal of humility *and* a strong sense of the importance and potential of this work that we present this edited volume.

This compilation of chapters aims to share an assortment of these interventions, presenting preliminary results as well as substantial discussion of the *process* of developing and implementing such approaches within college and university settings, including challenges faced and lessons learned. We see each of the approaches presented in this book as potentially part of a "portfolio of interventions" (Kazdin & Blasé, 2011) that collectively hold promise for creating substantial cultural change within higher education, with ripple effects into many if not all domains in society (see Chapter 11, this volume). Hunt and Eisenberg (2010) corroborate this potential in stating that college is the only life stage for many individuals when one setting comprises all of their main domains of functioning, including educational/professional, social, and health-related. They go on to state that campuses are also well-equipped "to develop, evaluate, and disseminate best practices. In short, colleges offer a unique opportunity to address one of the most significant public health problems among late adolescents and young adults" (p. 3).

Further, we believe that even for groups like non-traditional, commuter, and graduate-level students, colleges and universities offer unique potential for studying and intervening on critical behavioral health processes. It is also important to indicate that college campuses will do their best work serving in these essential roles if there is partnership across various units, including those that are academic and student services-based. For example, collaboration between faculty members and college counseling professionals is highly encouraged. Pistorello (2013) offers an outstanding volume detailing numerous ways to employ mindfulness- and acceptance-based approaches, mostly in the context of counseling centers. Professionals engaged in that critical setting, as well as those working with students within the classroom and other contexts discussed in this volume, would do well to put their heads and hands together in this essential work.

The Road Ahead

This chapter, along with others in Part I, provides context for the detailed, practice-specific, student-centered material in Parts II and III. In Chapter 2, McHugh, Sandoz, and Hooper skillfully provide a detailed explanation of various elements of relational frame theory, the theoretical framework that underlies ACT, as well as its relevance to higher education contexts. Since faculty have many points of contact with students (e.g., as instructors, advisors, mentors), Cardaciotto and Block-Lerner in Chapter 3 discuss ways that mindfulness- and acceptance-based interventions might be employed to assist faculty in navigating the stresses and challenges of juggling multiple roles within the interrelated contexts of one's department, university, and field/discipline.

Part II is specifically devoted to the training of aspiring behavioral health professionals, both within (Georgescu & Brock in Chapter 4) and outside (i.e., within clinical supervision, research mentoring, and other contexts; Roemer, Eustis, Williston, & Hayes-Skelton in Chapter 5) of the traditional academic classroom. In addition to this being our own "wheelhouse," so to speak, this topic felt particularly relevant to include, as it is clinicians-in-training who are often exposed to these approaches in the service of getting them ready to deliver them to their clients. The complexities involved in this training, including those related to requiring and evaluating experiential work and engaging in potential multiple relations with students across training contexts, are grappled with thoughtfully, with the authors of both chapters clearly embodying a stance toward their own emotional experiences consistent with mindfulness- and acceptance-based approaches.

Part III addresses mindfulness- and acceptance-based interventions with special student populations or in special contexts. Here we have asked authors to (flexibly) adhere to a structure that entails provision of an evidence-informed rationale for work with the particular population or in the particular context, and discussion of the following topics: (a) methods of their particular intervention or approach; (b) at least preliminary results, including perspectives from participants (e.g., qualitative responses); (c) challenges faced and lessons learned; and (d) recommendations for future research and/or applied work within the population or context. Authors were also encouraged to include supplementary materials such as handouts, worksheets, scripts for exercises, or sample homework assignments. We believe the latter really foster the creative approaches presented in the chapters "coming alive" in ways that will be useful to readers interested in engaging in this work.

In Chapter 6, Pistorello and colleagues detail their extraordinarily promising work incorporating ACT interventions into first-year experience seminars. Sandoz and Mullen, in Chapter 7, present innovative interventions for the challenging and critical population of academically-at-risk students. Danitz, Orsillo, Lenda, Shortway, and Block-Lerner in Chapter 8 target students in pre-professional programs other than those training to be behavioral health professionals; informed by the literature and their own work in various contexts, they usefully discuss trade-offs inherent in choices around the logistical parameters of interventions, including length/dose and whether participation should be required or voluntary. Wolanin and Gross in Chapter 9 strongly make the case for the use of mindfulness- and acceptance-based interventions with college student athletes, approaches that are often at odds with traditional assumptions around athletes' emotional experiencing. These authors discuss their own work with athletes across multiple settings, sharing helpful strategies for cultivating relationships with coaches and other athletic training staff and working with the athletes themselves. In Chapter 10, Marks, Block-Lerner, Barrasso-Catanzaro, and Kowarz review the literature on brief and non-traditional mindfulness- and acceptance-based interventions with undergraduate students, and highlight a host of remaining empirical questions about brief interventions. They also discuss their own work using curriculum-grounded workshops to study predictors of receptivity to these approaches. Finally, Cardaciotto, Hill, Block-Lerner, and Biglan conclude by considering the contents of this volume through the lens of prevention science.

A Final Note on Naming

It is important to note that we encouraged the authors who contributed to this volume to be intentional in their use of terms to describe interventions. We valued inclusiveness and flexibility in these choices, with some contributors clearly describing "ACT" or "dialectical behavior therapy" (Linehan, 1993) and others preferring broader terms like "acceptance-based behavioral therapies" or "contextual cognitive-behavioral therapies." As Roemer and Orsillo (2009) suggest, "names serve to highlight similarities and downplay distinctions among approaches with similar names and maximize distinctions and downplay similarities among differently named treatments" (p. 3). Part of what is exciting and promising about the approaches portrayed in this book has to do with their emphasis on principles versus protocols (even though some protocols are described). Ultimately, continued progress down the path of identifying active ingredients and mechanisms of action, especially at very molecular levels (see Kazdin, 2007) of these multifaceted interventions, may make the naming of packages less important.

Notes

1 While much of the focus of this chapter is on undergraduates, mental health issues are of concern for graduate- and professional-level students as well (e.g., Hyun, Quinn, Madon, & Lustig, 2006), to be addressed in several chapters to come.
2 See, for example, the website of the Association for Contextual Behavioral Science, https://contextualscience.org

References

Abramowitz, J. S., & Arch, J. J. (2014). Strategies for improving long-term outcomes in cognitive behavioral therapy for obsessive-compulsive disorder: Insights from learning theory. *Cognitive and Behavioral Practice, 21,* 20–31. doi:10.1016/j.cbpra.2013.06.004

American College Health Association (2009). American College Health Association—National College Health Assessment Spring 2008 reference group data report (abridged). *Journal of American College Health, 57,* 477–488. doi:10.3200/JACH.57.5.477-488

American College Health Association (2012). *National college health assessment. University of Iowa.* Retrieved from www.studenthealth.uiowa.edu/wellness/healthiowa-data

Arch, J. J., & Ayers, C. R. (2013). Which treatment worked better for whom? Moderators of group cognitive behavioral therapy versus adapted mindfulness based stress reduction for anxiety disorders. *Behaviour Research and Therapy, 51,* 434–442. doi:10.1016/j.brat.2013.04.004

Arnett, J. J. (2004). *Emerging adulthood: The winding road from the late teens through the twenties.* New York, NY: Oxford University Press.

Arria, A. M., Caldeira, K. M., Vincent, K. B., Winick, E. R., Baron, R. A., & O'Grady, K. E. (2013). Discontinous college enrollment: Associations with substance use and mental health. *Psychiatric Services, 64*(2), 165–172. doi:10.1176/appi.ps.201200106

A-Tjak, J. G. L., Davis, M. L., Morina, N., Powers, M. B., Smits, J. A., & Emmelkamp, P. M. G. (2015). A meta-analysis of the efficacy of acceptance and commitment therapy for clinically relevant mental and physical health problems. *Psychotherapy and Psychosomatics, 84,* 30–36. doi:10.1159/000365764

Bardeen, J. R. (2015). Short-term pain for long-term gain: The role of experiential avoidance in the relation between anxiety sensitivity and emotional distress. *Journal of Anxiety Disorders, 30,* 113–119. doi:10.1016/j.janxdis.2014.12.013

Barr, V., Rando, R., Krylowicz, B., & Winfield, E. (2010). The Association for University and College Counseling Center Directors Annual Survey. *Report of the Association for University and College Counseling Center Directors.*

Biglan, A., Flay, B. R., Embry, D. D., & Sandler, I. N. (2012). The critical role of nurturing environments for promoting human well-being. *American Psychologist, 67,* 257–271. doi:10.1037/a0026796

Biglan, A., Hayes, S. C., & Pistorello, J. (2008). Acceptance and commitment: Implications for prevention science. *Prevention Science, 9,* 139–152. doi:10.1007/s11121-008-0099-4

Blanco, C., Okuda, M., Wright, C., Hasin, D. S., Grant, B. F., Liu, S-M., & Olfson, M. (2008). Mental health of college students and their non-college attending peers: Results from the National Epidemiologic Study on Alcohol and Related Conditions. *Archives of General Psychiatry, 65,* 1429–1437. doi:10.1001/archpsyc.65.12.1429

Bond, F. W., Hayes, S. C., Baer, R. A., Carpenter, K. C., Guenole, N., Orcutt, H. K., . . . Zettle, R. D. (2011). Preliminary psychometric properties of the Acceptance and Action

Questionnaire – II: A revised measure of psychological flexibility and acceptance. *Behavior Therapy, 42,* 676–688. doi:10.1016/j.beth.2011.03.007

Bowen, S., & Marlatt, A. (2009). Surfing the urge: Brief mindfulness-based intervention for college student smokers. *Psychology of Addictive Behaviors, 23,* 666–671. doi:10.1037/a0017127

Brunner, J. L., Wallace, D. L., Reymann, L. S., Sellers, J.-J., & McCabe, A. G. (2014). College counseling today: Contemporary students and how counseling centers meet their needs. *Journal of College Student Psychotherapy, 28,* 257–324. doi:10.1080/87568225.2014.948770

Buchanan, J. L. (2012). Prevention of depression in the college student population: A review of the literature. *Archives of Psychiatric Nursing, 26,* 21–42. doi:10.1016/j.apnu.2011.03.003

Campbell-Sills, L., Cohan, S. L., & Stein, M. B. (2006). Relationship of resilience to personality, coping, and psychiatric symptoms in young adults. *Behaviour Research and Therapy, 44,* 585–599. doi:10.1016/j.brat.2005.05.001

Carr, P. G. (2015). *Letter from the commissioner of the National Center of Education Statistics.* Retrieved from http://nces.ed.gov/programs/coe/commissioner.asp

Chawla, N., & Ostafin, B. (2007). Experiential avoidance as a functional dimensional approach to psychopathology: An empirical review. *Journal of Clinical Psychology, 63,* 871–890. doi:10.1002/jclp.20400

Conley, C. S., Travers, L. V., & Bryant, F. B. (2013). Promoting psychosocial adjustment and stress management in first-year college students: The benefits of engagement in a psychosocial wellness seminar. *Journal of American College Health, 61*(2), 75–86. doi:10.1080/07448481.2012.754757

Corrigan, P. (2004). How stigma interferes with mental health care. *American Psychologist, 59,* 614–625. Retrieved from www.apa.org/pubs/journals/amp/

DeRosier, M. E., Frank, E., Schwartz, V., & Leary, K. A. (2013). The potential role of resilience education for preventing mental health problems for college students. *Psychiatric Annals, 43,* 538–544. doi:10.3928/00485713-20131206-05

DiGiuseppe, R. (2014, November). Discussion. In Z. Moore (Chair), *Innovative mindfulness- and acceptance-based interventions for college student mental health.* Symposium conducted at the annual meeting of the Association for Behavioral and Cognitive Therapies, Philadelphia, PA.

Eagan, K., Stolzenberg, E. B., Ramirez, J. J., Aragon, M. C., Suchard, M. R., & Hurtado, S. (2014). *The American freshman: National norms Fall 2014.* Los Angeles: Higher Education Research Institute, UCLA.

Eisenberg, D., Downs, M. F., Golberstein, E., & Zivin, K. (2009). Stigma and help seeking for mental health among college students. *Medical Care Research and Review, 66,* 522–541. doi:10.1177/1077558709335173

Eisenberg, D., Golberstein, E., & Hunt, J. B. (2009). Mental health and academic success in college. *The B. E. Journal of Economic Analysis & Policy, 9,* 40. doi:10.2202/1935-1682.2191

Eisenberg, D., Hunt, J., & Speer, N. (2012). Help seeking for mental health on college campuses: Review of evidence and next steps for research and practice. *Harvard Review of Psychiatry, 20,* 222–232. doi:10.3109/10673229.2012.712839

Eisenberg, D., Hunt, J., & Speer, N. (2013). Mental health in American colleges and universities: Variation across student subgroups and across campuses. *Journal of Nervous and Mental Disease, 201,* 60–67. doi:10.1097/NMD.0b013e31827ab077

Eisenberg, D., Hunt, J., Speer, N., & Zivin, K. (2011). Mental health service utilization among college students in the United States. *The Journal of Nervous and Mental Disease, 199,* 301–308. doi:10.1097/NMD.0b013e3182175123

Eisenberg, D., Speer, N., & Hunt, J. B. (2012). Attitudes and beliefs about treatment among college students with untreated mental health problems. *Psychiatric Services, 63,* 711–713. doi:10.1176/appi.ps.201100250

Gallagher, R. P. (2005). National survey of counseling center directors. (Monograph Series Number 8O). *Report of the International Association of Counseling Services, Inc.* Retrieved from www.collegecounseling.org/pdf/2005_survey.pdf

Gallego, J., Aguilar-Parra, J. M., Cangas, A. J., Langer, A. I., & Mañas, I. (2014). Effect of a mindfulness program on stress, anxiety and depression in university students. *The Spanish Journal of Psychology, 17,* 1–6. doi: 10.1017/sjp.2014.102

Golberstein, E., Eisenberg, D., & Gollust, S. E. (2009). Perceived stigma and help-seeking behavior: Longitudinal evidence from the healthy minds study. *Psychiatric Services, 60,* 1254–1256. doi:10.1176/ps.2009.60.9.1254

Greeson, J. M., Juberg, M. K., Maytan, M., James, K., & Rogers, H. (2014). A randomized controlled trial of Koru: A mindfulness program for college students and other emerging adults. *Journal of American College Health, 62,* 222–233. doi:10.1080/07448481.2014.887571

Hartley, M. T. (2013). Investigating the relationship of resilience to academic persistence in college students with mental health issues. *Rehabilitation Counseling Bulletin, 56,* 240–250. doi:10.1177/0034355213480527

Hayes, S. C., Luoma, J. B., Bond, F. W., Masuda, A., & Lillis, J. (2006). Acceptance and commitment therapy: Model, processes and outcomes. *Behaviour Research and Therapy, 44,* 1–25. doi:10.1016/j.brat.2005.06.006

Hayes, S. C., Strosahl, K. D., & Wilson, K. G. (1999). *Acceptance and commitment therapy: An experiential approach to behavior change.* New York, NY: Guilford Press.

Hayes, S. C., Strosahl, K. D., & Wilson, K. G. (2012). *Acceptance and commitment therapy: The process and practice of mindful change* (2nd ed.). New York, NY: Guilford Press.

Hayes, S. C., Wilson, K. G., Gifford, E. V., Follette, V. M., & Strosahl, K. (1996). Experiential avoidance and behavioral disorders: A functional dimensional approach to diagnosis and treatment. *Journal of Consulting and Clinical Psychology, 64,* 1152–1168. doi:10.1037/0022-006X.64.6.1152

Hunt, J., & Eisenberg, D. (2010). Mental health problems and help-seeking behavior among college students. *Journal of Adolescent Health, 46,* 3–10. doi:10.1016/j.jadohealth.2009.08.008

Hyun, J. K., Quinn, B. C., Madon, T., & Lustig, S. (2006). Graduate student mental health: Needs assessment and utilization of counseling services. *Journal of College Student Development, 47,* 247–266.

Johnston, L. D., O'Malley, P. M., Bachman, J. G., & Schulenberg, J. E. (2011). *Monitoring the Future national survey results on drug use, 1975–2010: Volume I, Secondary school students.* Ann Arbor, MI: Institute for Social Research, the University of Michigan. Retrieved from www.monitoringthefuture.org/pubs/monographs/mtf-vol1_2011.pdf

Kabat-Zinn, J. (1990). *Full catastrophe living: Using the wisdom of your body and mind to face stress, pain and illness.* New York, NY: Delacorte.

Kabat-Zinn, J. (1994). *Wherever you go there you are: Mindfulness meditation in everyday life.* New York, NY: Hyperion.

Kazdin, A. E. (2007). Mediators and mechanisms of change in psychotherapy research. *Annual Review of Clinical Psychology, 3,* 1–27. doi:10.1146/annurev.clinpsy.3.022806.091432

Kazdin, A. E., & Blasé, S. L. (2011). Rebooting psychotherapy research and practice to reduce the burden of mental illness. *Perspectives on Psychological Science, 6*(1), 21–37. doi:10.1177/1745691610393527

Keng, S. L., Smoski, M. J., & Robins, C. J. (2011). Effects of mindfulness on psychological health: A review of empirical studies. *Clinical Psychology Review, 31,* 1041–1056. doi:10.1016/j.cpr.2011.04.006

Keng, S.-L., Smoski, M. J., Robins, C. J., Ekblad, A. G., & Brantley, J. G. (2012). Mechanisms of change in mindfulness-based stress reduction: Self-compassion and mindfulness as mediators of intervention outcomes. *Journal of Cognitive Psychotherapy, 26,* 270–280. doi:10.1891/0889-8391.26.3.257

Jenks Kettmann, J. D., Schoen, E. G., Moel, J. E., Cochran, S. V., Greenberg, S. T., & Corkery, J. M. (2007). Increasing severity of psychopathology at counseling centers: A new look. *Professional Psychology: Research and Practice, 38,* 523–529. doi:10.1037/0735-7028.38.5.523

Khoury, B., Lecomte, T., Fortin, G., Masse, M., Therien, P., Bouchard, V., . . . Hofmann, S. G. (2013). Mindfulness-based therapy: A comprehensive meta-analysis. *Clinical Psychology Review, 33,* 763–771. doi:10.1016/j.cpr.2013.05.005

Kingston, J., Clarke, S., & Remington, B. (2010). Experiential avoidance and problem behavior: A mediational analysis. *Behavior Modification, 34,* 145–163. doi:10.1177/0145445510362575

Kolek, E. A. (2009). Recreational prescription drug use among college students. *NASPA Journal, 46,* 519–539.

Linehan, M. M. (1993). *Cognitive-behavioral treatment of borderline personality disorder.* New York, NY: Guilford Press.

Mermelstein, L. C., & Garske, J. P. (2015). A brief mindfulness intervention for college student binge drinkers: A pilot study. *Psychology of Addictive Behaviors, 29,* 259–269. doi:10.1037/adb0000040

Palmer, P. J., & Zajonc, A. (2010). *The heart of higher education: A call to renewal.* San Francisco, CA: Jossey-Bass.

Paul, N. A., Stanton, S. J., Greeson, J. M., Smoski, M. J., & Wang, L. (2013). Psychological and neural mechanisms of trait mindfulness in reducing depression vulnerability. *Social Cognitive and Affective Neuroscience, 8,* 56–64. doi:10.1093/scan/nss070

Pew Research Center. (2014). *The rising cost of not going to college.* Retrieved from www.pewsocialtrends.org/2014/02/11/the-rising-cost-of-not-going-to-college/

Pistorello J. (Ed.). (2013). *Mindfulness and acceptance for counseling college students: Theory and practical applications for intervention, prevention, and outreach.* Oakland, CA: New Harbinger.

Regehr, C., Glancy, D., & Pitts, A. (2013). Interventions to reduce stress in university students: A review and meta-analysis. *Journal of Affective Disorders, 148,* 1–11. doi:10.1016/j.jad.2012.11.026

Roemer, L., & Orsillo, S. M. (2009). *Mindfulness- and acceptance-based behavioral therapy in practice.* New York, NY: Guilford Press.

Rogers, H. B. (2013). Mindfulness meditation for increasing resilience in college students. *Psychiatric Annals, 43,* 545–548. doi:10.3928/00485713-20131206-06

Rogers, H., & Maytan, M. (2012). *Mindfulness for the next generation: Helping emerging adults manage stress and lead healthier lives.* New York, NY: Oxford University Press.

Rosen, L. D., Carrier, L. M., & Cheever, N. A. (2013). Facebook and texting made me do it: Media induced task-switching while studying. *Computers in Human Behavior, 29,* 948–958. doi:10.1016/j.chb.2012.12.001

Ruthig, J. C., Marrone, S., Hladkyj, S., & Robinson-Epp, N. (2011). Changes in college student health: Implications for academic performance. *Journal of College Student Development, 52,* 307–320. doi:10.1353/csd.2011.0038

Schwartz, V. (2013). College mental health at the cutting edge? *Journal of College Student Psychotherapy, 27*, 96–98. doi:10.1080/87568225.2013.766094

Segal, Z. V., Williams, J. M. G., & Teasdale, J. D. (2012). *Mindfulness-based cognitive therapy for depression* (2nd ed.). New York, NY: Guilford Press.

Shapiro, S. L., Brown, K. W., Astin, J. A. (2008). *Toward the integration of meditation into higher education: A review of research.* Prepared for the Center for Contemplative Mind in Society. Retrieved from www.contemplativemind.org/admin/wp-content/uploads/2012/09/MedandHigherEd.pdf

Silva, M., Dorso, E., Azhar, A., & Renk, K. (2007–2008). The relationship among parenting styles experienced during childhood, anxiety, motivation, and academic success in college students. *Journal of College Student Retention: Research, Theory, & Practice, 9*, 149–167. doi:10.2190/CS.9.2.b

Tucker, J. R., Hammer, J. H., Vogel, D. L., Bitman, R. L., Wade, N. G., & Maier, E. J. (2013). Disentangling self-stigma: Are mental illness and help-seeking self-stigmas different? *Journal of Counseling Psychology, 60*, 520–531. doi:10.1037/a0033555

Turchik, J. A., Garske, J. P., Probst, D. R., & Irvin, C. R. (2010). Personality, sexuality, and substance use as predictors of sexual risk taking in college students. *Journal of Sex Research, 47*, 411–419. doi:10.1080/00224490903161621

Twenge, J. M., Gentile, B., DeWall, C. N., Ma, D., Lacefield, K., & Schurtz, D. R. (2010). Birth cohort increases in psychopathology among young Americans, 1938–2007: A cross-temporal meta-analysis of the MMPI. *Clinical Psychology Review, 30*, 145–154. doi:10.1016/j.cpr.2009.10.005

Vogel, D. L., Wade, N. G., & Hackler, A. H. (2007). Perceived public stigma and the willingness to seek counseling: The mediating roles of self-stigma and attitudes toward counseling. *Journal of Counseling Psychology, 54*, 40–50. doi:10.1037/0022-0167.54.1.40

Watkins, D. C., Hunt, J. B., & Eisenberg, D. (2011). Increased demand for mental health services on college campuses: Perspectives from administrators. *Qualitative Social Work, 11*, 319–337. doi:10.1177/1473325011401468

2 Theoretical Underpinnings

Relational Frame Theory and Contextual Behavioral Science in a Higher Education Context

Louise McHugh, Emily K. Sandoz, and Nic Hooper

Introduction

It has been argued that psychological flexibility (PF) is a key ingredient in psychological health, as it enables individuals to cope in an uncertain, unpredictable world where novelty and change are the norm rather than the exception (Kashdan & Rottenberg, 2010). Although mindfulness-based interventions could potentially be understood through a number of conceptual, theoretical, philosophical, and psychological approaches, this chapter will focus on the contemporary contextual behavioral perspective and on the PF model. The PF model provides a theoretical account for the change processes in acceptance and commitment therapy (ACT) and mindfulness-based interventions more generally.

The Psychological Flexibility Model

Human beings have the potential to tolerate and effectively use emotions, thoughts, and behaviors to achieve most adaptive outcomes in varying situations. Research suggests that PF harnesses this potential (Kashdan & Rottenberg, 2010). PF can be defined as "the process of contacting the present-moment fully as a conscious human being and persisting in or changing certain behaviors in the service of chosen values" (Dahl, Stewart, Martell, & Kaplan, 2013; p. 92). A key mechanism that impacts PF is experiential avoidance (EA), or the unwillingness to experience difficult thoughts, feelings, or sensations even when avoiding these is damaging (Levin, Hildebrandt, Lillis, & Hayes, 2012). EA is strongly associated with depression, anxiety, and general psychological distress (Boulanger, Hayes, & Pistorello, 2010).

PF can be targeted through acceptance and mindfulness-based interventions such as ACT (Hayes, Strosahl, & Wilson, 1999, 2012). ACT is a form of cognitive behavior therapy that applies acceptance, mindfulness, and behavior change processes to develop PF and reduce EA (Levin et al., 2012). The approach is transdiagnostic and can help to develop resilience skills in the prevention and amelioration of a diverse range of psychological difficulties and enhance cognitive capacity (Hayes, Barnes-Holmes, & Wilson, 2013; Ruiz, 2010).

Acceptance and Commitment Therapy

ACT is theoretically based in contemporary behavior analysis (BA; Hayes & Wilson, 1993), and is one of a number of acceptance and mindfulness-oriented cognitive and behavioral approaches, a so-called "third wave" of these interventions, such as dialectical behavior therapy (Linehan, 1993) and mindfulness-based cognitive therapy (Segal, Williams, & Teasdale, 2001). The recently emerged "third wave" behavioral approaches combine techniques from cognitive-behavioral traditions with acceptance and mindfulness techniques (Baer, 2003).

ACT explicitly teaches clients to abandon attempts to control uncomfortable thoughts and feelings and instead to observe them non-judgmentally and accept them as they are, which is a process that is grounded in mindfulness (Baer, 2003). Mindfulness-based interventions have become increasingly prevalent over the last decade, and there is a large body of empirical research on the efficacy of mindfulness-based interventions to enhance psychological well-being and in the treatment of several psychological disorders (Baer, 2003; Hayes, Villatte, Levin, & Hildebrandt, 2011; Keng, Smoski, & Robins, 2011).

Science of Human Behavior: Behavior Analysis

The PF model and ACT are underpinned by contextual behavioral science (CBS), which studies psychological events through a behavior analytic framework. BA uses learning principles to effect behavior change. This branch of psychology is not concerned with mentalistic causes of behavior (e.g., id or ego of psychodynamics or visual-spatial sketch pad of cognitive psychology), rather it focuses on the behavior itself. From this perspective, though, prediction of behavior is not enough. It aims to provide accounts of behavior that allow both prediction and influence. A behavioral analysis must involve identifying variables that can be manipulated. This results in its emphasizing environmental variables, as only the environment can be manipulated to regulate behavior (see Törneke, 2010).

From the behavior analytic perspective, behavior can be examined at the level of the operant. Operant comes from the same origin as the word "operate," which means to perform a function; exert power, or influence. The three elements of any operant behavior can be thought of as the "ABCs" of human behavior (Ramnero & Törneke, 2011). The A is for *antecedents*; in everyday terms, these are the triggers for a given behavior. The B is for the *behavior* we are trying to understand. And C is for *consequences*. All behavior has consequences, and these tend to influence future behavior. This influence happens in one of two ways: consequences make the behavior either more or less likely to happen again—that is, the consequences act as a *reinforcement* or as a *punishment*.

Reinforcement means that the consequences of a behavior lead to it persisting or increasing over time. If a particular consequence leads to an increase in the behavior, then we say it is *reinforcing* (or appetitive). For example, Kori is more likely to attend her statistics class because doing so gives her a chance to talk to Pat.

Likewise, Dr. Plumb finds himself telling more and more stories about his children because his class looks more engaged during these stories. Punishment means that the consequences of a behavior lead to it decreasing or ceasing over time. If a particular consequence leads to a decrease in the behavior, then we say it is *punishing* (or aversive). For example, because his classmates roll their eyes and snicker when he asks questions, Bernard stops speaking up in class. Similarly, Dr. Shannon stops submitting grant proposals because reviews are poor without much feedback. Therefore, "operant learning" refers to responding to antecedents with a particular behavior and learning from the consequences of that behavior. Patterns of Kori's class attendance, Dr. Plumb's storytelling, Bernard's lack of participation, and Dr. Shannon's lack of submission were all learned from their consequences.

Examining the ABCs of behavior can result in a complex analysis, since antecedents can come from the environment or they can be internal in the form of thoughts, feelings, memories, and so on. For example, Kori's attendance in statistics might be even more likely when she's feeling sad about a bad date the evening before. Her sad feelings create a context in which talking to Pat is even more reinforcing. Likewise, Bernard might keep talking in his psychology class, because he remembers his teacher saying that students will be most successful if they participate in discussion. The memory of his teacher's instruction creates a context in which his classmates' snickering does not reduce his participation.

An even more complex analysis emerges as a result of the phenomenon of generalization. Generalization refers to a process within operant conditioning, when a conditioned response (CR) starts occurring in response to the presentation of other similar stimuli, not just the conditioned stimulus (CS). For example, Dr. Plumb gets reinforced for telling stories about his kids in his undergraduate developmental psychology class, and so then starts to bring stories about them into other undergraduate classes as well as one of his postgraduate ones.

Traditional behavior analytic accounts of internal antecedents (e.g., thoughts, feelings, memories) have been unsuccessful in creating a productive empirical research program (Hayes, Barnes-Holmes, & Roche, 2001). However, relational frame theory (RFT; Hayes et al., 2001) is a comprehensive behavior analytic account of language and cognition that may help to explain internal antecedents. Over the past thirty years, empirical support for this account has been growing. This theory of language and cognition is grounded in a philosophy of science called functional contextualism.

Philosophy of Science: Functional Contextualism

Functional contextualism, a holistic philosophy of science and a perspective aligned with pragmatism, considers events as ongoing actions that derive meaning from their context (Biglan, 1995; Hayes et al., 2011). Function and context are intimately connected. From the contextual behavioral science point of view, *function* refers to the effect or impact something has. For example, what is the function of running a marathon? It may be to raise money for charity, to get fit, or to please one's wife. In other words, the same behavior can have entirely different functions. Further, one cannot know the function of a behavior (i.e., anything a person does, including thinking, talking, and remembering) unless the *context* of the behavior, or the situation in which it occurs, is known. Following the last example, imagine a man's wife had expressed that she felt it was important that they engaged in more shared activities. The function of running the marathon in this case might be to support the needs of his wife.

From the functional-contextual perspective, the function of a behavior is more important than its form. In other words, behaviors are defined by the conditions under which they occur—their antecedents and consequences. Even though they look different from the outside, Kori's attendance and Dr. Plumb's behavior both function as attention-seeking. Likewise, Bernard's lack of participation and Dr. Shannon's lack of submission both function as escape. Further, changing the consequences of one behavior will impact other behaviors that are functionally similar. Pat's attention in statistics will not only increase Kori's attendance in that class, but will increase all behavior that could get Pat's attention. She might hang out in the lounge more often or attend tutoring in the learning center. From this perspective, understanding what the behavior is in the service of (i.e., its function, which depends upon context) allows for more effective interventions to influence behavior change.

The PF model reflects the philosophy of functional contextualism by its particular focus on the social and verbal (e.g., thoughts) contexts of psychological struggles. In treating language as acts in context, the PF model approaches thoughts from the point of view of what works (i.e., practical workability) in any given situation instead of its logical or literal truth (Hayes et al., 2011). For example, if a student who was struggling with an assignment said, "This essay is causing me lots of discomfort," although the *form* of the thought may be true, what is more important is its *function*, or how useful this thought is in moving the student toward his or her value of education.

Theoretical Framework: Relational Frame Theory

As previously noted, RFT (Hayes et al., 2001) is a contemporary behavior analytic perspective of language and cognition derived from functional contextualism. According to RFT, language and cognition can be understood in terms of the learned capacity to relate stimuli under arbitrary contextual control, referred to as relational framing (see Hayes et al., 2001). That is, humans can relate things together in arbitrary ways to make sense of them. From a CBS point of view, this relating is at the heart of human language and cognition.

Let's break it down by starting with what we mean by "relating," a form of activity that is a cornerstone of the RFT explanation of human language. Relating can be defined as responding to one thing because of its relationship with another (e.g., picking the bigger object from an array or selecting the name badge that matches your name). Many species can relate things based on physical properties (e.g., monkeys can see that two identical objects are the same or that two non-identical objects are different). This is non-arbitrary relating. However, humans alone have developed the ability to relate things in a way that does not depend on physical properties but on arbitrary contextual cues. This is arbitrary relational responding or *relational framing*.

Empirical evidence suggests that we humans learn to engage in relational framing from a very early age (Lipkens, Hayes, & Hayes, 1993; Luciano et al., 2007). We learn it through exposure to interactions with parents and others in our language community from an early age. The earliest and arguably most fundamental example of relational framing that children learn (and which probably emerges somewhere between 16 and 20 months) is the relation of coordination (sameness) between words and their referents. In this case, children learn to behave toward an object and its name (e.g., an actual cookie and the spoken sound "cookie") as if they are the same as each other, despite their lack of physical similarity, based on the presence of contextual cues such as the word "is." For example, a small child who has learned to relate a cookie to the sounds of the word "cookie" might clap and smile when mom says "cookie" in much the same way that she does when she sees a cookie. The child might begin to salivate. She might hold out her hand as if to grab a cookie. She might say "mine" or "please" just as she has to in order to get things she wants, like cookies.

Coordination (sameness) is only one type of relation that we learn. With continued exposure to the socio-verbal environment, we learn to relate words and objects in other ways also (i.e., we learn additional frames). Other relations include distinction (e.g., "Windows are different from doors"), opposition ("Quiet is opposite to noisy"), comparison ("My house is bigger than yours"), perspective ("I am here and you are there"), and hierarchy ("a Holstein is a type of cow"). See Hayes et al. (2001) for a more comprehensive list and description of characteristics of particular families of relational frames.

To understand the meaning of "arbitrary contextual control," imagine you have never met the authors of this chapter; we tell you that "Emily is taller than Louise," and when we ask who is shorter, you answer "Louise." Your reply is based not on formal properties (e.g., physical similarity) but on the arbitrary (i.e., based on social convention) contextual cue "taller." You can do this because you have previously learned to "relationally frame" stimuli in accordance with the relation of comparison in the presence of this cue and thus when you hear it, you frame Emily and Louise in this way and derive that Louise is shorter.

RFT researchers have provided an increasing quantity of empirical evidence showing the diversity of patterns of framing as well as how they can be established and influenced (e.g., Dymond & Barnes, 1996; Roche & Barnes, 1997; Steele & Hayes, 1991). According to RFT, humans learn to relationally frame based on exposure to contingencies of reinforcement in the socio-verbal environment. In the example of the small child above, she learned to relate a cookie with the sound of a word based on the presence of contextual cues such as the word "is." With continued exposure to the socio-verbal environment, humans gradually learn a variety of alternative frames, often based on learning the non-arbitrary counterpart first. For example, in the case of the comparative frame described above related to height, a child might initially learn to choose between different physical lengths when asked which is taller or shorter, and eventually his or her response generalizes so that the contextual cues alone control the response pattern, and the child can answer appropriately when asked a question such as that involving Emily and Louise (see Barnes-Holmes, Barnes-Holmes, Smeets, Strand, & Friman, 2004 for an empirical example of training the relational frame of comparison).

Despite the fact that there are many types of relational frames, all relational frames involve three defining features: mutual entailment, combinatorial entailment, and transformation of stimulus functions.

i   *Mutual entailment* refers to the fact that a relation in one direction between two stimuli entails or automatically gives rise to a second relation in the opposite direction. For example, if a verbally able child is given two previously unknown euro coins and told that a 1 euro coin is worth more than a 50 cent coin, then she may derive that the 50 cent coin is less than the 1 euro coin. In other words, the first relation entails the second one and this works whichever is trained first (i.e., it is mutual).

ii *Combinatorial entailment* involves the combination of two relations to form a third. For example, given three foreign coins, if the 1 euro coin is more than the 50 cent coin, and the 50 cent coin is more than a 20 cent coin, then a 1 euro coin can be derived as more than a 20 cent coin, and a 20 cent coin as less than a 1 euro coin.

iii *Transformation of function.* Entailment makes relational framing interesting to logicians; what makes it interesting to psychologists is the transformation of functions. As previously noted, function refers to the impact of some object or event on behavior. Thus, *transformation of function* means behavior change. Transformation of function is the key process according to which language can influence our behavior. In technical terms, if two stimuli, A and B, participate in a relation, and one stimulus (A) has a psychological function, then under certain conditions the stimulus functions of B may be transformed in accordance with that relation. For instance, imagine a young child has previously experienced buying candy in the store using a particular coin. Through basic conditioning processes, coins of this particular type (that before conditioning had no meaning/function) have acquired an *appetitive* function—they have come to elicit behaviors such as excitement or salivation, and have become reinforcing. If the child is then shown a new coin, told that a new coin is worth more than the first, and is then given a choice as to which she wants, she will likely choose the new one despite the desirability of the original coin and the fact that she has had no experience with the new one. This is because the appetitive psychological functions of the new coin have been transformed through comparative relations (i.e., worth "more than"). The new coin now elicits more excitement and is more reinforcing than the original coin. This is the process through which RFT suggests many of our behaviors are determined.

According to RFT, it is this relational framing and subsequent transformation of functions which render human psychological suffering so common (Hayes et al., 2001). For example, hearing someone talking about failing an exam or about an upcoming assignment can be anxiety-provoking for someone who has just experienced or is just about to experience something similar. The person is only exposed to words, but the words evoke thoughts and feelings as though it is a real event. Interestingly, similar thoughts may be evoked by the same person hearing about someone's successful grade on a paper: Hearing that someone received an A grade may equally bring to mind thoughts of one's own lesser grade on a paper (via a relation of distinction). Therefore, RFT provides a framework to assist learning in a way that is less language-driven and more sensitive to function/context (versus form; Boone & Cannici, 2013).

Contextual Behavioral Science in the Higher Education Context

In the section that follows we will outline three areas where relational framing and the subsequent transformation of functions are targets for behavioral change in a higher education setting. These are rule-following, values (i.e., motivation), and self-flexibility (i.e., developing perspective-taking relations).

Rule Following

Language and deriving stimulus relations allows humans to learn without having to be shaped by directly contacting behavioral consequences. For example, I can buy a piece of new equipment and use it based on the instructions provided in the package rather than having to rely on trial and error. This indirect learning is referred to in the behavioral literature as rule-following (Törneke, Luciano, & Valdivia Salas, 2008). Research suggests that rules can be powerfully influential to the extent that once control is established by a rule, subsequent behavior is likely to be in accordance with the rule and less likely to change when the antecedents and consequences specified by the rule change (e.g., Kaufman, Baron, & Kopp, 1966). For example, imagine that a 16-year-old secondary school student was instructed that a good essay must include his own opinion. As a good scholar, he follows that rule in every subsequent essay that he is assigned. However, when he reaches university, he is no longer allowed to write his opinion in essays (i.e., the contingencies for opinion giving change). He would learn the new rule more slowly than those students who were given no rule at all and simply learned from the direct contingencies (i.e., direct experience). In such circumstances, his behavior is said to be "insensitive" to the scheduled contingencies. The lack of sensitivity to contingencies (i.e., direct experience) often exhibited by humans in comparison to other species has been attributed to the role of rule-governed behavior (e.g., Catania, Matthews, & Shimoff, 1982; Galizio, 1979; Joyce & Chase, 1990). Exposure to rules, whether self-generated ("I have to get straight As") or generated by others ("Engineering is a male discipline"), produces responding that is resistant to change when the contingencies are changed (LeFrancois, Chase, & Joyce, 1988; Rosenfarb, Newland, Brannon, & Howey, 1992).

Baumann, Abreu-Rodrigues, and Souza (2009) found that exposure to one specific rule, or self-generated rule, produced insensitivity to changes in contingencies with change in responding occurring only when participants were provided with varied rules and self-generated rules, encouraging response variability. Similarly, Wulfert, Greenway, Farkas, Hayes, and Dougher (1994) presented participants with multiple rules, and divided them into high and low rigidity scorers based on a personality rigidity scale administered before the task. Both sets of rigidity scorers were provided with either accurate or inaccurate instructions in terms of how to respond during the task in order to receive points. The results revealed that when provided with accurate instructions, both the high and low scorers produced contingency sensitive responses. When, however, inaccurate instructions were administered, the high rigidity scorers continued to follow the instructions whereas the low scorers were more inclined to adapt their responses to the changing contingencies. The studies by Baumann, Abreu-Rodrigues, and Souza (2009) and Wulfert, Greenway, Farkas, Hayes and Dougher (1994) suggest that instructional control can impede sensitivity to changing contingencies when individuals are not provided with various rules to choose from. For example, students may struggle to adjust when they find themselves in a course that follows a programmed instruction or a flipped classroom format. The more rigid their rules about what behaviors will be effective in a regular class, the more trouble they will have developing new behaviors that work in the new course format. In addition, some may exhibit rigid personality traits that prevent them from adapting their responses in identifying a more effective response strategy.

According to RFT, there are functionally distinct patterns of rule-following that have been referred to as pliance, tracking, and augmenting (Hayes, Zettle, & Rosenfarb, 1989). Pliance is defined as "rule-governed behavior under the control of apparent socially mediated consequences for a correspondence between the rule and relevant behavior" (Hayes et al., 1989, p. 203). Non-technically speaking, pliance involves complying with a rule given by someone else because one has a history of reinforcement for complying with rules set by this person rather than because s/he has experienced the consequences of following the rule in the past. For example, if a parent tells a teenager to "empty the dishwasher," and the teenager does so because of a history of consequences for rule-following mediated by the verbal/social community (i.e., the parent has provided reinforcement such as praise or an allowance in the past for complying with his/her instructions), this is pliance.

The second unit of rule-following, "tracking" is defined as "rule-governed behavior under the control of the apparent correspondence between the rule and the way the world (environment) is arranged" (Törneke, 2010, p. 206). Non-technically speaking, tracking involves following a rule because one has been reinforced for doing so in the past. Using the previous example, if the teenager now empties the dishwasher in order to have clean dishes available to use for dinner, then this rule-following behavior may be termed tracking. In this case, the teenager makes contact with the relation specified in the rule (i.e., "If I empty the dishwasher then there will be clean dishes available to use"), and this in turn changes some aspect of his/her behavior (i.e., empty the dishwasher). In a sense, tracking is following a rule because the individual has a history where rules have worked.

The third unit of rule-following involves augmenting. Augmenting can be defined as "rule-governed behavior due to relational networks that alter the degree to which events function as consequences" (Hayes et al., 2001, p. 109). Augmentals change the reinforcing value of the consequences that are specified in the rule. When a relational network is put into a relation with a consequence, it changes the function of that consequence. For example, "If you want to be successful you need to get a university degree" can be followed via pliance. However, if the rule is followed because "getting a degree will result in being a success," then it is augmenting. Augmenting, as the name suggests, involves strengthening the power of consequences to control our behavior.

All three types of rule-following can be problematic. Pliance becomes problematic when a person continuously seeks reinforcers and avoids punishers in order to please others. For example, a young man who studies medicine primarily because it is what his parents want him to do may not actually enjoy the profession when he is in it. Consequences provided by others are not as predictable and controllable as other sources of reinforcement such as that from activities we engage in that we find enjoyable (Törneke, 2010). When an individual is guided primarily by pliance, he will be sensitive to the wants of others at the expense of contacting his own needs.

Tracking becomes problematic when the track does not result in the specified consequence. For example, imagine the rule "I only study well at night." The consequences derived from "studying well at night" (e.g., remembering definitions of key terms) will maintain this type of tracking; the consequences from studying at times other than at night will not. Therefore, tracking can be problematic when the short-term consequences specified in the rule maintain behavior that is not useful or limiting in the long term. In this case, tracking of reinforcing short-mid-term consequences (e.g., studying at night is effective) will block the tracking of long-term consequences (e.g., of studying throughout the day), and the result will be less time to study in the long term.

Augmenting is problematic as when it interacts with pliance and tracking it increases insensitivity to changing contingencies. For example, the abstract consequence "being a success" may have been established as the ultimate reward in the repertoire of an individual for her to feel "valid." That is, there is an augmented relation of coordination between "being a success" and "valid." This relation will heighten the consequences of not succeeding into punishers as long as not complying with "being a success" is established in a relation of coordination to "being valid."

Rule following has been demonstrated to result in rigid patterns of behavior, and the ACT model attempts to foster broad flexible behavioral repertoires. For college and university students, moving from pliant rule-following to tracking is critical in order to develop meaningful life choices. It is no longer useful to follow rules that credible speakers such as parents or educators provide to them. In any educational setting, it is vital that learners are aided in developing repertoires that allow them to track their environment so that they are behaving in line with consequences that are chosen by and desirable for them not just in the service of following the rule per se. For example, students first study because their parents have told them to (pliance). However, over time when they start to see the positive results of studying they may start to study in order to perform better on class tests (tracking).

The human ability to use language to generate and follow rules provides us with a powerful tool. However, as we have discussed, this tool can also promote rigid patterns of behavior that are out of contact with our direct experience. Mindfulness-based interventions provide an antidote to problematic rule-following, because they involve training attention in a deliberate, focused, and flexible way (Hayes et al., 2012). Mindfulness-based interventions focus on developing skills that allow the focus of attention to be on current experience, which reduces rigid rule-following that can dislocate one from the present moment.

Values (Motivation for Higher Education)

Hayes et al. (1999) define values as "verbally construed global desired life consequences" (p. 206), adding that they can be thought of as "verbally constructed contingencies . . . useful when the consequences of actions are remote, subtle, or probabilistic" (p. 207). More recently, Wilson has defined values as "freely chosen, verbally constructed consequences of ongoing, dynamic, evolving patterns of activity, which establish predominant reinforcers for that activity that are intrinsic in engagement in the valued behavioral pattern itself" (Wilson & DuFrene, 2009, p. 66; cf. Wilson & Sandoz, 2008). Values in ACT and other acceptance-based behavioral interventions serve as an organizational rubric for groups of activities that an individual perceives as reinforcing and as enhancing his/her quality of life. Values are assumed to be shaped by learning history, and they can be subdivided into domains such as intimate and social relationships, education, and career path (Dahl, Plumb, Lundgren, & Stewart, 2009). Values never refer to specific actions, but rather to overarching, guiding aspirations in the individual's life. Accordingly, a value for the education domain could be something like "enhancing my understanding of my area of interest." More specific actions like "not leaving assignments to the last minute" could be subsumed under such a value, but these actions would not comprise values in and of themselves. In fact, from the CBS perspective, it is important for individuals to clearly delineate specific goals within each value, as well as specific behaviors or sets of behaviors likely to achieve those goals.

The focus on values-driven behavior is implemented to bring individuals' behavior increasingly under the control of longer-term contingencies so that they pursue larger (perhaps more satisfying) later rewards rather than smaller sooner rewards. This might be predicted to result in higher levels of reinforcement for the individual over time According to Hayes, an extensive behavioral literature shows that "in the absence of verbal behavior, consequences are effective over only a very short timeframe: minutes to hours at most" (Hayes et al., 1999, p. 206). Essentially, the verbal rules known as values put human beings more under the control of desirable long-term consequences. For example, a student may value the pursuit of learning. In line with this value the student may get a PhD that will allow an academic or research job which would be congruent with his or her value.

Previous research has demonstrated that not living in accordance with values is associated with increased levels of psychological distress and depression (Plumb & Hayes, 2008). Michelson, Lee, Orsillo, and Roemer (2008) found differences in reports of active values between individuals diagnosed with general anxiety disorder relative to individuals not diagnosed with any anxiety disorders, with the anxious participants reporting less consistency in living their values. Hayes, Orsillo and Roemer (2010) targeted values, along with mindfulness, when examining the use of an acceptance-based behavioral therapy (ABBT) for generalized anxiety disorder. Hayes et al. (2010) found that change in both acceptance and engagement in meaningful activities predicted positive outcome of post-treatment status beyond that of change in worry. Support for the benefits of engagement with personal values also comes from the chronic pain literature, where McCracken and Yang (2006) found that reports of lower pain-related disability and anxiety correlated with greater accounts of success in living personal values. In fact, values clarification and engagement has received a lot of support in the area of behavioral medicine, with a large amount of the existing research pertaining to chronic pain (e.g. Vowles & McCracken, 2008).

In the original ACT text, Hayes et al. (1999) suggested that it may be functional for individuals to describe and record valued directions and values-consistent goals. Since this original suggestion, several values assessment and treatment tools have been developed to aid values clarification and the direction of goals related to the values process. One measure that has become increasingly popular in this regard is the Personal Values Questionnaire (PVQ; Blackledge & Ciarrochi, 2006). The PVQ aims to facilitate contact with values and to assess for aversive versus appetitive control. The PVQ considers valued living across nine values domains: family relationships, friendship/social relationships, romantic relationships, work/career, education, recreation, spirituality, community, and physical well-being. The PVQ categorizes the function behind reported values into three categories: social compliance (i.e., involving rigid and pliant rule-following), appetitive control (i.e., in the service of accessing higher levels of reinforcement), or avoidance (i.e., in the service of getting away from or reducing something that is aversive).

Hildebrandt et al. (2008, as cited in Plumb, Stewart, Dahl, & Lundgren, 2009) found that specific components of the PVQ, pliant (i.e. rigid rule-following) and avoidant values reasoning (i.e., reasoning in the service of reducing an unwanted internal experience rather than in the service of moving toward something that matters), demonstrated strong predictive power of poorer psychological health at baseline in a sample of teachers and substance abuse counselors. Plumb and Hayes (2008) similarly reported that these same components, pliant and avoidant reasoning, correlated with pre-treatment levels of depression. Taken together, results from these studies suggest that valued living that is sensitive to direct contingencies and guided by access to higher levels of long-term reinforcers rather than by reducing unwanted internal experiences, processes fostered by the interventions discussed in Part III of this volume, results in better psychological health.

More recently, Chase et al. (2013) investigated the impact of training goal-setting online with and without an ACT-based personal values component on undergraduate academic performance (i.e., grade point average [GPA]). Undergraduate students were randomly assigned to one of three groups (i.e., goal-setting training alone, values training plus goal-setting training, or a wait-list). The findings indicated that the combination of goal setting and values training significantly improved undergraduate GPAs in the following semester while no significant change in GPA was demonstrated for the other groups. From our account of CBS thus far we have seen the importance of coming under the control of long term reinforcers (e.g., values) rather than only short-term reinforcers (e.g., goals that have no values-based direction). Therefore it is not surprising that values plus goals produces better results than goals alone. That is, values motivate achieving goals.

Self-Understanding via Perspective Relations

Higher education is a significant time for personal growth. Self-esteem has been repeatedly demonstrated to be one of the strongest predictors of mental health problems for 12–25 year olds (Dooley & Fitzgerald, 2013). However, efforts to increase self-esteem in young people have not been fruitful. This is particularly evident from past interventions that directly targeted raising self-esteem to promote positive behavioral outcomes. For example, in California during the 1980s, politician John Vasconcellos argued that raising self-esteem in young people would reduce crime, teen pregnancy, drug abuse, school underachievement, and pollution. The Governor George Deukmejian organized a task force on self-esteem. A statewide project that aimed to boost self-esteem was developed. However, the findings from the project demonstrated a failure to produce desired outcomes. What did emerge, however, were higher levels of prejudice, discrimination, and defensiveness toward honest feedback and more importantly, no increase in overall well-being in the targeted adolescents (Baumeister, Campbell, Krueger, & Vohs, 2003). One reason for the failure of self-esteem interventions with adolescents is that self-esteem is an ill-defined concept. There is a need for a basic theoretical understanding of the development of self-understanding and related concepts such as self-esteem in order to design effective interventions that produce positive behavioral outcomes in adolescents and young adults.

One unique part of the ACT model is its approach to developing a flexible rather than purely optimistic self (McHugh & Stewart, 2012). From the CBS point of view, the ability for humans to narrate about their "self" is a uniquely human skill (McHugh & Stewart, 2012). Research has shown that this "self" makes a qualitative shift from adolescence to adulthood. Specifically, neuroscience data has indicated that brain structures relating to self-reflection are different for adolescents and adults, indicating that this is a formative time in the development of identity (Pfeiffer et al., 2009). Understanding the development of the self is of critical importance for this transition phase from adolescence into adulthood. According to CBS, the experience of self is a by-product of language. Therefore, in order to have a sense of self, a creature must be a language-user, and only humans are language users.

This basic understanding of how humans relate abstractly provided by RFT (detailed earlier in this chapter) provides an understanding of how humans learn about themselves. Imagine a college student is being bullied at university; she may start to relate university with fear. The physical functions of fear (heart racing, sweaty palms) will occur when on the campus of her university or even when she hears the word "university." If this person is told another word for a university is "ord," then "university" and "ord" will now be in a relation of sameness for this student. Therefore, later if she hears someone say "are you going to ord tomorrow?" she will experience some of the fear she has at university. Specifically, the functions of university (including fear) will transform via the relation of sameness to the word "ord."

Language involves responding to abstract relations, and the self is the product of learning to put one's own behavior into relation to others. More specifically, the self involves learning to verbally discriminate one's own behavior from others' behavior (McHugh & Stewart, 2012). This basic pattern of learning begins in early childhood. As a sense of self develops, so too does the ability to understand that others also have desires, beliefs, and wishes. From the CBS perspective, relating is a key language-based skill that underpins the development of empathy, a sophisticated sense of self, and transcendence. Children learn to relate their own behavior as different from that of others by learning three key "deictic" or "perspective" relations which are "I versus YOU," "HERE versus THERE," and "NOW versus THEN." They learn to respond appropriately to questions such as "What are YOU doing HERE?" "What am I doing NOW?" or "What was I doing THEN?" As children gradually learn to respond appropriately to these questions, and as they learn that whenever they are asked about their own behavior they always answer from the point of view of "I," "HERE," and "NOW." They will learn that this perspective is consistent and different from that of other people. For example, if you ask me about my behavior, I will always answer from the position of "I," "HERE," and "NOW" in response to your question asked by "YOU," "THERE" (where you are), and "THEN" (when you asked—a few seconds ago). "I" is always from this perspective here, not from someone else's perspective there. A sense of perspective is therefore abstracted through learning to talk about one's own perspective in relation to other perspectives.

Vilardaga and Hayes (2010) have outlined three steps to training a psychologically flexible self from the CBS point of view. Step 1 involves perspective relations (relational frames) that specify a relation in terms of the perspective of the speaker. The most important frames are I-YOU, HERE-THERE and NOW-THEN. Acquisition of these frames means learning to differentiate my behavior

("I") from that of others ("YOU"), and learning that my current responding is always "HERE" not "THERE" and "NOW" not "THEN." Training protocols have been developed that specifically target training this repertoire when deficient (see McHugh, Barnes-Holmes & Barnes-Holmes, 2009).

Step 2 involves empathy training via the transformation of emotional functions. Empathy has been defined as the ability to understand and share another person's emotional state. In general, it is thought to promote positive behavior such as helping to prevent or reduce antisocial behavior, including aggression and delinquency (Jolliffe & Farrington, 2009). Empathy involves the transformation of emotional functions via perspective relational frames. For example, imagine I told you I was feeling sad. If I then asked you, "If you were me how would you feel?" the emotional effects of the word "sad" would transform across the I-YOU relation and you would be able to respond that you would feel sad. In answering this question, some of the effects of the word sad would also transform from I to YOU. In non-technical terms, we adopt the perspective of others, and this allows us to "feel their suffering" and may prompt us to help them.

Step 3 of the Vilardaga and Hayes (2010) guide involves deictic (perspective) "self-as-context" training regarding one's own private events. This concept is based on the RFT approach to self, which is itself rooted in the relational frame conceptualization of deictic relational responding. The experience of self-as-context is the invariant in all perspective discriminations (i.e., "HERE and NOW"). Self-as-context can be thought of as a transcendence of psychological content that allows acceptance of that content. This includes acceptance of painful content produced through empathic responding to the suffering of others, which can support empathic responding. CBS suggests that, in combination with an extended relational repertoire, perspective-taking can establish three functionally different types of self. These are self as the *content* of verbal relations (conceptualized self); self as an ongoing *process* of verbal relations (knowing self); and self as the *context* of verbal relations (transcendent self).

Self-as-content (conceptualized self) consists of elaborate descriptive and evaluative relational networks that people construct about themselves and their histories over time. As soon as verbal humans become self-aware, they begin to interpret, explain, evaluate, predict, and rationalize their behavior. They organize these descriptions and evaluations into a coherent and consistent "self" network that persists across time and situations. This self is well-elaborated, touching on every verbally known aspect of life, and multi-layered, since contingencies support different depths of self-knowledge in different contexts. For example, an adolescent might explain why he failed an exam to his best friend in a very different way than he would explain it to his father.

Self-as-process (otherwise known as the knowing self) is the ongoing, verbal discrimination of psychological events as they occur in the moment (e.g., "I feel sad"). The knowing self feeds the conceptualized self. The knowing self is extremely useful in behavioral regulation both for the socio-verbal community as well as for the person themselves. Regarding the former, it allows other members of the verbal community to predict a person's behavior without knowledge of their learning history. For example, if someone says that she feels angry then this may allow others to predict how she might act in particular contexts. Self-as-process is also critical in the psychological development of the individual him/herself. In order to respond effectively to one's own responding, one must first be aware of the response and its impact. For example, understanding and responding to my thoughts and feelings about other people's behavior in a fluid and flexible manner is critical in the context of establishing personal relationships.

Self-as-context, or the transcendent self, is the invariant in all self-discriminations. If someone answers many different questions about themselves and their behavior, then the only aspect of their answering that will be consistent across time is the context from which the answer is given, that is, "I, HERE and NOW." Self-as-context is "content-less" and thus constant and unchanging from when it first emerges. It is itself a product of verbal responding, yet as a verbal category which applies to everything that a person has ever done, it incorporates both the non-verbal self (as behavioral stream resulting from direct experience) as well as the verbal self (as both object and process of knowledge gained through relational framing), and can thus provide the experiential link between non-verbal and verbal self-knowledge.

Developing a flexible sense of self is critical for those entering into the demands of higher education. This is a time of great social and emotional challenges. Being able to navigate the world with empathy and self-understanding during this challenging phase will likely result in less resistance to negative feedback and, ultimately, to longer-term outcomes like higher completion rates. Exercises to develop self as context involve getting the individual to notice that he or she is a perspective of all of his/her experiences rather than the evaluations or descriptions of the experience per se. One such exercise that is commonly employed is referred to as the "observer you" exercise. This exercise involves instructing the individual to bring to mind a number of life events (e.g., a time you were happy last summer, a time you were excited last year, a time you were embarrassed when you were a teenager, and so forth). Once the individual has recalled each event, he/she is instructed to notice that what is constant across all these events is that he/she was the perspective from which the events occurred rather than being the description or evaluation of any one of these events.

Conclusion

There is a movement in CBS that is now providing an understanding of human behavior. The insight that CBS provides can benefit individuals across the lifespan. This chapter has aimed to articulate the philosophical and theoretical framework offered by CBS and to provide clear examples of how this bottom-up account of human behavior can help to promote better well-being and a more effective learning environment for higher education students that involves effective rule-following, clear values guided action, and a flexible understanding of self. These are fast-moving times with an increasing number of students availing themselves of higher education. These are times when the type of scientifically grounded psychological insight and flexibility provided by CBS should be maximized in order to promote individual health in higher education and guide future generations, rather than in fearful and destructive directions, in positive and creative ones.

References

Baer, R.A. (2003). Mindfulness training as a clinical intervention: A conceptual and empirical review. *Clinical Psychology: Science and Practice, 10*, 125–143.

Barnes-Holmes, Y., Barnes-Holmes, D., Smeets, P. M., Strand, P., & Friman, P. (2004). Establishing relational responding in accordance with more-than and less-than as generalized operant behavior in young children. *International Journal of Psychology and Psychological Therapy, 4*, 531–558.

Baumann, A. A., Abreu-Rodrigues, J., & Souza, A. S. (2009). Rules and self-rules: Effects of variation upon behavioral sensitivity to change. *The Psychological Record, 59*, 641–670. Retrieved from http://opensiuc.lib.siu.edu/cgi/viewcontent.cgi?article=1041&context=tpr

Baumeister, R. F., Campbell, J. D., Krueger, J. I., & Vohs, K. D. (2003). Does high self-esteem cause better performance, interpersonal success, happiness, or healthier life-styles? *Psychological Science in the Public Interest, 4*, 1–4. Retrieved from http://files.clps.brown.edu/jkrueger/journal_articles/baumeister-2003-doeshigh.pdf

Biglan, A. (1995). *Changing cultural practices: A contextualistic framework for intervention research*. Reno, NV: Context Press.

Blackledge, J. T., & Ciarrochi, J. (2006, July). *Initial validation of the Personal Values Questionnaire. 2006.* Paper presented at the second World Conference for ACT/RFT, London, England.

Boone, M. S., & Cannici, J. (2013). Acceptance and commitment therapy (ACT) in groups. In J. Pistorello (Ed.), *Mindfulness and acceptance for counseling college students: Theory and practical applications for intervention, prevention, and outreach* (pp. 73–94). Oakland, CA: New Harbinger.

Boulanger, J. L., Hayes, S. C., & Pistorello, J. (2010). Experiential avoidance as a functional contextual concept. In A. Kring & D. Sloan (Eds.), *Emotion regulation and psychopathology* (pp. 107–136). New York, NY: Guilford Press.

Catania, A. C., Matthews, B. A., & Shimoff, E. (1982). Instructed versus shaped human verbal behavior: Interactions with nonverbal responding. *Journal of the Experimental analysis of Behavior, 38*, 233–248. Retrieved from www.ncbi.nlm.nih.gov/pmc/articles/PMC1347864/

Chase, J. A., Houmanfar, R., Hayes, S. C, Ward, T. A., Vilardaga, J. P., & Follette, V. M. (2013). Values are not just goals: Online ACT-based values training adds to goal setting in improving undergraduate college student performance. *The Journal of Contextual Behavioral Science, 2*, 79–84. doi:10.1016/j.jcbs.2013.08.002

Dahl, J., Plumb, J., Lundgren, T., & Stewart, I. (2009). *The art and science of valuing in psychotherapy*. Oakland, CA: New Harbinger.

Dahl, J., Stewart, I., Martell, C., & Kaplan, J. (2013). *ACT and RFT in relationships*. Oakland, CA: New Harbinger.

Dooley, B., & Fitzgerald, A. (2013). Methodology on the My World Survey (MWS): A unique window into the world of adolescents in Ireland. *Early Intervention in Psychiatry, 7*, 12–22. doi:10.1111/j.1751-7893.2012.00386

Dymond, S., & Barnes, D. (1996). A transformation of self-discrimination response functions in accordance with the arbitrarily applicable relations of sameness, more than, and less than: Erratum. *Journal of the Experimental Analysis of Behavior, 66*(3), 348–360.

Galizio, M. (1979). Contingency shaped and rule-governed behavior: Instructional control of human loss-avoidance. *Journal of the Experimental Analysis of Behavior, 31,* 28–46. doi:10.1901/jeab.1979.31-53

Hayes, S. A., Orsillo, S. M., & Roemer, L. (2010). Changes in proposed mechanisms of action in an acceptance-based behavior therapy for generalized anxiety disorder. *Behaviour Research and Therapy, 48,* 238–245. doi:10.1016/j.brat.2009.11.006

Hayes, S. C, Strosahl, K. D., & Wilson, K. G. (2012). *Acceptance and commitment therapy: The process and practice of mindful change* (2nd ed.). New York, NY: Guilford Press.

Hayes, S. C., & Wilson, K. G. (1993). Some applied implications of a contemporary behavior-analytic account of verbal behavior. *The Behavior Analyst, 16,* 283–301. Retrieved from www.ncbi.nlm.nih.gov/pmc/articles/PMC2733641/

Hayes, S. C., Barnes-Holmes, D., & Roche, B. (Eds.). (2001). *Relational frame theory: A post-Skinnerian account of human language and cognition.* New York, NY: Plenum Press.

Hayes, S. C., Barnes-Holmes, D., & Wilson, K. G. (2013). Contextual behavioral science: Creating a science more adequate to the challenge of the human condition. *Journal of Contextual Behavioral Science, 1,* 1–16. Retrieved from www.sciencedirect.com/science/journal/22121447/1/1-2

Hayes, S. C., Strosahl, K. D., & Wilson, K. G. (1999). *Acceptance and commitment therapy: An experiential approach to behavior change.* New York, NY: Guilford Press.

Hayes, S. C., Villatte, M., Levin, M., & Hildebrandt, M. (2011). Open, aware, and active: Contextual approaches as an emerging trend in the behavioral and cognitive therapies. *Annual Review of Clinical Psychology, 7,* 141–168. doi:10.1146/annurev-clinpsy-032210-104449

Hayes, S. C., Zettle, R. D., & Rosenfarb, I. (1989). Rule following. In S. C. Hayes (Ed.), *Rule-governed behavior: Cognition, contingencies, and instructional control* (pp. 191–220). New York, NY: Plenum Press.

Jolliffe, D., & Farrington, D.P. (2009). *The effects on offending of the community justice initiatives in Liverpool and Salford.* Available on request from the Ministry of Justice.

Joyce, J. H., & Chase, P. N. (1990). Effects of response variability on the sensitivity of rule governed behavior. *Journal of the Experimental Analysis of Behavior, 54,* 251–262. doi:10.1901/jeab.1990.54-251

Kashdan, T. B., & Rottenberg, J. (2010). Psychological flexibility as a fundamental aspect of health. *Clinical Psychology Review, 30,* 865–878. doi:10.1016/j.cpr.2010.03.001

Kaufman, A., Baron, A., & Kopp, R. E. (1966). Some effects of instructions on human operant behavior. *Psychonomic Monograph Supplements, 1,* 243–250.

Keng, S., Smoski, M. J., & Robins, C. J. (2011). Effects of mindfulness on psychological health: A review of empirical studies. *Clinical Psychology Review, 31,* 1041–1056. doi:10.1016/j.cpr.2011.04.006

LeFrancois, J. R., Chase, P. N., & Joyce, J. H. (1988). The effects of a variety of instructions on human fixed-interval performance. *Journal of the Experimental Analysis of Behavior, 49,* 383–393. doi:10.1901/jeab.1988.49-383

Levin, M. E., Hildebrandt, M. J., Lillis, J., & Hayes, S. C. (2012). The impact of treatment components suggested by the psychological flexibility model: A meta-analysis of laboratory-based component studies. *Behavior Therapy, 43,* 741–756. doi:10.1016/j.beth.2012.05.003

Linehan, M. M. (1993). *Cognitive behavioral therapy of borderline personality disorder.* New York, NY: Guilford Press.

Lipkens, G., Hayes, S. C., & Hayes, L. J. (1993). Longitudinal study of derived stimulus relations in an infant. *Journal of Experimental Child Psychology, 56*, 201–239.

Luciano, C., Gomez-Becerra, I., & Rodriguez-Valverde, M. (2007). The role of multiple-exemplar training and naming in establishing derived equivalence in an infant. *Journal of Experimental Analysis of Behavior, 87*, 349–365. doi:10.1901/jeab.2007.08-06

McCracken, L. M., & Yang, S. Y. (2006). The role of values in a contextual cognitive-behavioral approach to chronic pain. *Pain, 123*, 137–145. Retrieved from www.researchgate.net/publication/232481985_A_Contextual_Cognitive-Behavioral_Analysis_of_Rehabilitation_Workers'_Health_and_Well-Being_Influences_of_Acceptance_Mindfulness_and_Values-Based_Action

McHugh, L., & Stewart, I. (2012). *The self and perspective taking: Contributions and applications from modern behavioral science.* Oakland, CA: New Harbinger Publications. Retrieved from www.merriam-webster.com/dictionary/operate (n.d.).

McHugh, L., Barnes-Holmes, Y., & Barnes-Holmes, D. (2009). Understanding and training perspective-taking as relational responding. In R. Rehfeldt., & Y. Barnes-Holmes (Eds.), *Derived relational responding: Applications for learners with autism and other developmental disabilities* (pp. 281–300). Oakland, CA: New Harbinger.

Michelson, S. E., Lee, J. K., Orsillo, S. M., & Roemer, L. (2008, November). The relationship between values in symptom severity, experiential avoidance, and quality of life in generalized anxiety disorder. Poster session presented at the annual meeting of the Association for Behavioral and Cognitive Therapies, Orlando, FL.

Pfeiffer, J. H., Matsen, C. L., Borofsky, L. A., Dapretto, M., Fuligni, A. J., & Lieberman, M. D. (2009). Neural correlates of direct and reflected self-appraisals in adolescents and adults: When social perspective-taking informs self-perception. *Child Development, 80*, 1016–1038. doi:10.1111/j.1467-8624.2009.01314.x

Plumb, J. C., & Hayes, S. C. (2008). *An examination of personal values in depressed and non-depressed individuals.* (Unpublished master's thesis). University of Nevada, Reno, NV.

Plumb, J. C., Stewart, I., Dahl, J., & Lundgren, T. (2009). In search of meaning: Values in modern clinical behavior analysis. *The Behavior Analyst, 32*, 85–103.

Ramnero, J., & Torneke, N. (2011). *ABCs of human behavior: Behavioral principles for the practicing clinican.* Oakland, CA: New Harbinger & Reno, NV: Context Press.

Roche, B., & Barnes, D. (1997). A transformation of respondently conditioned stimulus function in accordance with arbitrarily applicable relations. *Journal of the Experimental Analysis of Behavior, 67*, 275–300. doi:10.1901/jeab.1997.67-275

Rosenfarb, I. S., Newland, M. C., Brannon, S. E., & Howey, D. S. (1992). Effects of self-generated rules on the development of schedule-controlled behavior. *Journal of the Experimental Analysis of Behavior, 58*, 107–121. doi:10.1901/jeab.1992.58-107

Ruiz, F. J. (2010). A review of acceptance and commitment therapy (ACT) empirical evidence: Correlational, experimental psychopathology, component and outcome studies. *International Journal of Psychology and Psychological Therapy, 10*, 125–162. Retrieved from www.ijpsy.com/volumen10/num1/256/a-review-of-acceptance-and-commitment-therapy-EN.pdf

Segal, Z. V., Williams, J. M. G., & Teasdale, J. D. (2001). *Mindfulness-based cognitive therapy for depression: A new approach to preventing relapse.* New York, NY: Guilford Press.

Steele, D. L., & Hayes, S. C. (1991). Stimulus equivalence and arbitrarily applicable relational responding. *Journal of the Experimental Analysis of Behavior, 56*, 519–555. doi:10.1901/jeab.1991.56-519

Törneke, N. (2010). *Learning RFT: An introduction to relational frame theory and its clinical application.* Oakland, CA: New Harbinger.

Törneke, N., Luciano, C., & Valdivia Salas, S. (2008). Rule-governed behavior and psychological problems. *International Journal of Psychology and Psychological Therapy, 8,* 141–156. Retrieved from www.ijpsy.com/volumen8/num2/191/rule-governed-behavior-and-psychological-EN.pdf

Vilardaga, R., & Hayes, S. C. (2010). Acceptance and commitment therapy and the therapeutic relationship stance. *European Psychotherapy, 9,* 117–140. Retrieved from http://cbsopenlab.com/wp-content/uploads/2012/12/2009-Vilardaga-et-al-ACT-and-the-therapeutic-relationship.pdf

Vowles, K. E., McCracken, L. M. (2008). Acceptance and values-based action in chronic pain: A study of treatment effectiveness and process. *Journal of Consulting and Clinical Psychology, 76,* 397–407. doi:10.1037/0022-006X.76.3.397

Wilson, K. G., & DuFrene, T. (2009). *Mindfulness for two: An acceptance and commitment therapy approach to mindfulness in psychotherapy.* Oakland, CA: New Harbinger.

Wilson, K. G., & Sandoz, E. K. (2008). Mindfulness, values, and therapeutic relationships in acceptance and commitment therapy. In S. F. Hick, & T. Bein (Eds.), *Mindfulness and the therapeutic relationship* (pp. 89–106). New York, NY: Guilford Press.

Wulfert, E., Greenway, D. E., Farkas, P., Hayes, S. C., & Dougher, M. J. (1994). Correlation between a personality test for rigidity and rule-governed insensitivity to operant contingencies. *Journal of Applied Behavior Analysis, 27,* 659–671. doi:10.1901/jaba.1994.27-659

3   The Person of the Professor

Applications of Mindfulness and Acceptance for Faculty Well-Being and Vitality

LeeAnn Cardaciotto and
Jennifer Block-Lerner

Introduction

Programs on college and university campuses have been developed to support students academically, socially, and psychologically (see Chapter 1, this volume). However, little attention has been given to the well-being of the faculty who teach, advise, and otherwise mentor them. Faculty experience stressors, all of which may not be in their control, and like students, they balance multiple roles and responsibilities. In addition to the degree of stress related to job demands and institutional factors (e.g., resources, enrollment pressures, and amount and types of communication from administrators), challenges at different stages of one's career have the potential to contribute to faculty job satisfaction, which is critical to the strength of higher education institutions. Therefore, finding ways of fostering academics' well-being and vitality is important. Although mindfulness- and acceptance-based programs have been implemented with a number of populations to reduce stress and improve quality of life, their potential has not been examined with faculty. This chapter explores this possibility, examining the roles, responsibilities, and challenges of being a faculty member in higher education; the psychological impact of the demands of the position; and how mindfulness- and acceptance-based approaches could be applied to foster well-being and vitality with this impactful population.

Being a Member of the Academy

A faculty member's life is often characterized by a "three-legged stool" consisting of teaching, scholarly activities, and service (e.g., Seldin & Miller, 2009). The balance of these activities may differ based on the nature of one's higher education institution and personal skills and preferences, but for full-time faculty members, there is an expectation that one will engage in all three for successful promotion through one's career. And although the focus tends to be on three legs, a centipede may be a better representation of faculty duties. Faculty also recruit and mentor students and colleagues, engage in administrative work, obtain funding for research and special projects, give guest presentations, participate in professional organizations, plan and convene conferences and workshops, provide clinical services, and engage in many other assorted tasks. National surveys indicate that faculty members work on average over 50 hours per week (US Department of Education, 2013).

While some academic duties, such as teaching, advising, and committee meetings have fixed hours that fall into the typical workday, other tasks, such as class preparation, scholarship, and responding to email have to be fit in whenever possible, leading to the demands feeling limitless (Jacobs & Winslow, 2004). These feelings likely are compounded by the increasing role of technology (e.g., email communication; online learning management systems) that essentially create a 24 hour/7 day per week position.

Faculty Burnout and Contributing Situational Stressors

Managing all of the roles, responsibilities, and demands of the job has been associated with burnout (e.g., Lackritz, 2004). Burnout is defined as "a prolonged response to chronic emotional and interpersonal stressors on the job, and is defined by the three dimensions of exhaustion, cynicism, and inefficacy" (Maslach, Schaufeli, & Leiter, 2001, p. 397). According to Maslach and colleagues, feelings of emotional exhaustion represent the individual stress component, whereby one feels overextended and personal resources feel drained. This prompts an individual to distance themself from their work; in higher education, this could be exhibited through less investment in teaching, disengagement from the larger community, or simply "going through the motions." Cynicism (also referred to as depersonalization) represents the interpersonal context dimension of burnout, and involves psychologically distancing oneself from others, such as through indifference. This could interfere with building and maintaining collaborative relationships with students, colleagues, and administrators. The last component, reduced efficacy or personal accomplishment, represents the self-evaluation component of burnout, and is associated with negative self-appraisal. Faculty who feel they are not accomplishing as much as they would like might believe they are incompetent and/or doubt themselves professionally. Feelings of burnout can have negative consequences, as they have been associated with job withdrawal (e.g., absenteeism, intention to leave), lower productivity, reduced commitment to the job or organization, and conflict with colleagues (Maslach et al., 2001).

In academia, the stressors that contribute to faculty burnout seem to stem from two sources. The first is workplace or job stress, which has increased over time in the academic sector (Khalil, Omar, & Dawood, 2014). Stressors that can contribute to this response include: time and resource constraints; long working hours with a rushed work pace and heavy workload; low pay; ineffective communication, poor work relationships, conflict with colleagues or administrators, and/or inadequate support; role ambiguity and overload; lack of recognition and respect; dealing with difficult students; promotion demands, including striving for publication and favorable student evaluations; teaching high numbers of students; job insecurity or lack of job control; and keeping up with technological advances (Khalil et al., 2014). Further, there are stressors specific to service-oriented professions (including education) such as acting as both a caretaker and a disciplinarian and teaching students with a wide range of needs (Sangganjanavanich & Balkin, 2013).

The second source of stress that may contribute to burnout is life balance, such as challenges finding time and energy for partners, children, exercise, hobbies, friends, and civic activities (Sorcinelli & Billings, 1993). Several authors (e.g., Austin & Pilat, 1990; Philipsen & Bostic, 2010) have written about this imbalance and how the demands of scholarly activities and pressures of tenure and promotion directly impact personal needs and self-care. This especially is an issue for early career faculty (and is described below in more detail).

The stressors that contribute to burnout can negatively impact all faculty. However, understanding the goals and demands at different career stages can help identify faculty's unique challenges and potential places for intervention.

Early Career

Early career faculty, also referred to as "junior faculty" or "new faculty," are typically defined as those within the first seven years of appointment to a faculty position or those who have not yet received tenure (Austin, Sorcinelli, & McDaniels, 2007). Two decades of research on these faculty confirm that the strongest impact on early career satisfaction has not changed: it is intrinsically driven. A multi-institutional study by Rice, Sorcinelli, and Austin (2000) examined the rewards and challenges facing early career faculty. They found that those new to academia report high levels of satisfaction related to the relative autonomy and flexibility of schedule and their ability to frame their own agendas; the opportunities for intellectual growth, discovery, and cognitive stimulation; the personal contact with students; and most simply their love of learning. New faculty even positively comment on the role of service in their career, specifically that it provides valuable insight and an outlet for action not always available in teaching or research (Sorcinelli & Billings, 1993).

However, research suggests that over time, what some hope and want for their work life does not match their actual experience. A study by Sorcinelli and Billings (1993) that used ethnographic and surveying methods to examine untenured faculty at the University of Massachusetts (Amherst) found that although new faculty morale was high from the second year through tenure and satisfaction remained in some areas (e.g., sense of accomplishment; being able to have a positive impact on others), the intrinsic rewards became less strong, and other areas of satisfaction took a downward turn (e.g., opportunities for continued learning). Work stress eroded job satisfaction (two-thirds of the sample reported their jobs to be "very stressful"); this trend has been supported by others (e.g., Olsen, 1993).

The challenges that contribute to early career dissatisfaction can be placed in one of three categories: performance expectations (particularly tenure), collegiality and community, and balancing professional and personal roles (Austin et al., 2007). Consistent with their high levels of motivation, new faculty tend to set high standards for themselves, feeling the responsibility of being prepared for class and motivating their students to learn (Sorcinelli & Billings, 1993). This occurs within the context of adjusting to the academic environment and learning new roles. Given multiple course preparations and the immediacy of course and administrative work, new faculty tend to spend more time on teaching than on scholarship (Sorcinelli & Billings, 1993). They also worry about vague and unclear expectations for performance (Rice et al., 2000), especially given that the reward structure of the tenure and promotion process typically gives more weight to research. Having unrealistic expectations and focusing on exceeding them can prevent faculty from effectively coping with the demands and practicing self-care.

Concerning the second issue faced by early career faculty, they enter their careers with a vision of a collegial culture, wanting support and mentorship from colleagues, a community where collaboration is respected and encouraged, and friendships across department lines (Austin et al., 2007; Sorcinelli & Billings, 1993). Faculty members' relationships with colleagues has been cited as a key predictor of satisfaction (Lacy & Sheehan, 1997). However, some early career faculty report feeling isolated, disconnected, and lonely, which can stem from a lack of time for informal or formal interactions, lack of mentoring and networking opportunities (particularly with senior colleagues), and the opportunity to work remotely (Austin et al., 2007).

The larger context of the new faculty member's life outside of his/her office is the third challenge. As noted earlier, research suggests balancing professional and personal lives is a challenge for all faculty. However, it appears to be even more difficult for new faculty who also are struggling with time management of their work-related responsibilities (e.g., Solem & Foote, 2006). Further, stressors from work and one's personal life can mutually impact each other. On the one hand, junior faculty report "negative spillover" of their work into personal time (Sorcinelli & Near, 1989). On the other, significant family responsibilities characteristic of faculty at this stage of their career (e.g., childbirth, raising young children) may disrupt the tenure timeline or take faculty away from opportunities to engage with colleagues on campus.

Mid-Career

The literature refers to faculty who have received tenure and who are expected to have a number of work years ahead as "mid-career." Mid-career is often a time of reassessment and reflection, perhaps when the questions, "What will I be doing for the rest of my career?" or "What do I want to be known for?" are raised. During this stage, following an initial period of professional growth and development, some faculty reach a career plateau, whereas others remain active until the end of their careers, using temporary plateaus as jumping off points for new, stimulating career goals (Baldwin, 1990). Why might some plateau and maintain the status quo? With only a small number of opportunities for promotion, external motivators decrease or disappear, and so there is an absence of professional aspirations or reward. Mid-career faculty can find themselves teaching the same courses for years, engaging in research pursuits that are no longer interesting, and/or experiencing difficulty staying current in their field (Austin, 2011).

Whether they feel tired, stagnant, stuck, or disengaged, faculty at this stage (and later) can become dissatisfied and disengage from decision-making, collaboration, and socialization (Huston, Norman, & Ambrose, 2007), all of which can negatively impact interactions with students and colleagues. Therefore, maintaining vitality is important not only for the faculty member's well-being, but for that of the institution.

Vitality, a term used widely but imprecisely, has been defined as "the optimal capability of the individual to make significant and meaningful contributions to their career goals and the institution's missions" (Viggiano & Strobel, 2009, p. 77). Baldwin (1990) described the "vital professor" as someone who is

> curious and intellectually engaged . . . . Perhaps most significant, vital professors grow personally and professionally throughout their academic career, continually pursuing expanded interests and acquiring new skills and knowledge. Adjectives that would apply to vital professors include: enthusiastic, caring, dedicated, vigorous, creative, flexible, risk-taking, and regenerative . . . .Vital professors may be campus leaders, inspiring teachers, prolific scholars, excellent advisors, but they do not necessarily perform all faculty roles with equal zest or skill. (p. 180)

Qualitative research studies (e.g., Baldwin, 1990) suggest that vital professors have more complex and multidimensional careers than their colleagues with access to more sources of professional stimulation and achievement. They also have more fluid careers that involve risk-taking, role change, and professional growth options. They are sensitive to the benefits and challenges of their environments. Further, they articulate specific professional goals and are less likely to get derailed by challenge or failure (Strage, Nelson, & Meyers, 2008).

Fostering Faculty Well-Being and Authentic Renewal

Although there are numerous articles and blogs that detail the joys of academia, these joys sit alongside stress and struggle. Mindfulness- and acceptance-based approaches have been applied with many populations, including college students at various levels and in many contexts (see Part III), to decrease suffering and bolster quality of life. However, to date, these approaches have not been examined in the context of faculty well-being. Examining other applications in related areas may provide illustrations of how such approaches could be utilized for faculty and evidence their potential success.

Acceptance and Commitment Therapy in the Workplace

As noted in other chapters in this volume, acceptance and commitment therapy (ACT; Hayes, Strosahl, & Wilson, 1999) is an empirically-based psychological intervention rooted in functional contextualism and based on relational frame theory (RFT; see Chapter 2 of this volume). ACT aims to foster contact with one's present-moment experience, promote willingness to experience whatever arises in each moment, and clarify one's values and action in accordance with them. Together, these processes allow an individual to have psychological flexibility (PF), enabling choices to be made that are in line with what is important to the individual and brings meaning. It fosters one's ability to prevent long-term desired qualities of life from taking a backseat to more immediate goals of being right, looking good, feeling good, and avoiding psychological pain (Hayes, Luoma, Bond, Masuda, & Lillis, 2006).

Although ACT was initially developed as a psychological intervention, since then, it has evolved to include applications outside of the therapy context, including in the workplace, which has been called acceptance and commitment training ("ACTraining;" Moran, 2010). ACT workshops encourage participants' willingness to experience undesirable internal experiences (e.g., anxiety, stress, burnout-related thoughts) that result from unalterable working demands in order to facilitate the pursuit of valued behavioral goals. Rather than altering the form or frequency of negative private events (e.g., encouraging positive thinking or stress-reduction techniques), ACT aims to alter the psychological context within which the thoughts and emotions occur (e.g., experiencing thoughts for what they are versus truths). Workshop components are based on the six core interactive processes of ACT (acceptance, defusion, contact with the present moment, self-as-context, values, and commitment to values-based action; Hayes et al., 1999). The training involves a wide range of experiential exercises and techniques designed to help participants develop these skills and promote PF.

The first study to evaluate the efficacy of ACT in the workplace for stress management was conducted by Bond and Bunce (2000). Results showed that it significantly improved employees' general mental health, depressive symptomatology, and innovation potential, with psychological acceptance as a mediator. Since then, several studies have been published on ACT in the context of stress, burnout, and productivity at work (e.g., Bond, Flaxman, & Bunce, 2008; Flaxman & Bond, 2010; Hayes et al., 2004), and other workplace topics have been investigated, including adopting best practices (e.g., Varra, Hayes, Roget, & Fisher, 2008), leadership (Moran, 2010) and self-efficacy (Biglan, Layton, Jones, Hankins, & Rusby, 2013). Taken together, these studies suggest that workplace ACT interventions make positive contributions to employees' well-being and increase their willingness to perform effectively.

ACT workplace workshops foster greater PF, increasing workers' sensitivity to performance-related contingencies of reinforcement in their work environment, because they are not expending attentional resources trying to control or avoid their internal experiences (Bond, Flaxman, van Veldhoven, & Biron, 2010). In other words, PF increases the opportunity to come into contact with what matters at work (e.g., performing at one's best; producing quality work products; maintaining work relationships), allowing workers to do their jobs more effectively and have better mental health (because they are engaging in behaviors that are meaningful). In addition, workers with more PF may be better at noticing the degree to which they have control in a given situation and seizing their capacity to exert influence, ultimately enhancing performance, mental health, and the ability to learn (Bond, Hayes, & Barnes-Holmes, 2006).

ACT workplace workshops also help participants to clarify their values, defined as "chosen qualities of purposive action that can never be obtained as an object but can be instantiated moment by moment" (Hayes et al., 2006, p. 8). In the absence of connection with values, behaviors can be dominated by being right or looking good in the eyes of others, seeking other reinforcers, or by avoidance, contributing to rigid and inflexible behavior that might not be best in the long run. In the midst of high-stress work demands, understanding and engaging in action consistent with one's values has been found to promote job satisfaction. For example, even though 76% of child welfare workers scored in the moderate to high range of emotional exhaustion (one component of burnout), 90% self-reported at least moderate levels of job satisfaction (Stalker, Mandell, Frensch, Harvey, & Wright, 2007). This finding might be explained by the importance of having a sense of mission or commitment, particularly in the service of others (Stalker et al., 2007).

Mindfulness for Teachers

A second body of research that could inform the application of mindfulness- and acceptance-based approaches with faculty relates to teachers, given the overlap in responsibilities and the fact that teachers also experience significant levels of stress (Travers, 2001). Similar to faculty in higher education, teachers' academic preparation does not include tools for fostering self-awareness and managing psychological distress that results from the rigor and demands of their work, and there are few resources available to them to alleviate it. To help with this, studies have begun investigating the application of mindfulness with this population.

One of the most frequently cited definitions of mindfulness is by Kabat-Zinn (1994): "paying attention in a particular way: on purpose, in the present-moment, and non-judgmentally" (p. 4). Most conceptualizations of mindfulness include two components: awareness (i.e., the continuous observation of one's here-and-now experiences) and acceptance (i.e., coming into contact with those experiences with willingness, openness, and/or curiosity). The practice of mindfulness can take place informally during daily activities or formally through meditation. Regularly practicing mindfulness allows one to notice experiences as events that unfold with each moment (versus as what the mind says they are), helping to break the habitual pattern of believing thoughts as if they were their own entities and reacting (versus responding with intention) to experience. In other words, despite how automatic internal experiences are, they do not have to be so influential (Moran, 2010). Dozens of therapies exist that utilize or integrate mindfulness in some way, and review studies (e.g., Keng, Smoski, & Robins, 2011) document the benefits of mindfulness on psychological health.

Experiential learning programs have been created to foster teachers' development of mindfulness. For example, the Cultivating Awareness and Resilience in

Education (CARE; www.garrisoninstitute.org) program includes mindfulness practices to help pre-K–12 teachers be more aware, present, and engaged, and preliminary results illustrate improvement in mindfulness, well-being, and the ability to maintain supportive relationships with students (Jennings, Snowberg, Coccia, & Greenberg, 2011). Results from four focus groups with teachers who participated in CARE suggested that participants developed greater self-awareness, including recognizing the need for self-care, and showed improvements in being less emotionally reactive, although they were less likely to articulate improvements in teaching efficacy (Schussler, Jennings, Sharp, & Frank, 2015). The Mindfulness-Based Wellness Education (MBWE; Soloway, Poulin, & Mackenzie, 2011) program was designed as a 9-week elective course for teachers-in-training. The curriculum examines wellness and teaching strategies through the lens of mindfulness. After the course, participants reported increases in mindfulness, life satisfaction, and teaching self-efficacy (Poulin, Mackenzie, Soloway, & Karayolas, 2008).

In addition to these larger programs, other studies have examined mindfulness training for teachers. For example, Franco, Mañas, Cangas, Moreno, and Gallego (2010) found that "Flow Meditation," a 10-week mindfulness training program consisting of body-scan meditations, mindful breathing, and metaphors/exercises corresponding to different topics, was effective in reducing psychological distress in 68 secondary school teachers in Spain. Roeser et al. (2013) conducted a randomized, wait-list control field trial of an 8-week, 11-session program that met for a total of 36 hours. The program included a variety of approaches to foster mindfulness and self-compassion, and results showed that 87% of teachers completed the program and evidenced greater mindfulness, focused attention, working memory capacity, occupational self-compassion, and reduced occupational stress and burnout.

Programming for Faculty Through Faculty Development

One means to apply mindfulness- and acceptance-based approaches to foster faculty well-being is through university-wide faculty development programming. Current faculty development activities often focus on the changing nature of higher education and pedagogical methods related to topics such as instructional technology, adult learners, and underprepared students (McKee & Tew, 2013). Instead of solely focusing on pedagogical development, faculty development programming could include topics related to faculty well-being and vitality at each phase of the academic career, especially since those who feel stressed or burned-out may be less likely to be innovative or give their best efforts in the classroom or to their scholarship.

As previously noted, for early career faculty, work stress has the potential of eroding job satisfaction over time, and faculty academic preparation does not include tools for fostering self-awareness and managing psychological distress. Occupational health psychologists advocate the reduction of workers' exposure to stress; however, some sources of stress are not completely avoidable (e.g., deadlines), and personal life stressors may result in increased feelings of stress at work (Bond et al., 2010). Therefore, it is unlikely that stress can be eliminated entirely. Mindfulness training can help faculty notice internal experiences of stress without attempts (e.g., procrastination, overeating, substance use) to avoid them. Being more sensitive to the present-moment also may help faculty recognize when self-care is needed. Further, doing something worthwhile, such as engaging in activities that lead to tenure and promotion, will likely create uncomfortable feelings at times; mindfulness- and acceptance-based exercises would teach faculty how to actively feel natural feelings without defending against or avoiding them, fostering opportunities for effective action versus waiting to feel less anxious or more assured and confident (Moran, 2015).

For mid-career faculty, the literature provides evidence that self-renewal and vitality are fostered through the development of practical goals and plans by which to achieve them, providing a sense of purpose and meaning (Strage & Merdinger, 2014). From an ACT framework, these goals would be developed in the context of the faculty member's values, which may need ongoing clarification, especially if s/he is entering a different career phase. Values clarification would help faculty to engage in projects and service activities that have meaning (refer to Chapter 5, this volume), especially since there may not be the same degree of external reward. Further, fostering of committed action is important, as those faculty who reported being engaged were less likely to be discouraged by challenge or failure (Strage et al., 2008). Also, having a sense of mission and commitment appears to mediate feelings of exhaustion and job satisfaction (Stalker et al., 2007).

Although structures are in place in colleges and universities to implement faculty development programs related to fostering faculty well-being and vitality, barriers and challenges likely would exist. For example, workshops that target well-being may not be a priority for administrators or well-received by faculty. To address this issue in the workplace context, Flaxman and Bond (2010) explained how they marketed ACT workshops to organizations, using empirical outcomes that demonstrate relationships between PF and important organizational outcomes, and to individual participants, using in-house contacts to advertise the workshops. Further, they considered participant-specific factors in the planning process, which would also be relevant in higher education: participants' psychological functioning (50% of their participants reported clinical levels of distress); attrition due to work scheduling, absenteeism, turnover, vacations, and forgetting (reminders reduced attrition by 20%); and confidentiality and privacy, which could impact engagement. Last, the authors highlighted the need for the ACT workshops to be part of a larger effort by the organization to manage workplace stress; in higher education, the workshops could be part of both employee well-being and faculty development programs.

Concerning barriers and challenges related to faculty mindfulness training, one of the challenges facing research on K–12 teacher mindfulness programs (and perhaps mindfulness programs in general) is the absence of a clearly articulated mechanism of change. This would help to identify aspects of mindfulness training such as the core interventions or practices, the amount of practice necessary, expected short- and long-term outcomes, and scope of programming (e.g., attention training versus promotion of emotional well-being). Other barriers include determining who on campus would be qualified to teach mindfulness or if an external teacher should be appointed, as well as the logistics for structuring the training (length, duration, frequency) to maximize participation and prevent attrition. Consultation with organizations or firms specializing in workplace mindfulness training may be warranted, since workplace programs have been adapted to be more conducive to the environment (e.g., shorter classes, shorter daily practice recommendations, courses ranging in length, online programming) without painting the picture of a "quick fix" (Hyland, Lee, & Mills, 2015).

The Mindful Educator

This chapter has explored the challenges and struggles of working in the professoriate and the application of mindfulness- and acceptance-based approaches to address these struggles and promote faculty well-being and vitality. However, as faculty who teach in practice-oriented programs at institutions that prioritize teaching and learning, we would be remiss if we did not characterize a "mindful educator." A mindful educator is a mindful *person*, engaging continual practice in cultivating a mindfulness-based approach to teaching, research, service, and living as a whole (O'Haver-Day & McNelis, 2012). S/he is aware of self (e.g., feelings of stress; pulls to check email), others (e.g., the learner's level of experience; a colleague's downtrodden expression), and context (e.g., the end of the semester; college/university culture). This awareness gives space for choice and intentional responding rather than immediate, habitual reaction.

For us in the classroom, this level of awareness helps to intentionally foster a student-centered learning environment, allowing us to be sensitive to nuances, connect with and nourish our students' curiosities, and foster their growth. As (aspiring) mindful educators, we aim to create a physical, mental, and emotional space for exchange and engagement without adding unnecessary authority. We find circular or U-shaped seating arrangements, spending time with students before and after class, and seeing value in students' participation (no matter how on- or off-target it might be) helps to foster this space. As much as possible, we ask reflective questions and engage in mindful inquiry to foster curiosity and model "not-knowing;" this is contrasted with Socratic questions, whereby the questioner often already holds the answer. The empathy and compassion that comes from mindfulness practice enables us to have patience for imperfection (both our own and that of our students). Being mindful also helps us to slow down our pace and experience the joys of teaching and seeing students come into their own. And consistent with an ACT framework, practicing mindfulness is in the service of our values, in which our students are paramount to our work. This sentiment is echoed in other methods of "teaching" such as mentorship and supervision (see Chapter 5, this volume).

When we teach, we bring our full self (physical, intellectual, emotional, all influenced by our professional and personal lives) into the classroom, and this is the place from which we teach. As a result, we may have moments of feeling vulnerable, insecure, or exhausted (especially during particular chapters of our personal/family lives). However, these feelings can be noticed with curiosity, unfold just as all other experiences do, and even be "grist for the mill," helping us better empathize and have compassion for when our students feel the same way. We also identify with Kahane's (2011) journey in becoming a mindful educator when he wrote:

> My teaching, especially starting out, tended to be about covering up what I didn't know, about coming across as accomplished, about performing seamless knowledge in order to stave off the ever-present spectre of humiliation. I taught from a deep-seated lack . . . The alternative that I experience more often now is a pedagogy of plenty. My anxiety as a teacher is not gone . . . But I am more able to work with it: to embrace groundlessness and uncertainty as the heart of learning. (p. 17)

Ironically, teaching from a place of curiosity and compassion has enabled us to give up the struggle of "having to know" and covering inadequacies with content. Also, as Kahane notes, "clinging to competence can make us boring" (p. 20).

Conclusion

The literature on implementing mindfulness- and acceptance-based approaches with faculty members on college and university campuses is not even in its infancy, and thus is an area for future exploration. The studies and models reviewed in this chapter on the stresses of different stages of academic careers, as well as the value of mindfulness- and acceptance-based interventions with related populations, suggests that they hold great promise for the well-being of faculty members. Further, fostering well-being in this critical population has significant implications for student learning, the health and vitality of the larger institution and, even more broadly, the state of higher education.

References

Austin, A. E. (2011). Supporting faculty members across their careers. In K. J. Gillespie, D. L. Robertson, & Associates (Eds.), *A guide to faculty development* (pp. 363–378). San Francisco, CA: John Wiley & Sons.

Austin, A. E., & Pilat, M. (1990). Tension, stress, and the tapestry of faculty lives. *Academe, 76*, 38–42. doi:10.2307/40249663

Austin, A. E., Sorcinelli, M. D., & McDaniels, M. (2007). Understanding new faculty: Background, aspirations, challenges, and growth. In R. P. Perry, & J. C. Smart (Eds.), *The scholarship of teaching and learning in higher education: An evidence-based perspective* (pp. 39–89). Dordrecht, the Netherlands: Springer.

Baldwin, R. G. (1990). Faculty vitality beyond the research university: Extending a contextual concept. *The Journal of Higher Education, 61*, 160–180. doi:10.2307/1981960

Biglan, A., Layton, G., Jones, L. B., Hankins, M., & Rusby, J. C. (2013). The value of workshops on psychological flexibility for early childhood special education staff. *Topics in Early Childhood Special Education, 32*, 196–210. doi:10.1177/0271121411425191

Bond, F. W., & Bunce, D. (2000). Mediators of change in emotion-focused and problem-focused worksite stress management interventions. *Journal of Occupational Health Psychology, 5*, 156–163. doi:10.1037/1076-8998.5.1.156

Bond, F. W., Flaxman, P. E., & Bunce, D. (2008). The influence of psychological flexibility on work redesign: Mediated moderation of a work reorganization intervention. *Journal of Applied Psychology, 93*, 645–654. doi:10.1037/0021-9010.93.3.645

Bond, F. W., Flaxman, P. E., van Veldhoven, M. J. P. M., & Biron, M. (2010). The impact of psychological flexibility and acceptance and commitment therapy (ACT) on health and productivity at work. *Contemporary Occupational Health Psychology: Global Perspectives on Research and Practice, 1*, 296–313. doi:10.1002/9780470661550

Bond, F. W., Hayes, S. C., & Barnes-Holmes, D. (2006). Psychological flexibility, ACT, and organizational behavior. *Journal of Organizational Behavior Management, 26*, 25–54. doi:10.1300/J075v26n01_02

Flaxman, P., & Bond, F. W. (2010). A randomized worksite comparison of acceptance and commitment therapy and stress inoculation training. *Behavior Research and Therapy, 48*, 816–820. doi:10.1016/j.brat.2010.05.004

Franco, C., Mañas, I., Cangas, A. J., Moreno, E., & Gallego, J. (2010). Reducing teachers' psychological distress through a mindfulness training program. *The Spanish Journal of Psychology, 13*, 655–666. doi:10.1017/S1138741600002328

Hayes, S. C., Bissett, R. T., Roget, N., Padilla, M., Kohlenberg, B. S., Fisher, G., Masuda, A., . . . Niccolls, R. (2004). The impact of acceptance and commitment training on stigmatizing attitudes and professional burnout of substance abuse counsellors. *Behavior Therapy, 35*, 821–835. doi:10.1016/S0005-7894(04)80022-4

Hayes, S. C., Luoma, J., Bond, F., Masuda, A., & Lillis, J. (2006). Acceptance and Commitment Therapy: Model, processes, and outcomes. *Behavior Research and Therapy, 44*, 1–25. doi:10.1016/j.brat.2005.06.006

Hayes, S. C., Strosahl, K. D., & Wilson, K. G. (1999). *Acceptance and commitment therapy: An experiential approach to behavior change.* New York, NY: Guilford Press.

Huston, T. A., Norman, M., & Ambrose, S. A. (2007). Expanding the discussion of faculty vitality to include productive but disengaged senior faculty. *The Journal of Higher Education, 78*, 493–522. doi:10.1353/jhe.2007.0034

Hyland, P. K., Lee, R. A., & Mills, M. J. (2015). Mindfulness at work: A new approach to improving individual and organizational performance. *Industrial and Organizational Psychology*, Advance online publication. doi:10.1017/iop.2015.41

Jacobs, J. A., & Winslow, S. E. (2004). The academic life course, time pressures and gender inequality. *Community, Work, & Family, 7*, 143–161. doi:10.1080/1366880042000245443

Jennings, P. A., Snowberg, K. E., Coccia, M. A., & Greenberg, M. T. (2011). Improving classroom learning environments by cultivating awareness and resilience in education (CARE): Results of two pilot studies. *Journal of Classroom Interaction, 46*, 37–48. doi:10.1037/spq0000035

Kabat-Zinn, J. (1994). *Wherever you go, there you are: Mindfulness meditation in everyday life.* New York, NY: Hyperion.

Kahane, D. (2011). Mindfulness and presence in teaching and learning. In I. Hay (Ed.), *Inspiring academics: Learning with the world's great university teachers* (pp. 17–22). London: Open University Press.

Keng, S. L., Smoski, M. J., & Robins, C. J. (2011). Effects of mindfulness on psychological health: A review of empirical studies. *Clinical Psychology Review, 31*, 1041–1056. doi:10.1016/j.cpr.2011.04.006

Khalil, A. I., Omar, T. Y., & Dawood, E. S. (2014). Perceived work-related stressors and its relationship with the physiological and psychological well being of nursing faculty members. *Journal of Education and Practice, 5*, 64–75. Retrieved from www.iiste.org/Journals/index.php/JEP/article/view/18560

Lackritz, J. R. (2004). Exploring burnout among university faculty: Incidence, performance, and demographic issues. *Teaching and Teacher Education, 20*, 713–729. doi:10.1016/j.tate.2004.07.002

Lacy, F. J., & Sheehan, B. A. (1997). Job satisfaction among academic staff: An international perspective. *Higher Education, 34*, 305–322. doi:10.1023/A:1003019822147

Maslach, C., Schaufeli, W. B., & Leiter, M. P. (2001). Job burnout. *Annual Review of Psychology, 52*, 397–422. doi:10.1146/annurev.psych.52.1.397

McKee, C. W., & Tew, W. M. (2013). Setting the stage for teaching and learning in American higher education: Making the case for faculty development. *New Directions for Teaching and Learning, 2013*(133), 3–14. doi:10.1002/tl.20041

Moran, D. J. (2010). ACT for leadership: Using acceptance and commitment training to develop crisis-resilient change managers. *International Journal of Behavioral Consultation and Therapy, 6*, 341–355. doi:10.1037/h0100915

Moran, D. J. (2015). Acceptance and commitment training in the workplace. *Current Opinion in Psychology, 2*, 26–31. doi:10.1016/j.copsyc.2014.12.031

O'Haver-Day, P., & McNelis, A. (2012). The mindful educator. In G. Sherwood, & S. Horton-Deutsch (Eds.), *Reflective Practice: Transforming education and improving outcomes* (pp. 63–77). Indianapolis: Sigma Theta Tau International.

Olsen, D. (1993). Work satisfaction and stress in the first and third year of academic appointment. *The Journal of Higher Education, 64*, 453–471. doi:10.2307/2960052

Philipsen, M. I., & Bostic, T. B. (2010). *Helping faculty find work–life balance: The path toward family-friendly institutions.* San Francisco, CA: Jossey-Bass.

Poulin, P. A., Mackenzie, C. S., Soloway, G., & Karayolas, E. (2008). Mindfulness training as an evidence-based approach to reducing stress and promoting well-being among human services professionals. *International Journal of Health Promotion and Education, 46*, 35–43. doi:10.1080/14635240.2008.10708132

Rice, R. E., Sorcinelli, M. D., & Austin, A. E. (2000). *Heeding new voices: Academic careers for a new generation.* Washington, D.C.: American Association for Higher Education.

Roeser, R. W., Schonert-Reichl, K. A., Jha, A., Cullen, M., Wallace, L., Wilensky, R., . . . Harrison, J. (2013). Mindfulness training and reductions in teacher stress and burnout: Results from two randomized, waitlist-control field trials. *Journal of Educational Psychology, 105*, 787–806. doi:10.1037/a0032093

Sangganjanavanich, V. F., & Balkin, R. S. (2013). Burnout and job satisfaction among counselor educators. *The Journal of Humanistic Counseling, 52*, 67–79. doi:10.1002/j.2161-1939.2013.00033.x

Schussler, D. L., Jennings, P. A., Sharp, J. E., & Frank, J. L. (2015). Improving teacher awareness and well-being through CARE: A qualitative analysis of the underlying mechanisms. *Mindfulness*, Advance online publication.doi:10.1007/s12671-015-0422-7

Seldin, P., & Miller, J. E. (2009). *The academic portfolio: A practical guide to documenting teaching, research, and service.* San Francisco, CA: Jossey-Bass.

Solem, M. N., & Foote, K. E. (2006). Concerns, attitudes, and abilities of early-career geography faculty. *Journal of Geography in Higher Education, 30*, 199–234. doi:10.1080/03098260600717299

Soloway, G. B., Poulin, A., & Mackenzie, C. S. (2011). Preparing new teachers for the full catastrophe of the 21st century classroom: Integrating mindfulness training into initial teacher education. In A. Cohan, & A. Honigsfeld (Eds.), *Breaking the mold of pre-service and in-service teacher education* (pp. 221–227). Lanham: R and L Education.

Sorcinelli, M. D., & Billings, D. A. (1993, April). *The career development of pretenure faculty: An institutional study.* Paper presented at the Annual Meeting of the American Education Research Association, Atlanta, Georgia. Retrieved from http://eric.ed.gov/?id=ED359875

Sorcinelli, M. D., & Near, J. P. (1989). Relations between work and life away from work among university faculty. *The Journal of Higher Education, 60,* 59–81. doi:10.2307/1982111

Stalker, C., Mandell, D., Frensch, K., Harvey, C., & Wright, M. (2007). Child welfare workers who are exhausted yet satisfied with their jobs: How do they do it? *Child & Family Social Work, 12,* 182–191. doi:10.1111/j.1365-2206.2006.00472.x

Strage, A., & Merdinger, J. (2014). Professional growth and renewal for mid-career faculty. *Journal of Faculty Development, 28*(3), 41–50. Retrieved from www.ingentaconnect.com/content/nfp/jfd/2015/00000029/00000001/art00005

Strage, A., Nelson, C., & Meyers, S. (2008). "Stayin' alive!": Meeting faculty mid-career professional renewal needs. *Metropolitan Universities, 19,* 71–83.

Travers, C. J. (2001). Stress in teaching: Past, present, and future. In J. Dunham (Ed.), *Stress in teaching* (pp. 130–163). Philadelphia, PA: Whurr.

U.S. Department of Education (2013). Digest of Education Statistics. *Institute of Education Sciences, National Center for Education Statistics.* Retrieved from https://nces.ed.gov/pubsearch/pubsinfo.asp?pubid=2015011

Varra, A. A., Hayes, S. C, Roget, N., & Fisher, G. (2008). A randomized control trial examining the effect of acceptance and commitment therapy on clinician willingness to use evidence-based pharmacotherapy. *Journal of Consulting and Clinical Psychology, 76*(3), 449–458. doi:10.1037/0022-006X.76.3.449

Viggiano, T. R., & Strobel, H. W. (2009). The career management life cycle: A model for supporting and sustaining faculty vitality and wellness. In T. R. Cole, T. J. Goodrich, & E. R. Gritz (Eds.), *Faculty health in academic medicine: Physicians, scientists, and the pressures of success* (pp. 73–82). Totowa, NJ: Humana Press.

Part II

Mindfulness- and Acceptance-Based Approaches in the Training of Behavioral Health Professionals

4 A Contextual Cognitive-Behavioral Therapy Approach to Clinical Professional Training

Inside the Classroom

Sandra Georgescu and Martin Brock

Introduction

Contextual cognitive-behavioral therapy (C-CBT) or "third wave" therapy (Hayes, Villatte, Levin, & Hildebrandt, 2011) training has for the most part taken place in academic departments that have strong behavioral/CBT backgrounds. Outside of this context, much of the training has been disseminated to graduate students and postgraduate practitioners via workshops, conferences, and supervision/consultation. Emerging empirical support for, and thereby increased popularity of C-CBTs over the years has led to a desire to train graduate-level trainees in a number of programs (including research, professional and organizational) across a wider range of academic settings (Plumb, n.d.). Some have integrated this training within existing core courses while others have included it in specialized or seminar courses. While anecdotal evidence suggests that is a generally welcomed addition by both students and faculty, the integration of C-CBTs (with their emphasis on mindfulness, acceptance, and their experiential approaches) into pre-existing standard academic curricula calls for some practical and ethical consideration. This chapter will therefore outline what we know about C-CBT training and highlight some of the areas that we, as educators, have stumbled upon and thought to be important when incorporating C-CBTs within the academic setting. We use C-CBT as a general umbrella term to refer to numerous approaches that emphasize values-driven mindfulness and acceptance processes, and utilize a functional contextual perspective vis-à-vis private events (for a more detailed description, see Hayes et al., 2011).

Mixed Methods Training

Clinical training in the classroom has typically been carried out through didactic instruction where competencies are assessed via quizzes, essays, and case conceptualizations/treatment planning. Outside of clinical seminars (introductory courses where students learn basic micro-skills including active listening and interviewing) or in-house supervision teams (in programs with onsite training clinics), the more applied nature of student learning in academia is typically limited to inclusion of in-class role-plays or mock therapy projects where various models are applied to simulated clients as an intellectual exercise. Practica and internships are intended to further build and generalize skills, and help trainees learn the *how* of therapy while making use of self-practice and self-reflection (Bennett-Levy & Thwaites, 2007), often under the supervision of individuals who work from divergent theoretical orientations. From a training perspective, C-CBTs are particularly sensitive to intersections among orientations; deviations from the underlying functional contextual philosophy (see Chapter 2, this volume) can significantly impact clinical decision-making (Holmes, Georgescu, & Liles, 2006). Thus, while we may use interventions connected with other traditions, we suggest training be rooted in one philosophical/theoretical camp to avoid unnecessary conflicts, increase coherence, and optimize trainees' delivery of care.

Consistent with functional contextual assumptions, the training of acceptance and commitment therapy (ACT) and its psychological flexibility (PF) model has been at the forefront of mindfulness- and acceptance-based behavioral approaches, and will be used as the primary example of mixed methods training inside the classroom. While recognizing the value of including didactic presentation of information, the typical acceptance and commitment *training* (AC*T*) emphasizes experiential learning that enhances trainees' experience with clinical interventions by "trying them on" for themselves (Luoma, Hayes, & Walser, 2007). As such, AC*T* teaches learners the *how* of therapy (hexaflex process engagement) in vivo by inviting them to fully engage their thoughts and feelings in a mindful, accepting, and values-driven way. The Association of Contextual Behavioral Science (ACBS), the professional home for many C-CBTers, has shown its commitment to empirical verification through studies that support and recommend future steps in the assessment and development of this training approach.

Broadly speaking, empirical literature on acceptance, mindfulness, and ACT in particular seems to show beneficial results for these hands-on types of training. Studies show that ACT can be effective in a time-limited experientially-based format, and that the increased knowledge and PF gained by the trained clinicians are maintained at follow-up (Hayes et al., 2004; Lappalainen et al., 2007; Luoma & Vilardaga, 2013; Masuda et al., 2007; Strosahl, Hayes, Bergan, & Romano, 1998). Earlier studies showed that adding AC*T* to existing didactic instruction increased clinician implementation and the sense of personal accomplishment, and improved client outcomes (Luoma et al., 2007; Strosahl et al., 1998). Further, experiential AC*T* workshops seem to be more effective than didactic or multicultural control conditions for reducing counselors' mental health stigma (Hayes et al., 2004; Masuda et al., 2007). One study investigating the training of beginning ACT practitioners showed that clinician skill levels remained relatively low post work-shop and were subsequently augmented through ongoing consultation and supervision (Walser, Karlin, Trockel, Mazina, & Taylor, 2013). In the case of students as trainees, preliminary investigation of the impact of experiential work seems to indicate that students moved in desired directions on measures of mindfulness, acceptance, and stigma (Spyrka & Georgescu, 2013; Stafford-Brown & Pakenham, 2012).

Taken together, initial literature on training in these C-CBT models seems to indicate that hands-on practice helps clinicians and students become more empathic, present, and psychologically flexible but, much like their professional counterparts, trainees may need ongoing consultation to master the use of theory-based interventions. Incorporating experiential learning of C-CBT into the graduate school experience (within and outside the classroom; also see Chapter 5, this volume) therefore seems like a perfect fit for mixed-method approaches since students are already in a system that provides the consultative/supervisory components.

Students in Sandra Georgescu's advanced intervention C-CBT group class that focused on teaching dialectical behavior therapy (DBT; Linehan, 1993) and ACT experientially have repeatedly (albeit anecdotally) reported their gratitude in having learned how to organize, facilitate, and think about managing experiential (intra- and interpersonal) processes within the classroom setting before or while they were jumping into individual and group therapy experiences at their external training sites. Further, students have also courageously shared what they learned in the experiential group class with supervisors at their practicum sites, who have typically welcomed these evidence-based approaches into their settings.

C-CBT-Based Experiential Learning

Kolb's (1984) first modern definition of experiential learning described a "process whereby knowledge is created through the transformation of experience. Knowledge results from the combination of grasping and transforming experience" (p. 41). Relational frame theory (RFT) which underpins ACT (Törneke, 2010) would support Kolb's definition of experiential learning while providing an account of the verbal processes at work in activities such as experiential training. A participant experiencing the thought, "If I engage in role-play I will make a fool of myself" might well experience a strong urge to avoid being involved in role-play so as to avoid the feared consequence of looking foolish (anxiety, shame etc.). An RFT perspective suggests that the stimulus function of role-play has been transformed through verbal behavior described above and the event framed relationally, may yield a "If I do role-play then it will be bad for me" rule.

From a C-CBT perspective, we would say that experiential training helps increase participants' PF by establishing a context where they are invited to directly contact select (verbal/symbolic) contingencies, observe their response, and draw conclusions about the impact of their response on behaviors (both private and public). To follow-up with the previous example, the participant may note the rule ("role-plays makes me look foolish") and consider its impact on the broader desire of developing competence (assumed to be valued if s/he is in a training) if it is to be taken literally (fused). In essence, training helps by establishing a context for perspective-taking, key to developing PF, the fundamental outcome of C-CBT (McHugh & Stewart, 2012). This approach is easily contrasted with other training methods that focus on outlining, at a descriptive level, those same contingencies or rules, yet abstain from direct engagement of participants' experience in vivo.

Metaphorically, contrasting didactic and experiential methods is much like contrasting just listening to the instructions of one's global positioning system (GPS) versus getting in the car and actually driving the path. Therapists in training, much like drivers on a road, are helped if the GPS also talks them through the steps in real-time, while they learn to make increasingly finer discriminations about what is encountered and how to adjust to get to their destination. Subsequent supervision augments these skills by creating a space where supervisees can share attempts and obstacles, receive feedback, and experiment with a wider selection of interventions in an open, engaging, and accepting context (see Chapter 5, this volume).

In ACT and other therapies that target experiential avoidance (EA) as the root of inflexibility and augment acceptance and behavioral change-based skills, experiential training initiates learners to the actual in vivo process of approaching private experience in a training context prior to engaging clients in these activities (Brock, Batten, Walser, & Robb, 2015). Much like clients who may struggle with denigrating thoughts about themselves or others, clinical trainees are generally more stressed then their non-clinical student counterparts and report this struggle to be directly associated with clinical training (Pakenham & Stafford-Brown, 2012; Skovholt & Ronnestad, 2003; Stafford-Brown & Pakenham, 2012). More specifically, they are known to struggle with doubts about their competence and worries about meeting clients' needs (Rodolfa, Kraft, & Reilley, 1988), and can get tangled up in all sorts of rules about "what to do or not to do" (Bach and Moran, 2008; Wilson and DuFrene, 2009). It has been found that developing perspective-taking and PF not only enhances clinicians' therapy skills but also leads to increased openness to using evidence-based interventions (e.g. Varra, Hayes, Roget, & Fisher, 2008). Furthermore, expanding training methods to include experiential learning also opens up room for creativity and variability of instructions and future intervention. Through the use of metaphor, mindfulness exercises, guided imagery, modeling of intentional self-disclosure, and guided debriefing activities, trainers progressively coach an ongoing approach/acceptance stance to potentially difficult (and sometimes joyful) content while persistently pointing to values and effective actions so that trainees can begin to experiment for themselves and broaden the clinical repertoires they import into therapy.

Given that much of the experiential training in psychology has historically come out of the psychodynamic/existential traditions (e.g., Grant, 2006), it is worth highlighting that while different theoretical orientations may share a common function in using experiential training (to increase clinicians'/trainees' effectiveness with clients), the nature of the training differs significantly. From a dynamic/existential perspective, experiential training in academia is generally group-based and interpersonal in nature (Yalom & Leszcz, 2005), whereas in the C-CBTs, much of the work focuses on the intrapersonal or the trainees' relationship with their own private experience (thoughts, feelings, sensations, urges) and associated behaviors (which does have implications for interpersonal functioning). Fundamental differences are tied to the orientation's underlying theories and hypothesized processes of change. With regard to the interpersonal domain, exchanges from a C-CBT perspective are typically oriented to the active enhancement of prosocial behaviors.

The typical ACT workshop therefore broadly includes a blend of didactic components that explain/inform participants about the processes underlying the PF model and multiple opportunities to engage in these processes directly through the use of mindfulness-like exercises, metaphors, and discussions. These offer participants the chance to practice willingness, openness, and acceptance while orienting to that which is professionally meaningful (Batten & Santanello, 2009). Participant-to-participant interactions are intentionally set up by leaders to be validating, supportive, and empowering by using prompts such as, "Please share with your partner what you liked about what he or she did," or "Thank your partner for engaging." Interpersonal exchanges are purposeful in eliciting, maintaining, and reinforcing an accepting, compassionate stance toward oneself and connection, empathy, and generosity toward others as trainees engage in prosocial connections with their fellow human beings. This actual practice of watching and sharing one's ability to engage in the process as it occurs in a reinforcing environment helps to build acceptance and compassion skills that are at the heart of experiential learning of C-CBT (more on this below).

An experiential approach can also be utilized to teach didactic-type groups. For example, students in the primary author's C-CBT group class were invited to partake in an abbreviated skills training group (outlined below) while picking a behavior that they wanted to intervene on for the duration of the class. They were given the option of keeping the specific behavior private when sharing their work, and the training was experiential to the extent that students were invited to engage in mindfulness exercises, role-plays, and mild "group interfering behaviors" so that they had a chance to observe how a leader/co-leader would intervene. Students were regularly asked for their observations and coached to tie these back to C-CBT theory. The group would always close with a statement about what they had noticed and what they would take away from that class; again, this was aimed toward reinforcing contact with process and minimizing content.

A C-CBT-based Course: Practical Considerations

Aligning the Course With the Program Curriculum

Given that individuals both self-select entry to graduate work and are chosen by a particular faculty member, lab, or committee, programmatic clarity and disclosure to prospective students about the role and extent of experiential training prior to entry into the program is key, especially if experiential work is a *required* component of the program. From a programming perspective, multiple options are available, whether requiring a class that includes experiential work (e.g., Argosy University in Chicago requires all first years in the doctoral program to partake in a year-long group class), asking students to partake in external experiential workshops (as do some PhD programs), or simply offering optional classes on acceptance-based approaches sprinkled with varying degrees of experiential work (as did the Chicago School). Decisions about sequencing, amount of training, and extent of experiential work embedded in each class or experience are best considered in the broader programmatic context. For example, at one end of the continuum one may decide that a simple didactic overview of acceptance-based behavioral therapies that informs students of these approaches alongside a number of other more classically oriented cognitive-behavioral therapies (CBTs) may be sufficient given the program's mission. Alternately, some have opted for a C-CBT (or "mindfulness- and acceptance- based interventions" course) that again provides an introductory level instruction into these therapies. In this case, the amount of experiential training during the course may be minimal, and the location of the course in the curriculum would be most flexible. Advanced intervention courses in this area are also possible, with higher emphasis on experiential learning, as exemplified below. Given students' struggles and hurdles during graduate training, the key consideration in terms of course alignment is to remain mindful of the broader curricular context and to ensure that positioning of courses allows for scaffolding (Pea, 2004) and the creation of a supportive environment that maximizes student learning, especially if more experiential.

Course Sequencing Process

Sequencing a course at the more micro/class level is another area to be considered. Depending on the number of weeks in the semester and content needed to provide for program-specific competency evaluation, courses can be designed to increase experiential work in a progressive manner. Classes can easily follow the typical psychoeducational structure where a teach-model-practice-debrief sequence (Linehan, 1993) can be used, both over the course of the semester and/or in each individual class. Weighing the amount of didactic and experiential work, role-plays, and debriefing time in each class would probably depend on the broader objectives, class time, and professor/trainer expertise. Generally speaking, experiential training is process-oriented, and makes use of didactic instruction as a context for and a bridge between learning by doing exercises: a form of learn and play. For instructors teaching C-CBT courses, the bulk of this (more experiential) work is in creating a context where students have ample opportunities to contact direct verbal/symbolic contingencies, whether through guided exercises, debriefing, and/or the use of metaphors, which may come to serve as cues for practice. Observational and approach skills are strengthened as students learn from engaging in the training and sharing their experiences relative to their ability to stay present, open, and aware. While trainers should weigh the ratio of instruction with debriefing of the experiential exercises, we encourage trainers to broadly opt for a "less is more" approach. Said another way, it is generally better to ensure that one has ample time to properly debrief even if at the expense of a few experiential exercises. Instructors' fusion and avoidance of their own anxiety (yes, we all have this to varying degrees!) also sometimes pulls for over-preparing, over-packing, and a speedy delivery. Linking experience to theory (for them and for us as instructors in planning this process) provides further reinforcement for the processes.

Below, we provide one way to organize a more advanced curriculum that represents a mix of two acceptance-based therapies, which seamlessly lend themselves to scaffolding the students' deepening experience over the course of the semester. We would encourage those interested in designing acceptance-based courses to think through and sequence out progressive exposure to relevant concepts while maintaining flexibility with the various models available in this area. As an example, we describe a course that utilizes psychoeducational skills training (from DBT) and ACT experiential training as vehicles for teaching C-CBT oriented group processes. Because the class was open to students from multiple theoretical orientations, the rationale for organizing content in this manner was to help students learn in very basic terms the mindful/observational stance that is part of both approaches. Furthermore, via the early introduction of DBT mindfulness skills, students learned up front the distinction between urges and action, and were encouraged to use the WHAT and HOW mindfulness skills (Linehan, 1993) as a format for discussing their experiences when debriefing. This initial instruction and subsequent shaping provided consistently during the four DBT weeks was sufficient for them to learn an accepting stance toward private experience as well as a way to disclose at the level of process rather than content. Once this format was in place, and students knew *how* to talk, they were prompted to begin thinking about *why* (the function of) they were talking (or not) and encouraged to consider the consequences for their and the entire group's processes. Although this scaffolding approach makes logical sense, we recognize that the proposed need/benefit for scaffolding the curriculum this way in the C-CBTs ultimately remains an unanswered empirical question.

Otherwise, with regard to sequence, the instructor is encouraged to be creative in designing the class based on his/her strengths, style, and students' needs. The typical ACT workshop generally includes some didactic presentation of the PF model, including the role of EA and the automaticity of language, and engagement in creative hopelessness exercises to highlight current behavior in the context of workability and long-term valued directions. Instructors can tailor and make use of preferred exercises and metaphors, many of which can be found in books, chapters, and among the many protocols provided by ACBS.[1] For example, some guided exercises like the observer exercise (Hayes, Strosahl & Wilson, 2012) verbally fly participants across time and roles while pointing their attention to the physical, cognitive, and emotional content that would accompany each image; at the end of each segment, the participant is asked to notice who is remembering, envisioning, and observing, and invited to consider the longitudinal sense of the observer. Variations on this longer exercise can be used to evoke and help the trainees contact a wider array of experiences from various "I/here/now" and "then/there" perspectives, drawing their attention to nuances, subtle changes, and points of contact with material. After debriefing the exercise, some didactic instruction would link this experience to the self-as-context process of the PF model. For the novice instructor (both in terms of general teaching and more specifically with regard to C-CBTs), we would recommend looking at various protocols on stress and anxiety, which usually fit with a graduate school experience, especially in the mental health professions.

Designing the Course

Students who enrolled in the sample class (below) had satisfied a Basic Intervention: CBT required course, were in their third or fourth year of a Clinical PsyD program and active on a therapy or advanced therapy practicum. As such, they had acquired basic clinical interviewing and assessment competencies as well as familiarity with various therapy models, at least at an introductory level. About a third of the students enrolled usually selected this class as an elective that satisfied the group class requirement for Master's-level licensure. Class size at its largest included 25 students. The overall course objectives were to (a) introduce students to overall group design for various populations/organizations, (b) familiarize students with didactic and experiential CBT group processes using DBT and ACT as vehicles, and (c) orient students to working with multi-problem clients from a C-CBT perspective. The class sequence was therefore designed as follows:

- 2 didactic classes—introduction to traditional CBT and C-CBT group work; group student presentations on the evidence base for DBT and ACT
- 4 classes DBT experiential skills group trainings
  - Review guidelines for skills training mindfulness definitions
    - Wise mind, "What" skills, "How" skills
  - When to use crisis survival skills
    - Overview: Crisis survival skills. Overview: Radical acceptance skills
  - Emotion regulation: What emotions do for you
    - Model for describing emotions. Overview: Reduce vulnerability to emotion mind—Building a life worth living
  - Interpersonal effectiveness: Overview
    - Clarifying goals, "Dear Man," "Give," "Fast"
- 1 didactic class conceptually bridging between DBT and ACT
- 2-day weekend ACT experiential training (equivalent of 15 hours of group/class time excluding breaks)—can be spread out throughout the semester (experiential role-plays focus predominantly on intrapersonal rather than interpersonal relating)
  - Group rules
  - Review of hexaflex / PF model (didactic)
  - Values of being in the helping profession
  - The ubiquity of suffering and RFT intro and the automaticity of language
  - Thought suppression, the problem-solving stance, and the associated costs
  - Acceptance, defusion, and self-as context
  - Revisiting values and committed action
  - Q&A/feedback
- 1 didactic wrap up class and final quiz.

See Appendix A for a resource list of readings and possible assignments.

Setting the Table for Participation

Different acceptance-based approaches conducted in group form may have different rules for group participation. For example, in DBT, the *Guidelines for Skills Training* handout is typically reviewed with new members (Linehan, 2015, p. 12). In ACT, most groups start off with an outline inviting participation, engagement, and willingness to challenge oneself in areas that are potentially difficult. The group leader also usually invites people to listen closely to their personal limits, emphasizing that "saying no" is a well-respected and honored way to observe one's limits (Walser & Pistorello, 2004). Particularly with large classes, one way of achieving this is to invite students to be aware of personal content privately (quietly) and only share or discuss key points of their learning. In other words, share what showed up as barriers to maintaining present-moment focus without necessarily divulging the personal material itself. Participants are encouraged up front to notice and choose their (verbal) actions in the face of urges to over-disclose. In this vein, we recommend that instructors mention the potentially avoidant function of over-talking/sharing, and encourage participants to notice if they are holding rules about participating too tightly, clarifying that "more talking" is not necessarily the goal. Given that the course is delivered in an educational setting where people will continue to work together on an ongoing basis and different levels of power exist, observing one's disclosure limits explicitly may be prompted by inviting students to use a veto card and reinforcing limit-setting behavior by respecting students' overt "no" responses to queries when they are not willing to disclose.

As leaders, we take opportunities to also model these processes and may self-disclose around our tendency to talk more and at a higher frequency as a means to avoid our own anxiety. Through this modeling, the instructor establishes a context for acknowledging and validating that we all struggle with thoughts, feelings, and urges that hook us while also practicing staying connected to the meaningful versus socially desirable across life domains. Sharing information about oneself and one's struggles is at the heart of human intimacy, human connection, and relationship building (Kohlenberg, Kohlenberg, & Tsai, 2009). At the same time, given the context of this work and what is being achieved, students are cautioned to keep an eye out for the function of their disclosures, prioritizing agency and intentional choice-making in interactions with others. While more room for personal disclosure is probably typical in supervisory or consultative context (Batten & Santanello, 2009; Follette & Batten, 2000), in an academic context this balance is usually communicated by queries about students' ability to hold whatever showed up, to let go of judgments, and to see what their hearts would tell them would be meaningful action in the service of living a value in their role as participants in the training.

The above are some suggestions to help raise awareness and shape both the type and amount of disclosures during training. Some evidence exists that in "setting the table" as mentioned above, participants in a one-day ACT workshop reported that they did not disclose more than usual, nor did they feel pressured to disclose more than they wished (Richards et al., 2011), thereby demonstrating their ability to maintain their professional limits and respect the integrity of their roles.

Debriefing Exercises

Theoretically speaking, debriefing from exercises usually involves a description of the student's ability to apply observational, defusion, and acceptance skills, notice hooks and urges toward over-learned automatic behaviors, and choose context-specific meaningful action. For example, during debriefing of the Sweet Spot exercise (Wilson & DuFrene, 2009), one may talk about what was meaningful in what came up and how s/he was able to hold this content (e.g., "Did you feel yourself push against what bubbled up at all?"). If the answer to such a question is "yes," students are often coached to "breathe into" the experience and see if they are able to expand present-moment awareness to their experience and maintain contact in a gentle fashion, as if they were holding a thrush's egg in their hands.

It is not unusual for people to also think of all the missed opportunities for closeness, caring, and connection when going through the Sweet Spot exercise, so students may be cued to think about what they would like to be doing that would really be in line with who they want to be. During exercises where students are engaged to contact more difficult material, like having the thought that one is alone or broken in some way, debriefing can also be kept private by having them write the content of what showed up on a piece of paper and then just sharing the present-moment impact of what they wrote (e.g., "It feels overwhelming and sad to think about the heaviness of my stuff").

During the debriefing exercise, instructors can also model self-disclosure around the types of content one may choose to share if they were in different situations. For example, one of us (Sandra Georgescu) often talks about the sense of disconnect and sadness that she feels in contacting bits of her history while only vaguely sharing the details of that history. Then she follows up by sharing the effort made to get close, especially when everything in her says "disengage." A link to the conceptual PF model is maintained by using defused language when sharing. At other times, direct/in the moment links between exchanges in the room and the model can be helpful. Students therefore become privy to a process that on the one hand acknowledges the struggle and on the other hand exemplifies values-driven behavior in the training context rather than engaging (reinforcing) sharing of the story/content of disclosures. From a place of caring, students can also be prompted to identify their own hooks and ways of avoiding, alongside possible values-based alternative behaviors with their training colleagues and/or with clients.

In tying this work back to their role as clinicians, it is worthwhile to repeatedly query students about application of exercises that they practiced during the training, with prospective clients. One way to ensure the transfer between training and the clinical session is to ask students to discuss how they would envision or even role-play applying a similar exercise with a given client. Subgroups of dyads or triads, where the third person can act as observer/process commentator and provide formative feedback to their peers can help make this more interactive. Spending some time talking through barriers and steps that they can take to augment their effectiveness can again make the link from training to practice. In light of the slightly varying ethical standards that surround clinical and academic training, the functional similarities and differences between the consultation room and the classroom environment are worth highlighting (out loud with students as well) as another instance of discrimination training. For example, in order to help them choose their disclosures more mindfully, students may be engaged in perspective-taking exercises where they are asked to jot down the role-specific response to a particular cue (if they were in the role of client, role of consultee, role of trainee, role of friend or acquaintance, and so forth). Then they could think through the function of each disclosure, consider actively chosen limits versus avoidance strategies, and learn to make increasingly refined functional discriminations.

Assessing for Competence

Assessment for academic and clinical suitability is initially done upon entrance into graduate school, where committees or faculty bodies make decisions about accepting students into programs. At this point, prospective students typically need to demonstrate both past academic abilities and interpersonal qualities suited for the helping profession. The admission process usually includes a full review of application materials and an interview.

Once admitted into a program, competency assessment in the academic context typically entails instructors entering a final grade at the end of the term that is a reflection of students' ability to absorb and apply the information received. This task is readily carried out with didactic/declarative type of information where professors can test recall, comprehension, and application via assignments and examinations. Programs also evaluate clinical suitability and professional development, and usually have procedures/guidelines for tracking and helping students in times of struggle. At the level of the department/program, therefore the existing gatekeeping avenues, when well in place, are assumed to be sufficient to monitor students' progress in the program, whether or not it includes experiential training.

For the purposes of a typical classroom setting, instructors can rely on assessing knowledge via conceptualizations, tests, and quizzes. Engagement in role-plays and recorded mock sessions that train up students' micro-skills (or communication/active-listening skills) are generally found in interviewing courses, and target instruction or rule-based therapeutic relational skills while assessing for "relational competencies" (Ridley, Kelly, & Mollen, 2011). Given this context and culture, we encourage instructors to limit student evaluations to presentations, papers, and exams rather than in-class participation whether as "mock clients" or professionals in training during experiential components of the class. Removing the performance evaluation component from experiential work frees trainees up to engage with the material in an authentic way by eliminating potentially punishing contingencies (real or imagined). A safe space can therefore be created where students can show up as professionals who are also people with histories and patterns of engagement. Exposure to this kind of work in an evaluative context is more likely to be restrictive and shift the focus from process to outcome, thereby defying the course's stated objective of teaching process from the inside out. Prioritizing the integrity of the work (and safety of the space) over evaluative procedures in this context is done with the reassurance that, if problems were to arise in an experiential context, they would probably also be seen outside of this particular training, such as in seminars, supervision, classes and other professional settings. We therefore see no additional benefit to adding evaluation of participation to experiential training.

We do, however, advocate that some form of evaluation is needed or desired on competencies with process-level interventions learned during experiential training in the classroom context. For this, instructors can opt to make use of Luoma, Hayes, and Walser (2007) process-specific examples and queries for therapist action, which probe these abilities while protecting the live process. Their *Learning ACT* book outlines and explains the PF model processes, and provides vignettes with example interventions. Readers are then asked to discriminate between ACT-consistent and inconsistent responses and also generate their own response for a different case. An accompanying CD demonstrates role-played interventions, where the audience is engaged in the same discrimination task. One could use these end-of-chapter exercises to assess the students' ability to come up with their own ACT-consistent responses, and provide feedback and grades based on this (or similar instructor developed) homework assignment.

The Ethics of Experiential Training in Academia

The following section lists several ethical considerations to be thought through as educators attempt to integrate experiential, process based-training into the classroom. For the purpose of guidance, we will highlight parts of the American Psychological Association (APA; 2010) *Code of Ethics* for each of the areas that seem directly relevant to this integration, while inviting the interested reader to seek out the actual wording from their degree/field specific code of ethics as they prepare for this journey.

7.02 Descriptions of Education and Training Programs

This section of the ethics code generally asks that program descriptions include an up-to-date account of the content of each class as well as course requirements of individual students. Some thought is warranted on whether to make an experiential course a required component of the curriculum or whether to organize it as an elective, thereby giving students the option to select or opt out of such training experiences. Either way, programs are required to accurately articulate their position.

2.01 Boundaries of Competence (When Teaching C-CBTs)

One of the most common sentences overheard at conferences and in consultation groups is the reminder that "ACT *is* a behavioral therapy." Given that C-CBTs are theory-driven and instructors interested in teaching clinical graduate-level courses often come to this work from a wide variety of professional and theoretical backgrounds, we encourage instructors to consider their familiarity with behavioral principles, including those consistent with RFT (see Chapter 2, this volume), and interventions (like contingency management, exposure, skills training, and so forth). Recent evidence has shown that RFT can be directly tied to clinical interventions, and is useful in enhancing clinical work by clarifying/specifying direct relational interventions, reinforcing certain types of frames, using augmentals, and moving beyond traditional self-instructional rule development (Luciano, Valdivia Salas, Cabello-Luque, & Hernandez, 2009, Törneke, 2010, Villatte, Villatte & Hayes (2015). While instructors do not necessarily need to be experts in this theory, basic knowledge of foundational principles and ongoing professional development in it should enhance training abilities. Much like speaking a primary language, familiarity with core behavioral theory will help link the processes with committed action-oriented behavioral interventions (like skills training) while modeling a theoretically consistent home base, and help students to conceptualize/apply interventions with flexibility.

Instructors interested in developing and potentially becoming peer reviewed in this work are invited to actively engage with ACBS, which offers recommendations and avenues for "training the trainer."[2] While the competencies needed to engage in such work are continuously being developed, clarified, and organized (Hayes, Strosahl, & Wilson, 2012), professionals interested in training can access tools that help with self-assessment, guided self-learning, connection to consultative/mentoring communities, and receiving peer-reviews that offer feedback, guidance, and resources should they choose to undergo community recognition.

7.04 Student Disclosure of Personal Information

The helping profession has in many ways formulated a wide variety of implicit and explicit rules and regulations around self-disclosure (Stricker, 1990) and its role and use for training purposes. With the intention of protecting trainees, the *APA Ethics Code* explicitly states that we refrain from *requiring* "students or supervisees to disclose personal information in course- or program-related activities" (APA, 2010) except if this requirement has been clearly articulated in the program description or in the event that such disclosure is related to evaluating students' competence for a job. The astute reader will hear the echoes of informed consent, and will be challenged to negotiate trainees' self-disclosure during training. Welcoming the totality of students' experience as a vehicle for learning and simultaneously helping them be mindful of their disclosure was discussed above, and we therefore only highlight the ethical importance of establishing a framework for sharing that also reinforces students for observing their privacy limits.

7.05 Mandatory Individual or Group Therapy

The ethics code explicitly states that if therapy is to be required by a training program, students should have the option of selecting providers not affiliated with

Table 4.1 C-CBT Experiential Training Versus Psychotherapy

Training in Academia	Psychotherapy
• **Purpose:** to build more advanced clinical skill/competencies and augment service delivery to others • **Assessment:** Competency-based, relative to standards established by the program/profession; may be course specific • **Fit:** Standardized: Assumed level of academic/professional suitability (through program admissions and gatekeeping) that allows for provision of a program-wide curriculum to all students; accommodations contingent on documented disability that would impact learning program-wide skills/competencies acquisition • **Disclosure:** Option #1: A priori consent in the event that program *requires* disclosure of sensitive personal information. Option #2: Electives provided so students can select out of experiential classes; content of personal disclosure are de-emphasized; teaches process level disclosure and actively trains the maintenance of professional limits • **Tailoring:** No/minimal individual tailoring of structured experiential exercises, slightly more flexible tailoring when shaping disclosures and debriefing • **Delivery:** usually in group format (class), individual supervision may augment • **Duration:** Predetermined, time-limited and only slightly flexible at programmatic level (most programs have a time in program cap); classes are time-limited • **Benefits:** Enhance knowledge of psychological interventions and their delivery; enhance clinical skills/competencies to better deliver interventions with clients	• **Purpose:** identify, assess, conceptualize, target problem with client or family; therefore to relieve "psychopathology" so that client(s) can regain quality and meaning in life • **Assessment:** In-house individually tailored and/or supplemented (based on need); possible ancillary assessment including pharmacological, neurological or other • **Fit:** Individualized: Service matched to type and degree of problem severity and incapacitation (e.g. outpatient, intensive outpatient, partial or inpatient hospitalization) • **Disclosure:** Disclosure of personal information/ struggle with presenting issue is an essential part of ongoing therapy; failure to disclose may be therapy interfering • **Tailoring:** Client/problem-specific treatment plan; highly individualized tailoring of experiential work, even in group settings where this may be done according to presenting problem (e.g. group for depression) • **Delivery:** individual and/or group depending on presenting problem, resources, and client willingness • **Duration:** is variable and based on presenting problem, progress and treatment effectiveness; ethically bound for referral if therapy is deemed ineffective • **Benefits:** Personal benefit (symptom decrease), increase in quality of life and functioning

the program, to avoid multiple relationships and the possibility of coercion/abuses of power. The question of whether experiential training counts as "provision of therapy" usually comes up in a context where a trainee struggles with the format of training, whereby the solution may be to abandon or lighten the training. We have considered and consulted the literature, other trainers, and academics on this, and as a result propose that C-CBT experiential training that increases PF (thereby enhancing personal development) *in the service of better serving clients* mirrors much of the other work carried out in graduate school that is also personally and professionally enhancing (e.g., diversity training, assessment/therapy seminars, or advising). Furthermore, the ubiquity of suffering (Hayes, Strosahl, & Wilson, 2012) among human beings recontextualizes the distinction between us as "normal" and clients as "abnormal" in some way. Psychotherapy, functionally speaking, therefore becomes a service that is provided to individuals who struggle with a certain *degree* of problems (that significantly impair functioning). If our gatekeeping processes are well in place, individuals who struggle to an elevated extent (either at admissions or during the course of the program) would likely be reviewed by committees much in the same way as if a supervisee struggled with issues that came up with a client, albeit with more discretion (as mentioned above) if the training occurs in group format. After all, the ability to sit with one's own (sometimes difficult) private experience is a common occurrence in clinical work (yes, our buttons get pushed too), and repeated elevated degrees of struggle with one's private content and reactions (and its impact of professional functioning) may occasionally necessitate additional action or even pose readiness/clinical suitability questions. Hence, in our view, experiential training and its purpose is different from the provision of therapy. Table 4.1 summarizes our view of differences between experiential training in academia and psychotherapy.

Closer consideration of each type of "service" highlights their distinction; we suggest that while growth-promoting (much like education in general), C-CBT experiential classroom training has an entirely different function than psychotherapy (namely, building profession-specific competencies). As previously mentioned, increased observational capacity and acceptance, concurrent with effective client-focused action, have been shown to augment clinician effectiveness at the levels of both self-care and enhancing client outcomes.

3.05 Multiple Relationships

The last ethical consideration relates to the possible multiple relationships that are present during one's tenure as faculty. After all, in addition to being course instructors, many of us are also advisors, dissertation chairs and readers, supervisors, mentors, committee members, and potentially administrators. The one role that we *do not* wear with our students is that of therapist, and more seasoned faculty members know how to limit students' disclosures and seek/receive/provide consultation (formal or informal) on addressing the potential breach of such a limit (which is probably most at risk in the advisor or supervisory roles). In the case of experiential training, we therefore advise that simple protections, such as purposely excluding the evaluation of student participation in experiential work or using pre-existing exercises for the assessment of competencies, are workable substitutes. Occasionally, we may encounter instances of over-sharing (e.g., if a student has shared information about a personal situation in an exercise debriefing that may relate to his or her competency in another area of the program) or other unprofessional behaviors for which we recommend following the typical consultative/department specific steps to determine the most helpful and ethical course of action. Otherwise, comportment issues that are likely to arise, if at all given the limits established early on, are not likely to be any different from those within other training experiences, such as mentorship, seminars, supervision, or diversity training (Barnett, 2008). The same ethical/institutional/departmental procedures are therefore recommended to serve as checks and balances, especially when making disciplinary decisions, usually within various committees.

Conclusion

This chapter is intended to encourage those seeking to bring C-CBT approaches into the classroom to do so in thoughtful and research-informed ways. Evidence shows that experiential training is beneficial for therapists, students, and their clients. Some data point to clinicians' need for follow-up consultation post experiential training; students have the particular advantage of being surrounded by ongoing supervision as part of their programs, making it an ideal time to receive this training at no extra cost. This chapter has provided some guidance and ethical food-for-thought should faculty choose to incorporate such training into their classrooms. In Appendix A we provide some of the resources and a template for a two-day workshop-style training that we have found to be beneficial in teaching ACT in the classroom and in workshops. These are intended for practical purposes, and we encourage those interested to tailor their teaching to best suit the needs of the department and scaffold the work so it matches the level of familiarity of the students. We have outlined one possible approach to this (by starting off with DBT skills training and building on with an ACT workshop) so that students who are entirely new to C-CBTs can learn in a step-wise fashion. Different combinations may also be possible (for example, more MBSR-focused up front followed by ACT); individual tailoring is encouraged.

Notes

1 See www.contextualscience.org
2 See http://contextualscience.org/training_standards

References

American Psychological Association (2010). *Ethical principles of psychologists and code of conduct.* Retrieved from: www.apa.org/ethics/code/principles.pdf
Bach, P. A., & Moran, D. J. (2008). *ACT in practice: Case conceptualization in acceptance and commitment therapy.* Oakland, CA: New Harbinger Publications.

Barnett, J. E. (2008). Mentoring, boundaries, and multiple relationships: Opportunities and challenges. *Mentoring & Tutoring: Partnership in Learning, 16*, 3–16. doi:10.1080/13611260701800900

Batten, S. V., & Santanello, A. P. (2009). A contextual behavioral approach to the role of emotion in psychotherapy supervision. *Training and Education in Professional Psychology, 3*, 148–156. Retrieved from doi:10.1037/1931-3918.a0014801

Bennett-Levy, J., & Thwaites, R. (2007). Self and self-reflection in the therapeutic relationship. In P. Gilbert & R. L. Leahy (Eds.), *The therapeutic relationship in the cognitive behavioral psychotherapies* (pp. 255–281). New York, NY: Routledge.

Brock M. J., Batten S. V., Walser R. D., & Robb, H. B. (2015). Recognizing common clinical mistakes in ACT: A quick analysis and call to awareness. *Journal of Contextual Behavioral Science*. Retrieved from www.sciencedirect.com/science/article/pii/S2212144714000921

Chiles, J. A., & Strosahl, K. D. (2004). *Clinical manual for assessment and treatment of suicidal patients*. Arlington, VA: American Psychiatric Publishing.

Follette, V., & Batten, S. (2000). The role of emotion in psychotherapy supervision : A contextual behavioral analysis. *Cognitive and Behavioral Practice, 7*, 306–312. doi:10.1016/S1077-7229(00)80088-7

Grant, J. (2006). Training counselors to work with complex clients: Enhancing emotional responsiveness through experiential methods. *Counselor Education and Supervision, 45*, 218–230. doi:10.1002/j.1556-6978.2006.tb00144.x

Hayes, S. C, Strosahl, K. D., & Wilson, K. G. (2012). *Acceptance and commitment therapy: The process and practice of mindful change* (2nd ed.). New York, NY: Guilford Press.

Hayes, S. C., Villatte, M., Levin, M., & Hildebrandt, M. (2011). Open, aware, and active: contextual approaches as an emerging trend in the behavioral and cognitive therapies. *Annual Review of Clinical Psychology, 7*, 141–168. doi:10.1146/annurev-clinpsy-032210-104449

Hayes, S.C., Bissett, R., Roget, N., Padilla, M., Kohlenberg, B.S., Fisher, G., . . . Niccolls, R. (2004). The impact of acceptance and commitment training and multicultural training on the stigmatizing attitudes and professional burnout of substance abuse counselors. *Behavior Therapy, 35*, 821–835. doi:10.1016/S0005-7894(04)80022-4

Holmes, P., Georgescu, S., & Liles, W. (2006). Further delineating the applicability of acceptance and change to private responses: The example of dialectical behavior therapy. *The Behavior Analyst Today, 7*, 311–324. doi:10.1037/h0100157

Kohlenberg, R. J., Kohlenberg, B., & Tsai, M. (2009). Intimacy. In M. Tsai R. J. Kohlenberg, J. W. Kanter, B. Kohlenberg, W. C. Follette, & G. M. Callaghan (Eds.), *A guide to functional analytic psychotherapy: Awareness, courage, love and behaviorism* (pp. 131–144). New York, NY: Springer

Kolb, D.A. (1984). *Experiential learning: Experience as the source of learning and development*. Englewood Cliffs, NJ: Prentice Hall. Retrieved from http://academic.regis.edu/ed205/kolb.pdf

Lappalainen, R., Lehtonen, T., Skarp, E., Taubert, E., Ojanen, M., & Hayes, S. C. (2007). The impact of CBT and ACT models using psychology trainee therapists: A preliminary controlled effectiveness trial. *Behavior Modification, 31*, 488–511. doi:10.1177/0145445506298436

Linehan, M. M. (1993). *Skills training manual for treating borderline personality disorder*. New York, NY: Guilford Press.

Linehan, M. M. (2015). *DBT skills training handouts and worksheets*. New York, NY: Guilford Press.

Luciano, C., Valdivia Salas, S., Cabello-Luque, F., & Hernandez, M. (2009). Developing self-directed rules. In R. A. Rehfeldt & Y. Barnes-Holmes (Eds.), *Derived relational responding: Applications for learners with autism and other developmental delays* (pp. 335–354). Oakland, CA: New Harbinger Publications.

Luoma, J. B., & Vilardaga, J. P. (2013). Improving therapist psychological flexibility while training acceptance and commitment therapy: A pilot study. *Cognitive Behaviour Therapy, 42*, 1–8. doi:10.1080/16506073.2012.701662

Luoma, J. B., Hayes, S. C., & Walser, R. D. (2007). *Learning ACT: An acceptance and commitment therapy skills training manual for therapists.* Oakland, CA: New Harbinger.

Masuda, A., Hayes, S. C., Fletcher, L. B., Seignourel, P. J., Bunting, K., Herbst, S. A., . . . Lillis, J. (2007). Impact of acceptance and commitment therapy versus education on stigma toward people with psychological disorders. *Behavior Research and Therapy, 45*, 2765–2772. doi:10.1016/j.brat.2007.05.008

McHugh, L., & Stewart, I. (2012). *The self and perspective taking: Contributions and applications from modern behavioral science.* Oakland, CA: New Harbinger Publications. Retrieved from www.merriam-webster.com/dictionary/operate (n.d.).

Pakenham, K. I., & Stafford-Brown, J. (2012). Stress in clinical psychology trainees: Current research status and future directions. *Australian Psychologist, 47*(3), 147–155. doi:10.1111/j.1742-9544.2012.00070.x

Pea, R. D. (2004). The social and technological dimensions of scaffolding and related theoretical concepts for learning, education, and human activity. *The Journal of the Learning Sciences, 13*, 423–451. doi:10.1207/s15327809jls1303_6

Plumb, J. (n.d.). *Academic Training and Research Labs.* Retrieved from https://contextual science.org/research_labs_and_academic_training

Richards, R., Oliver, J. E., Morris, E., Aherne, K., Iervolino, A. C., & Wingrove, J. (2011). Acceptance and commitment therapy training for clinicians: An evaluation. *The Cognitive Behaviour Therapist, 4*, 114–121. doi:10.1017/S1754470X11000043

Ridley, C. R., Kelly, S. M., & Mollen, D. (2011). Microskills training evolution, reexamination, and call for reform. *The Counseling Psychologist, 39*, 800–824. doi:10.1177/0011000010378438

Rodolfa, E. R., Kraft, W. A., & Reilley, R. R. (1988). Stressors of professionals and trainees at APA-approved counseling and VA medical center internship sites. *Professional Psychology: Research and Practice, 19*, 43–49. doi:10.1037/0735-7028.19.1.43

Skovholt, T., & Ronnestad, M. (2003). Struggles of the novice counselor and therapist. *Journal of Career Development, 30*, 45–58. doi:10.1023/A:1025125624919

Spyrka, S., & Georgescu, S. (2013, July). The impact of experiential training versus didactic training on experiential avoidance, thought suppression, and stigma in graduate students. Poster presented at the Association for Contextual Behavioral Science (ACBS) World Conference 13, Sydney, Australia.

Stafford-Brown, J., & Pakenham, K. I. (2012). The effectiveness of an ACT informed intervention for managing stress and improving therapist qualities in clinical psychology trainees. *Journal of Clinical Psychology, 68*, 592–513. doi:10.1002/jclp.21844

Stricker, G. (1990). Self-disclosure and psychotherapy. In G. Stricker, & M. Fisher (Eds.), *Self-disclosure in the therapeutic relationship* (pp. 277–290). New York, NY: Plenum Press.

Strosahl, K. D., Hayes, S. C., Bergan, J., & Romano, P. (1998). Assessing the field effectiveness of acceptance and commitment therapy: An example of the manipulated training research method. *Behavior Therapy, 29*, 35–63. doi:10.1016/S0005-7894(98)80017-8

Törneke, N. (2010). *Learning RFT: An introduction to relational frame theory and its clinical applications.* Oakland, CA: New Harbinger.

Varra, A. A., Hayes, S. C., Roget, N., & Fisher, G. (2008). A randomized control trial examining the effect of acceptance and commitment training on clinician willingness to use evidence-based pharmacotherapy. *Journal of Consulting and Clinical Psychology, 76*(3), 449–458. doi:10.1037/0022-006X.76.3.449

Villatte, M., Villatte, J. L., & Hayes, S. C. (2015). *Mastering the clinical conversation: Language as intervention.* New York, NY: Guilford Press.

Walser, R. D., Karlin, B. E., Trockel, M., Mazina, B., & Taylor, C. B. (2013). Training in and implementation of acceptance and commitment therapy for depression in the Veterans Health Administration: Therapist and patient outcomes. *Behaviour Research and Therapy, 51*(9), 555–563. doi:10.1016/j.brat.2013.05.009

Walser, R. D., & Pistorello, J. (2004). ACT in group format. In S. C. Hayes & K. D. Strosahl (Eds.), *A practical guide to acceptance and commitment therapy* (pp. 347–390). New York, NY: Springer Publishing.

Wilson, K. G., & DuFrene, T. (2009). *Mindfulness for two: An acceptance and commitment therapy approach to mindfulness in psychotherapy.* Oakland, CA: New Harbinger.

Yalom, I., & Leszcz, M. (2005). *The theory and practice of group psychotherapy* (5th ed.). New York, NY: Basic Books.

5 An Acceptance-Based Behavioral Approach to Clinical Professional Training

Outside the Classroom

Lizabeth Roemer, Elizabeth H. Eustis,
Sarah Krill Williston, and Sarah Hayes-Skelton

Introduction

This chapter presents some reflections on how an acceptance-based behavior therapy (ABBT) perspective informs aspects of graduate training outside the classroom (i.e., mentoring, clinical supervision, advising). We draw heavily from our own experiences:

- Lizabeth Roemer (LR), a professor who has provided mentoring and supervision to clinical doctoral students for eighteen years;
- Sarah Hayes-Skelton (SHS), an assistant professor who received this supervision/mentorship as a postdoctoral fellow and now provides it to her own students; and
- Elizabeth H. Eustis (EHE) and Sarah Krill-Williston (SKW), two doctoral students who have received both clinical supervision and mentorship from the other two authors, and have provided mentorship to undergraduate students.

Although the doctoral program we are part of does not have a shared emphasis on acceptance-based behavioral principles, there is a shared emphasis on social justice values, which overlaps with some of the principles we derive from an ABBT perspective and the way we each enact these principles.

Acceptance-based behavioral therapy (ABBT; e.g., Roemer & Orsillo, 2009) refers to a class of treatment approaches, based in a cognitive-behavioral tradition, that explicitly incorporate (a) the cultivation of a decentered (the ability to observe thoughts and feelings as objective events in the mind rather than personally identifying with them; Safran & Segal, 1990), compassionate relationship to internal experiences, (b) acceptance rather than rigid avoidance of internal experiences, and (c) the intentional engagement in actions that are important to the individual (i.e., valued action, Wilson & Murrell, 2004) with awareness. Our work in this area is heavily informed by acceptance and commitment therapy (ACT; Hayes et al., 2012), mindfulness-based cognitive therapy (MBCT; Segal, Williams, & Teasdale, 2012), dialectical behavior therapy (DBT; Linehan, 1993a, 1993b), and cognitive-behavioral therapy (CBT; e.g., Borkovec & Sharpless, 2004). Just as ABBT builds on cognitive-behavioral therapy, rather than replacing or contradicting it, an ABBT-informed approach to graduate mentoring builds on Klepac and colleagues' (2012) guidelines for CBT training. Here, we focus on aspects that are emphasized explicitly in an ABBT-informed approach and have not been discussed elsewhere in the literature, to our knowledge. The principles and practices we describe apply to all levels (e.g., Master's) and disciplines of professional clinical training (e.g., within social work, counselor education). Nonetheless, our specific experiences are grounded within the context of a clinical psychology PhD program, which affects the ways we apply these general principles. For instance, we have weekly individual mentor-mentee and supervision meetings, which may not be possible in other contexts when faculty have many more supervisees or mentees.

Rather than providing a set of guidelines for all people to follow, we focus here on how this approach has influenced our own mentoring and supervision (both giving and receiving) in ways that are meaningful and important to us, in the hopes that our experiences may be beneficial to others. We supervise beginning therapists in the context of our program, as well as more advanced therapists in the context of our research; many of our reflections on clinical supervision relate to our work with beginning therapists. An acceptance-based behavioral approach has influenced the nature of the mentoring/supervisory relationship, our (the coauthors') shared attitude toward clinical work, research, and professional development, and the content of our mentoring and supervision meetings. Specifically, an emphasis on (a) values-driven behavior, (b) awareness and acceptance of the humanness of suffering, (c) mindfulness, and (d) compassion (toward self and others), all of which relate to and influence each other, affects mentorship in the clinical, research, and professional development realms. We first talk about each of these areas in general, and then follow with some specific examples from each realm: clinical supervision, research and scholarship, and professional development. Throughout, we include the voices of our trainee coauthors to capture the impact of this approach to mentoring and supervision, in addition to our intention in providing it.

ABBT Principles in Graduate Training

Values-Driven Behavior

A central aspect of ABBT is working with clients to clarify what matters to them and helping them to move toward acting in line with these values, rather than choosing actions in service of avoiding distress and discomfort. As ABBT therapists and researchers, we regularly reflect on what matters to us and use that to guide the choices we make in our personal and professional lives. We guide students in this process so that they are able to discover what they value about their work across domains (clinical, research, and other professional development contexts) and to find ways to do their work with an emphasis on how it matters to them, as opposed to having a central focus on external sources of validation.

This reflection process allows me (LR) to clarify what matters to me in each aspect of my job. Human connection, teaching, and being part of meaningful growth for other people are three of the things I value most across contexts, making mentoring and supervisory relationships a particularly rewarding and meaningful aspect of my job. I am deeply grateful for the growth I experienced in the context of my graduate mentoring relationship (with Tom Borkovec), which led me to appreciate the opportunity to be part of a similar process for others. As such, I am always aware of how precious the time I spend with trainees, particularly in one-on-one contexts, is to me. This helps me to continually return to being the kind of mentor and supervisor I want to be, again and again, regardless of whatever thoughts, feelings or reactions arise (such as the human, inevitable fears of inadequacy, time pressure concerns, hurt feelings, or other kinds of reactivity). My awareness of how much mentoring matters to me helps me to bring an attitude of appreciation and gratitude to the substantial time I spend with mentees and supervisees, which affects the quality of that time and my relationships with the people I mentor. I also explicitly express this value to the students I work with, which allows them to know that the time with them is of value to me.

Because I (SHS) was mentored in an ABBT approach, choosing to be a mentor/supervisor was a values-based decision for me and this allowed me to deeply reflect on the kind of mentor/supervisor that I wanted to be before taking on these roles. I am profoundly appreciative of the amazing mentors I have had (and continue to have) at each stage of my training, who have each taken a personal investment in me as a person, providing the support, care, encouragement, and guidance that I needed to develop into the psychologist I am today while modeling for me how to successfully negotiate this career path. Mentoring/supervising provides me with an opportunity to honor these mentors while providing the support, care, encouragement, and guidance to the next generation as I contribute to their growth and learning. An ABBT-based mentoring approach also allows me to appreciate the richness and diversity of my trainees/supervisees as I learn from each of their unique characteristics and values, which expands my thinking and experiences. Particularly as a new mentor and supervisor, taking the time to think through my values and who I wanted to be in these roles helped not only with the insecurities and other reactions that LR mentioned above, but also with how to make the many in-the-moment decisions that I had not had to face before.

The impact on students of this values clarity in supervisors and mentors is illustrated in SKW's reflection on mentoring:

> What stands out to me in my experience of acceptance-based mentoring and supervision is my mentor's and supervisor's values clarity in their own lives, particularly in the personal and professional domains. This model of values clarity provides the structural framework for my learning experiences and serves as a jumping off point for my own values-clarification process, as a clinician and scientist. Behaviorally, both my mentor and supervisor communicated explicitly early on (and throughout) how important the mentor and supervisory relationship is to them. While the content of their values has certainly shaped my experience, I think their own clarity has been the

most central modeling experience for me. My mentor and supervisor initi-
ated conversations explicitly about how and why they value mentoring and
teaching and supervising, and some of the principles they value (i.e., collaboration, kindness, genuineness, community engagement in professional contexts, commitment to scientific method, commitment to social justice). We
also meet each week face-to-face. Mentoring/supervision time is taken seriously, and protected from other administrative, social, or practical aspects of
my training. For example, mentors do not check email, answer phone calls, or
schedule over our meetings, and the time spent is dedicated to my learning and
development. Further, rather than time being project- or deadline-focused,
our meeting time is focused on my development as a clinician or researcher
and content is focused on issues that relate to my development in different
clinical, professional/developmental, and research-related domains. All these
behaviors are clearly related to their mentoring and supervision values. This
reinforces my motivation to learn, and creates an atmosphere where trust is
cultivated and a relationship as a platform for learning develops.

My (LR) value of genuine human connection, coupled with my understanding
that experiential avoidance (EA), which can be caused by the kind of self-
presentation of "strength" and invulnerability that often feels encouraged in graduate school, causes suffering, lead me to disclose vulnerability and my own human
reactions as a model to my mentees. Through these disclosures, I aim to cultivate
a genuine relationship with students in which we are both people who struggle
with thoughts, feelings, and sensations related to perceptions of inadequacy, self-
doubt, or reactivity. I hope this allows them to feel more comfortable sharing their
vulnerabilities with me, and helps them to accept the range of their own internal
experiences as part of the human experience of being in graduate school.

In our work with clients, we help them to clarify their values and enact valued behaviors across three domains: (a) relationships, (b) work/school/household
management, and (c) self-nourishment and community engagement (Roemer &
Orsillo, 2009). Similarly, in our own lives, we acknowledge the importance of each
of these domains and make choices so that we are engaging in actions that are
consistent with the way we want to be in each domain. In my (LR) ongoing work
with mentees and supervisees, I make sure that I ask about other areas of their
lives and help them to fit their graduate work into a context that also attends to
important relationships and their own self-care and community engagement. I
also try to model this approach by sharing my own decision-making when I make
choices to prioritize family, friends, or self-nourishment, rather than engaging
in work. For me, this is an important complement to modeling how to engage in
work that is rewarding and consistent with my values. Although I often address
this in my individual meetings with students, I have also found that providing
this kind of modeling in a group context can have a more widespread, positive
impact. Most recently, I made the choice to include photos of my collaborators
and students at my wedding at the end of a professional presentation I gave on my
wedding anniversary at a "Graduate Summit" focused on learning from "Leaders

in Clinical Psychology" sponsored by Division 12 of APA. This modeled the full relationships I have with my colleagues and students while showing that a "leader" in psychology could also be celebrating her wedding anniversary later that day, suggesting the values I hold across domains in the same moment. Both LR and SHS also intentionally model balancing our values and having full relationships with colleagues when we are teaching courses or in group supervision contexts.

Our field is filled with models of people who seem to always be working and often people seem to hide the times they spend disengaged from work as though this is the goal or what it means to be an "accomplished psychologist." Making this balance more transparent can help students to see a viable, full life in their mentors and supervisors, and also allows them to feel comfortable having conversations about the challenges of balancing personal and professional lives. At the same time, clarification of the values inherent in our work helps us to spend extensive time working because of its value, rather than as a sense of obligation or due to fear of being judged by others or falling "behind." In our experiences, this intrinsic motivation leads to better work and more life satisfaction. This conversation about balance recognizes that balance is a dynamic process. It does not mean that at every moment there is an equal divide across valued domains, but rather that different valued domains are acknowledged even when it is a period when the majority of time is spent in a single domain. For example, in academia, there is traditionally a larger focus in the work domain during the academic year whereas during summer the balance shifts. In our mentoring, even if an upcoming deadline may shift the focus temporarily for our mentees, we would talk with them about how they can creatively be attending to the family and self-care domains in smaller pieces, trusting and planning for when the balance can shift again.

The conversations that I (SHS) had with my mentor about values and balance were and still are the cornerstone of how I navigate through my professional career. With all of the pressures and requests of being a new academic, thinking through how each request or decision fits with my values helps me both turn toward aspects of my work that feel meaningful, but also helps me tolerate the less intrinsically meaningful aspects or helps me to recognize when I should say no to tempting requests to ensure some self-care or time with family. Connecting with my values allows me to appreciate some of the less appealing tasks because I can see their value of moving me toward tenure, as being part of having a complete academic identity, or by recognizing the ways that the university would not operate without faculty sharing in some of the less glamorous responsibilities.

Awareness and Acceptance of the Humanness of Suffering

ABBT approaches emphasize the naturalness and inevitability of human suffering and distress. Clinically, an important component of meaningful change occurs as therapists validate and accept the thoughts, emotions, sensations, and memories that clients share with them, approaching them with compassion, care, and understanding rather than the judgment and rejection that clients fear (Roemer & Orsillo, 2014). Similarly, within mentoring and supervisory relationships, we communicate how understandable and human a whole range of responses are. As noted above, modeling is one way of communicating this acceptance. Another is genuinely validating any expressions of distress from students. Students have often previously received messages that suggest they are not supposed to feel (or express) their fears or uncertainties, so this validation provides an important new learning experience that they can carry into other contexts. Because supervisors and mentors loom large as professional models, their communications of understanding and compassion are particularly powerful tools in promoting acceptance of suffering and distress.

Just as we use psychoeducation in therapy as one strategy to help clients develop a more decentered, compassionate, accepting relationship with their own internal experiences, I (LR) regularly refer to the context of graduate school and our professional field, as well as natural human tendencies, as explanations for the inevitable distress and uncertainty that students experience and express. For instance, I will talk to students about how the process of being accepted to graduate school encourages the perception that our value is determined by products (such as publications, conference presentations, GRE scores) rather than the process of our learning and engagement or our ability to relate to others with respect and care (which I see as more closely tied to success in graduate school and beyond). I also discuss how competitive thoughts and reactions are a natural by-product of the context of graduate school and the field, as well as human tendencies toward comparison and past experiences of being at the "top" of one's class that often led to admission to graduate school in the first place. As I get to know mentees better, I may also make connections to their specific contexts and histories that naturally lead to the kinds of responses they are sharing with me. For instance, with students who identify as people of color or with other marginalized statuses, I will draw connections to how experiences of discrimination and systemic inequity contribute to the thoughts and feelings that arise in the context of their work, helping them recognize, have compassion for, and decenter from these inevitable reactions, in order to reduce internalized stigma. Similarly, I will validate the reality of systemic inequities in economic burden for students, which can make aspects of their work process more challenging both practically and emotionally, particularly in the context of other students or colleagues with more privileged status. This validation and awareness can help students decenter and also problem-solve, which addresses practical barriers more effectively (e.g., finding part-time positions that are in line with their interests and values). I will also draw connections to family contexts when they are relevant as another way to better understand responses. This enhanced awareness and understanding helps students to cultivate acceptance of their own responses and also naturally leads to enhanced compassion, as discussed below.

Mindfulness

Mindfulness skills ("open-hearted, moment-to-moment, nonjudgmental awareness"; Kabat-Zinn, 2005, p. 24) are often practiced in the context of ABBTs in order to cultivate acceptance and to alter the nature of clients' relationships to their internal experience so that they are more decentered and less judgmental or reactive.

In the context of treating anxiety, an emphasis on the present moment counters the habitual future focus of worry (Roemer & Orsillo, 2013). Similarly, within the context of graduate training where future steps (e.g., obtaining a practicum site, accruing clinical hours, internship applications, completing a thesis or a dissertation) often loom large, repeatedly bringing awareness back to the present moment can be extremely helpful as an overall strategy. I (LR) often remind students that the kinds of activities they are currently engaged in are very closely related to the kinds of activities they plan to pursue in their career, so rushing through these training opportunities to get to those future responsibilities does not make sense. At the same time, I validate the unique stressors of graduate training (e.g., limited financial compensation, extensive external evaluation) that can make these moments particularly challenging. Cultivating spacious, curious awareness of experiences as they arise can also help students to make room for the thoughts and feelings that naturally occur and allow them to experience that these thoughts and feelings come and go, rather than being permanent and unending. This, combined with the expression of validation and compassion described above, can help students to notice their reactions without trying to control or remove them, which helps to reduce the duration and intensity of distress while promoting decentering so that distressing thoughts and feelings are not experienced as defining and overwhelming. My approach to applying mindfulness in my mentoring and supervision has involved largely informal practice: I apply mindfulness skills in all my interactions, repeatedly bringing my own awareness back to the present moment and to what is arising for me and what I notice in my students. This process, and our discussions, encourages the same approach in them. One could also use more formal practices and exercises for this purpose; I am more likely to use formal practices in a group setting to help each individual settle into her or his own expansive, curious, compassionate awareness.

Being aware in the present moment, with compassion, also helps trainees to respond more skillfully in therapy (as described in more detail below), and to engage in more skillful, valued actions throughout all aspects of their training and in their lives more broadly. Mindfulness skills help us all to notice when we are distracting ourselves from our work in ways that inevitably make us feel worse later, or when we are responding to a peer, friend, or partner in a way that is not consistent with how we want to interact with these people. Practicing awareness while in a mentoring or supervision meeting helps us to stay on task and meet the needs of our agenda, while also helping us to notice if we have avoided a particularly charged topic, or are having a strong reaction that we should explore and address. A shared commitment to cultivating awareness helps both mentors/supervisors and mentees/supervisees to continually practice these skills together, which stands to benefit all.

Compassion

Many ABBTs explicitly or implicitly cultivate self-compassion, as well as compassion toward others (Tirch, 2010). As described above, recognizing the humanness and widespread nature of suffering helps to promote compassion toward these experiences and reduces self-criticism and judgment, widespread human experiences that often accompany experiences of graduate school. Being put into so many new contexts and learning new skills naturally elicits fears and thoughts of inadequacy and self-doubt. Mindfulness and validation help students to develop compassion for these experiences and repeated exposure helps them to learn that they can *feel* unable to succeed in a new context or have *thoughts* that they will fail and yet still *experience* success and reward in these contexts. Mentors and supervisors can draw attention to these processes in order to enhance the general learning of adequacy regardless of thoughts and experiences, as well as the experience of learning from mistakes, rather than mistakes indicating permanent failure.

As Zen teacher Josh Bartok describes (personal communication, July 11, 2014), awareness of our own reactivity naturally leads not only to compassion for ourselves but also to compassion for others who also experience reactivity. As students become aware of their own thoughts and feelings and the non-defining nature of these reactions, they are also able to recognize the same processes in others, even when these processes lead to behaviors that can naturally evoke negative reactions. In my (LR) mentoring relationships, I often share my own realizations regarding the humanness of others and how compassion for them helps me to be the person I want to be in relation to them. One of the most gratifying experiences I have with my graduate students is watching them act with kindness and care toward their peers and particularly toward other members of our research or clinical team and more broadly when enacting our program's social justice mission. While graduate school and the field provide contexts that can promote competition and a desire to do better than the people around one, my students and I find that when we experience genuine joy at others' achievements, we enjoy our work together, and are able to be more successful as a group as well. These expressions of appreciative joy (*mudita*; Bernhard, 2013) are a particularly salient feature of our lab relationships and my students often go on to create similar contexts in their future work as well.

SKW discusses how awareness/acceptance of the humanness of suffering and compassion have played a role in her experiences in training:

> The acceptance-based process of relating to suffering in an open-hearted way stands out to me as another key aspect of acceptance-based mentoring and supervision. Behaviorally, supervisors and mentors model self-compassion and compassion for others. I observe this through how they communicate to me about how they are feeling, and how they communicate with one another in professional spaces I observe. Here, they model that it is acceptable to struggle with an issue, project, or personal concern and that struggles will be met with kindness and compassion by one another and oneself. This also translates into mentors and supervisors using time in our meetings to inquire about how I am doing and feeling in a genuine way. Additionally, early on in our meetings, they initiated conversations about the boundaries around what we could discuss in our meetings. In that conversation, they explicitly invited

in discussion about human suffering (including either my own personal and/ or familial concerns, or that of my clients or classmates) to communicate that mentoring and supervision is a space where you can be a whole person. Here, struggles (with a variety of stressors) are normalized as a part of common human experience. This taught me that not only will we teach mindfulness and/or self-compassion as a clinical competency but we will engage in behavior consistent with these principles in our mentoring, supervisory, and professional relationships. In these conversations about our own or our client's suffering, we also often incorporate compassionate behavioral conceptualizations of how these problems were developed, maintained, and may be relieved. In this way, these principles translate into valued actions in our relationships with one another and as a general approach to research and clinical work.

ABBT Principles in Clinical Supervision

Within the context of clinical supervision, ABBT principles guide the approach to providing clinical care, the attitude toward clients, and the nature of the supervisory relationship, in addition to the obvious impact on the therapy provided. Before we provide some examples of our intentions in providing clinical supervision, EHE describes the way ABBT principles affected her training as a therapist:

> ABBT supervision and mentoring provides me with experiential learning, which has been particularly helpful within my own clinical work. During supervision and mentoring meetings we discuss ABBT principles such as self-compassion, valued action, mindfulness, and decentering in relation to clients, research, and also in relation to our own lives. This deep understanding of ABBT principles and the integration of these principles into my professional and personal life has had a large impact on my clinical work. For example, when I talk with clients about various concepts such as decentering, I have a deeper understanding of the concept and what it means than if I had only read about it in a book or article. When I talk with clients about clarifying their values, and the challenges around values conflicts and working to balance their values, I can empathize with their experiences, since I am aware of times in my own life when two/multiple values are in conflict, and I have to make a decision about which action to take in that moment. From this perspective, I am better able to explain concepts to clients, to validate the challenges associated with practicing many of the new skills that I hope to help my clients foster, and therefore troubleshoot any barriers that arise. This strong training in ABBT principles across contexts allows me to apply ABBT principles and skills with fidelity, but also with great flexibility based on the client, the presenting problem(s), and cultural and contextual variables, therefore likely providing more effective and culturally competent and sensitive individualized treatment.

The ABBT training that I have received is grounded in traditional cognitive-behavioral therapy, and is guided by a strong case conceptualization based on the individual's learning history, biological predispositions, and context. This perspective also develops compassion for clients and a way of conceptualizing individuals' experiences in ways that are less stigmatizing. For instance, there is an understanding, as with other cognitive and behavioral approaches, that individuals' behaviors, thoughts, and feelings are shaped by their learning history, and that behaviors, whether they are deemed to be adaptive or maladaptive, are all attempts to serve a function. In addition, this lens includes a strong belief that humans can learn new ways of being and responding to their internal experiences through continued practice. Being supervised by psychologists who model this type of understanding of clients' experiences has helped me to develop my conceptualization skills, and to be able to openly share conceptualizations with clients.

One of the many aspects of ABBT that stands out to me, particularly within the context of the social justice focus of our program, is that it encompasses the ability to try to understand the client's contextual factors and their own values, not those imposed on them by dominant society. This perspective means that one focus of treatment is to determine how the client's anxiety or other symptoms are getting in the way of how they want to be in the world, and helping them to determine how they can live more in line with what is important to them, which is often an empowering experience. This focus promotes discussion about the client's contextual factors, the inequities within our society, and the fact that we live in an unjust world. Awareness of our values and actions that are in line with our values can be helpful here in our own lives as well as our clinical work if we can acknowledge external barriers to valued action and recognize that these barriers, such as discrimination across a variety of marginalized identities, exist in society, and not inside ourselves.

As supervisors, we incorporate an emphasis on values-driven behavior by exploring with supervisees what is meaningful to them about providing therapy and the type of therapist they want to be. Clarification of these values helps new therapists connect to these intentions as they face the inevitable anxiety that arises in taking on this new, challenging role. This helps trainees to engage in the valued actions of being present with their clients, listening to them, and empathically connecting to them, as well as preparing for sessions and developing a treatment plan, despite the distress and urges to avoid they may experience. Our emphasis on valued action across domains also leads us to specifically address other areas of supervisees' lives, such as self-care, to be sure they are finding ways to integrate the role of therapist into their broader lives and attending to their emotional well-being, an important aspect of ethical practice (Knapp & VandeCreek, 2012).

Attention to our own values also helps us as supervisors; both LR and SHS value the process of helping new therapists grow and learn, as well as helping people who are struggling emotionally. We keep this in mind (or, more accurately, return to it again and again) while we are listening to countless hours of therapy sessions, consulting on cases, and meeting with supervisees and noticing the ways that supervision takes up our time and energy so that we have less time for other things. By repeatedly choosing to engage in these activities because of how much we enjoy and are rewarded by the process of supervision, we experience less resentment and frustration with the time it takes and instead are more connected with how meaningful it is to watch the beginning therapists grow and develop.

Awareness and acceptance of the humanness of suffering is a significant theme in our clinical supervision. This shapes the way we conceptualize cases, as EHE describes above, leading to an empathic, destigmatizing case conceptualization. We see clients as struggling with some of the same natural human processes (like reactivity to internal experiences, EA, and constriction in valued actions) that we as supervisors and therapists also struggle with. This stance leads us to help trainees relate to their clients from a place of shared experience, rather than in a "one up" position that is commonly associated with the role of therapist. At the same time, we teach trainees to maintain boundaries and to keep the focus of sessions on the client's concerns, only using very intentional disclosures to model the humanness of suffering and target clients' self-criticism and EA.

This acceptance of distress is also important in the way we as supervisors talk to our supervisees about the emotional impact of therapy. Often new therapists believe that being a skilled therapist and having appropriate boundaries means not being affected by their clients or not "taking them home" with them. These therapists are then alarmed when they find themselves reacting strongly to a traumatic disclosure or the pain a client shares with them. We talk about the inevitability of these kinds of reactions, as well as the ways to cultivate an ability to "set down" our thoughts and feelings about our clients when we leave for the day or to intentionally plan to engage in other aspects of our lives after seeing clients. This allows therapists to fully engage with clients while with them and also disengage following sessions, even if that means practicing disengaging repeatedly because sometimes it can be hard to let go of the distress someone shares. Normalizing and validating these reactions helps to reduce the judgments and criticism that often arise for therapists, and also makes them more likely to share their distress in supervision, which is important both for trainees' learning and for ethical care.

EHE reflects on a similar focus in her mentoring of undergraduate students, illustrating the broad applicability of an ABBT approach to mentoring:

> Since self-care and self-compassion are important topics within ABBT, when students I mentor are faced with challenging clinical, volunteer, or other experiences I am able to validate their experiences, and highlight that it's not something within them that makes this work hard and it's not that they are responding abnormally to it, but that the nature of the work we do is challenging and that in fact it would be unnatural to not have a response to it. From there we can discuss ways that we can respond to these challenges, such as self-compassion, using both formal and informal mindfulness exercises, and practicing skills such as decentering from thoughts.

Acceptance of distress also guides our approach to therapists' reactions to therapy more broadly. Because we model and describe the ways that it is natural to experience anxiety around therapy and to have reactions to our clients based on our own lives, we hope that supervisees will be comfortable sharing these reactions as they arise. This sharing is an essential part of effective, ethical supervision. It allows us to validate the naturalness of responses and reactions, which reduces the judgment and EA that can intensify, prolong, and muddy reactions. By clarifying responses through awareness and acceptance, supervisees can more skillfully and intentionally respond therapeutically to clients, rather than responding from their own reactivity. This is an essential component of developing as a skillful therapist and we feel that this kind of openness and acceptance on the part of the supervisor is an essential component of clinical training.

Mindfulness skills in therapists have been connected to positive therapeutic outcomes, and there are many theoretical links between mindfulness and skillful therapy (see Fulton, 2013, for a review). Cultivating mindfulness, either informally or formally, is therefore a natural component of therapist training. One example of this application is encouraging therapists to notice their own reactivity (particularly when they are first starting out) and then repeatedly bring their attention back to the client. This practice of repeatedly attending to the client gives new therapists a strategy to help them to be the kind of therapist they want to be (responsive to the client, rather than self-focused). Supervision that predicts that self-focus will occur, validates it, and suggests that in each moment the therapist can again, gently, turn attention to the client, can help therapists to encounter this challenging experience with skill and models that this is a skill that can be addressed in supervision rather than a deficit within oneself. The acceptance cultivated by this approach counters the self-criticism, reactivity, and EA that can accompany this self-focus, allowing more skillful attention and engagement. The natural reinforcement of human engagement with the client then maintains this attentive response, so that eventually it becomes habitual and automatic.

Clearly, compassion is an integral component of clinical work, whether one is explicitly operating from an ABBT perspective or not (e.g., Hays, 2007). In our work with trainees, we often use case conceptualization to help them understand and empathize with challenging clients so that behaviors or reactions that naturally elicit responses of frustration or anger can instead be met with empathy and compassion. We also discuss how trainees can cultivate compassion for themselves in the process of providing therapy. Often supervision can evoke feelings of self-criticism as trainees who are deeply committed to helping their clients recognize that they missed something that was said, that they had a response that may have been experienced as invalidating, or that clients are not progressing in the way they had hoped. The shared understanding that we are all human and that we will inevitably make many, many mistakes can help trainees to take in this feedback and learn from it, without engaging in a spiral of self-criticism that interferes with their effectiveness. To facilitate this process, we often point out that it is exponentially easier to notice patterns or have a new perspective when listening to or watching a session (or even hearing about a session), as opposed to when being in a session and having to respond to a client. So we can notice things as supervisors that we would miss as a therapist. These observations are shared to help supervisees see that the discrepancy between our perspective and theirs is not due to deficits in their inherent skill or ability as a therapist, but has to do with the context we are each in. In doing so, we hope this fosters compassion for oneself for not knowing and therefore allows for an exploration of what else can be learned.

ABBT Principles in Research and Scholarship

SKW provides examples of how ABBT principles have applied to her professional development, particularly in the domain of research:

> My mentor and supervisor's modeling of values clarification also facilitates my own values clarification process in the professional domain. In terms of research, projects are explored from a personal values-perspective, both to motivate and focus me as a learner. My mentor encourages me to generate theoretically relevant questions, driven by my sense of personal values (which center on commitments to social justice and empowerment for marginalized populations) that personally matter to me. Here discussions are often focused on separating my personal values from imposed expectations, such as pressure to produce a certain amount of research. Relatedly, the decision to engage in research projects such as publications, posters, or symposia are often based in personal values-clarity: How can we create something that matters to us? Here, the focus is on meaningful work, rather than the magnitude of work.

Perhaps the most salient implication of ABBT principles for our mentoring of scholarship and research comes from this values-driven focus. Academic research is surrounded by external demands and "indicators" of success such as quantity of publications or presentations, grant funding, and ranking of journals that may or may not reflect individual's values. In mentoring meetings, we explore the reason that students have chosen clinical psychology and the type of impact they personally want to have on the field. For many of our students, given the focus of our doctoral program as a whole, one central motivation is social justice. Many students have a desire to impact clinical practice through promoting culturally-responsive interventions, increasing access to evidence-based treatments, and improving clinical training. Others want to make contributions associated with better understanding the process of meaningful change, or the factors that lead to clinical distress. Still others want to improve assessments and better represent the voices and experiences of people who have been underrepresented in the literature. By connecting to the values and meaning underlying their work, students are able to choose activities like grant and manuscript writing or conference presentations because of their desire to communicate their findings, or fund more extensive research, rather than because of the apparent demands of the increasingly competitive, product- rather than process-focused field. Students are also encouraged to find their own paths, rather than to feel compelled to follow the paths of their mentors, so that the research questions they address are personally-relevant (as long as the necessary expertise is available to competently mentor the proposed project).

Attending to the value of the work we do helps us all to focus on the quality and purpose of our work, rather than solely on quantity. It leads us at times to publish in journals or other contexts that reach a clinical audience, where we feel we can have a meaningful impact, rather than solely focusing on methods and outlets that are highly esteemed in the academic realm. At the same time, for those of us who value influencing the academic realm itself, we pursue grants and high profile publications so that we can have a meaningful impact on that realm as well. However, the intention behind these efforts is not to "measure up" to others by criteria that we do not consider meaningful. Instead, our focus is on having the impact on the field that is important to us.

This attention to values also helps us to be flexible and to evolve in our research endeavors. We pay attention to whether the work we are doing feels meaningful and important and we make adjustments, or add additional projects, when we feel unsatisfied with the value of our scholarship. We recognize that at different developmental stages we make different choices, so a student may choose a study that is feasible for a Master's thesis, and is somewhat connected to what the student cares about, while putting off a study that would be more centrally meaningful, but would either require too much sacrifice in other domains of life, or slow down progress so much that it would interfere with other stages of training. A values approach can help with identifying how learning a particular method or making a connection with a particular sample can be a step in the direction of the kind of work the student wants to contribute, even though each specific study does not accomplish all we would like to do. We encourage our students to connect with what they are learning and the process of discovery rather than focusing on getting projects finished or holding on too rigidly to outcomes. In this way, we are helping our students shift to a focus on enacting their values rather than focusing on the perceived goals of success.

As already described above, acceptance of the humanness of distress and suffering, mindfulness, and compassion can help students to address all the natural reactions that occur in the course of research. Research is, in its nature, a long-term, future, and outcome-focused endeavor, so practice in recognizing the value of each step in the process, letting go of attachment to outcomes, and noticing, decentering from, and accepting the inevitable reactions that arise in the course of each stage is an important part of one's professional development and growth. This focus on letting go of outcomes along with accepting and decentering from reactions (e.g., feelings of inadequacy) can be especially helpful in weathering the disappointments and external rejections that will inevitably arise throughout grad school. Mentoring meetings often focus on the process of research, as well as its content, in order to provide guidance and help students to find their own way of managing the stress associated with research. The aspect of compassion also helps us all to remain connected to the experience of our participants and to make our central concern their well-being, so that we practice ethical research and treat participants with respect and care, while conducting rigorous, scientifically sound research, so that we can make meaningful contributions to the literature.

ABBT Principles in Professional Development

In addition to all the considerations described above, an ABBT-informed approach to mentoring helps us to remember that students need to choose their own professional path. We explicitly encourage students to make choices based on the careers they want to have (while acknowledging that they are still in the process of figuring out what they want these careers to look like). We communicate our valuing of all aspects of clinical psychology and are equally proud of our students who choose purely clinical careers as we are of those who choose purely academic careers. We also talk about how these choices involve consideration of values across domains and contextual factors, such as valued actions related to family and financial concerns, in addition to interests and skills. We insure that all our students are competent in all aspects of their training, because that competence is an essential part of any trajectory in clinical psychology, and yet we encourage them to develop depth in areas that matter most to them. We work in our mentoring relationships to help students choose their trajectories by moving toward what is most meaningful to them, rather than moving away from what scares them. So we make sure that perceived preferences are not disguised avoidance or fears of not being able to have a successful research career while also living a balanced life, for instance.

EHE describes how an ABBT-based lab environment has shaped her experience of training and her professional development more broadly:

> I have found our lab environment to be one where individuals demonstrate compassion for others, strive to be in the present moment, are genuinely excited and curious about others' work and projects, and aim to make decisions about actions based on their values. This is not to say that there are never challenges or struggles, but the lens that ABBT provides is always present within the context. When there are challenges or struggles the same skills or lens can be applied, and there is support from mentors and supervisors as well as peers. This kind of an environment takes a strong commitment and a considerable investment of time from the mentor and a commitment from all of its members. However, when it is in place, it offers a unique model of training that can be very different from mainstream academia. In my experience, training in this kind of environment increases individuals' productivity whether individuals are working on their own or collaborating with others. Sometimes taking time for self-care can then help us to be more productive in another domain later. These are not just things that are talked about in meetings with my mentor and supervisors; supervisors and mentors model them. In my experience, this type of context provides an atmosphere that promotes well-being, collaboration, self-care, and ultimately productivity that is sustainable in the long-term. In thinking about my own professional

goals long-term, academia and research can seem like daunting career paths, yet the ABBT model provided by my mentor and supervisors as well as other advanced doctoral students in the lab allows me to see a way to sustain this type of career path, while practicing self-care and also making substantial contributions to the field and the advancement of the field. I believe that this type of a model would be beneficial for many graduate students trying to develop habits and practices that will help to sustain them throughout their careers and prevent burnout from long hours, high demands, and the challenging and emotional nature of work in clinical psychology.

Challenges to Enacting This Approach

Although all of us have benefitted significantly from this approach to our work, it should be noted that we have also encountered challenges in enacting it. One challenge is that not all training contexts take a similar approach, so students have to adapt to other contexts. For instance, SKW notes:

> While acceptance-based mentoring and supervisory relationships within my graduate program have been extremely meaningful and empowering in my training, I have found it difficult to shift to other training/ research contexts in which the principle of acceptance of and compassion for suffering is not as explicitly incorporated. It is challenging to observe stigmatization, and social distancing that may arise in these contexts, as well as figure out how to build professional relationships when these principles are not core features. Certain training contexts outside of the program have been confusing to navigate, especially around boundaries between personal well-being and challenges, and task-focused (as opposed to values-focused) work (e.g., research papers, clinical case conceptualizations). Here, I found I had to re-assess boundaries and shift to different norms. However, using a values-framework was helpful for me to understand what different training centers, institutions, supervisors, and mentors valued in order to adapt to the new setting, even if values may not be explicitly discussed in those settings.

Similarly, all of us operate within contexts that often emphasize external indices of success, rather than internal evaluations of meaning and value. As such, we mentor students to adhere to the external expectations (e.g., number of practicum hours needed to be competitive for internships where they will get the training that they value, thinking strategically about publications), while also considering personal meaning (e.g., choosing practica that will allow them to work in a meaningful context and learn meaningful skills, paying attention to what is meaningful in each publication, regardless of its scope and centrality to their work). Mentoring discussions often involve weighing the costs and benefits of specific decisions, given the student's overall values and priorities, which may lead to missing a family event in order to work on an important manuscript as the time for job applications draws near, and may lead to putting aside a manuscript that is less necessary professionally and less meaningful to spend more time with family at another time. These decisions do not follow any rigid formula (in our lives as well), yet we can guide students in the process of thinking them through so that they make intentional choices, rather than reactively avoiding feared outcomes on either side of the balance in their careers.

Applying ABBT Principles When Challenges to Academic Progress Arise

The doctoral students we typically work with tend to have highly developed tendencies toward productivity and achievement, an emphasis that is continually strengthened by the academic context, which is why we have focused here on the ways we validate the importance of other areas as well, to achieve balance. However, an acceptance-based approach can also be helpful in mentoring students who are struggling to complete their academic work. In these contexts, we might explore what the student values about earning a PhD, or academic work more broadly, so that s/he can connect to the motivation for engaging in academic work and why s/he may want to choose this work over self-care or time with families during certain periods. This exploration may also involve cultivating awareness, understanding, and compassion for the fears and other internal obstacles that arise surrounding approaching academic work, so that the student can decenter from these natural reactions and do the work that matters to her/him. This mentoring may also mean having frank conversations about whether getting a PhD is actually in line with a student's values or whether a different career/degree option may be more in line with what matters to her/him. In our experience, although these conversations can be challenging, they are essential in helping students to intentionally choose their academic path.

In addition, ABBT skills can be helpful when students face external barriers in their lives. For example, bringing awareness to situations where individuals experience discrimination or microaggressions based on their race, ethnicity, sexual orientation, social class, or gender identity can help students see that these barriers and inequities are external and systemic, and not due to anything about them, which can help to decrease internalized stigma. Students may face a range of external barriers, for example financial stress and family responsibilities, including childcare. Across these situations, ABBT skills such as awareness, mindfulness, compassion, and valued action can help students recognize these external, systemic challenges and keep students from internalizing them. Valued action can allow students to make choices in response to these types of barriers, such as choosing to take action in the face of inequality, enhancing social support to deal with external stressors, finding meaning in their actions within external constraints, and working to balance their values across time.

Conclusion

We have focused here on the process of our mentoring and supervision, in an effort to capture the ways that ABBT principles shape our mentoring/supervisory relationships and the guidance we hope to provide to the students we have the fortune of sharing this professional journey with. Students provided illustrations of their experiences of these efforts and the role they have played in their training thus far. All of this is conducted in the context of our shared commitment to using the scientific process to understand and ameliorate clinical distress that interferes with people living meaningful lives; because so much has been written about scientist-practitioner training, we did not include that content here, but it is inherent in all of the processes described above.

We hope that the experiences we have shared here have encouraged you to think about ways to further incorporate your values, as well as mindfulness and compassion, into mentoring and supervision. While we recognize that there are many demands on supervisors' and mentors' time, we encourage you to think about ways you can apply these skills even with limited time. For example, you could set aside five minutes to practice a mindfulness of breath exercise before supervision or a mentoring meeting to practice returning to the present moment,[1] you could practice informal mindfulness by returning again and again to the present moment during your meeting when your mind wanders (naturally) to other tasks you need to do, or you could spend ten minutes writing about how you would like to be in an area of your life that is important to you (e.g., "How do you want to be in your mentoring relationships?" "What kind of mentor would you like to be?" "What do you value about your job?"), and thinking about a small action you can take over the next week that is in line with the values you identify. Each of these actions (and many other similar ways of cultivating awareness, acceptance, compassion, and intention) can help to deepen and enrich the experience of mentoring and supervision for all involved.

Acknowledgments

Liz R. thanks Sue Orsillo, Josh Bartok, and Tom Borkovec, as well as all of her mentees over the years, including the three who coauthored this chapter, for the support, wisdom, and care they have provided, shaping her approach to this valued area of her life.

Elizabeth H. E. thanks her research mentors and clinical supervisors, particularly Lizabeth Roemer, Sarah Hayes-Skelton, and Tracey Rogers, for their strong commitment to training and the well-being of graduate students; the undergraduate students she has had the pleasure of mentoring; her lab-mates for providing a supportive context for professional and personal development; and Andrew Versaw for his support of these values across all areas of her life.

Sarah K. W. thanks her research mentors and clinical supervisors, and especially Lizabeth Roemer, Sarah Hayes-Skelton, Tracey Rogers, and Deb Cohen, for their dedication, as well as her lab-mates for their support and encouragement.

Sarah H-S thanks all of her many mentors and supervisors, but in particular Deb Hope, Sue Orsillo, and Liz Roemer for helping her discover the mentor and supervisor that she wants to be and all of her mentees and supervisees for being patient with her as she has practiced enacting these values.

Note

1 See "http://mindfulwaythroughanxiety.com/"mindfulwaythroughanxiety.com for downloadable recordings of mindfulness exercises.

References

Bernhard, T. (2013). *How to wake up: A Buddhist-inspired guide to navigating joy and sorrow*. Somerville: Wisdom Publications.

Borkovec, T. D., & Sharpless, B. (2004). Generalized anxiety disorder: Bringing cognitive-behavioral therapy into the valued present. In S. C. Hayes, V. M. Follette, & M. M. Linehan (Eds.), *Mindfulness and acceptance: Expanding the cognitive-behavioral tradition* (pp. 209–242). New York, NY: Guilford Press.

Fulton, P. (2013). Mindfulness as clinical training. In C. K. Germer, R. D. Siegel, & P. R. Fulton (Eds.), *Mindfulness and psychotherapy* (2nd ed., pp. 59–75). New York, NY: Guilford Press.

Hayes, S. C., Strosahl, K. D., & Wilson, K. G. (2012). *Acceptance and commitment therapy: The process and practice of mindful change* (2nd ed.). New York, NY: Guilford Press.

Hays, P. A. (2007). *Addressing cultural complexities in practice*. Washington, DC: American Psychological Association.

Kabat-Zinn, J. (2005). *Coming to our senses: Healing ourselves and the world through mindfulness*. New York, NY: Hyperion.

Klepac, R. K., Ronan, G. F., Andrasik, F., Arnold, K. D., Belar, C. D., Berry, S. L., . . . Strauman, T. J. (2012). Guidelines for cognitive behavioral training within doctoral psychology programs in the United States: Report of the Inter-organizational Task Force on Cognitive and Behavioral Psychology Doctoral Education. *Behavior Therapy, 43*(4), 687–697. doi:10.1016/j.beth.2012.05.002

Knapp, S. J., & VandeCreek, L. D. (2012). *Practical ethics for psychologists. A positive approach*. Washington, DC: American Psychological Association.

Linehan, M. M. (1993a). *Cognitive-behavioral treatment of borderline personality disorder*. New York, NY: Guilford Press.

Linehan, M. M. (1993b). *Skills training manual for cognitive behavioral treatment of borderline personality disorder*. New York, NY: Guilford Press.

Roemer, L., & Orsillo, S. M. (2009). *Mindfulness- and acceptance-based behavioral therapies in practice*. New York, NY: Guilford Press.

Roemer, L., & Orsillo, S. M. (2013). Mindfulness- and acceptance-based behavioral treatment of anxiety. In C. K. Germer, R. D. Siegel, & P. R. Fulton (Eds.), *Mindfulness and Psychotherapy* (2nd ed., pp. 167–183). New York, NY: Guilford Press.

Roemer, L., & Orsillo, S. M. (2014). An acceptance-based behavioral therapy for generalized anxiety disorder. In D. H. Barlow (Ed.), *Clinical handbook of psychological disorders: A step-by-step treatment manual* (5th ed., pp. 206–236). New York, NY: Guilford Press.

Safran, J. D., & Segal, Z. V. (1990). *Interpersonal process in cognitive therapy*. New York, NY: Basic Books.

Segal, Z.V., Williams, J.M., & Teasdale, J.D. (2012). *Mindfulness-based cognitive therapy for depression* (2nd ed.). New York, NY: Guilford Press.

Tirch, D. D. (2010). Mindfulness as a context for the cultivation of compassion. *International Journal of Cognitive Therapy, 3*, 113–123. doi:10.1521/ijct.2010.3.2.113

Wilson, K. G., & Murrell, A. R. (2004). Values work in acceptance and commitment therapy: Setting a course for behavioral treatment. In S. C. Hayes, V. M. Follette, & M. M. Linehan (Eds.), *Mindfulness and acceptance: Expanding the cognitive-behavioral tradition* (pp. 120–151). New York, NY: Guilford Press.

Part III

Application of Mindfulness- and Acceptance-Based Approaches in Higher Education

Special Populations and Contexts

6   ACT-Based First Year Experience Seminars

*Jacqueline Pistorello, Steven C. Hayes,
John Seeley, Antony Biglan, Douglas M.
Long, Michael E. Levin, Derek Kosty,
Jason Lillis, Jennifer L. Villatte, Chelsea
MacLane, Roger Vilardaga, Susan
Daflos, Steven Hammonds, Robert Locklear,
and Elisa Hanna*

Introduction

A recent survey with 150,000 first-year students from more than 200 universities in the United States found that only about half of the students—the lowest number since the survey began—rated their emotional health as "above average or highest 10%," whereas the number reporting "frequently feeling depressed in the past year" rose to almost 10%—a 3.4 percentage point increase relative to five years ago (Eagan et al., 2014). The college years, although a time of intellectual, emotional, and social growth, are laden with subtle and overt pressures: learning to individuate from parents, succeeding academically, getting along with roommates, exploring sexuality, fitting in, fulfilling extracurricular demands, feeling pressure to perform optimally given the high costs of a college education, surviving financial challenges, and finding identity amidst an increasingly diverse campus (Kadison & DiGeronimo, 2004). Several of these pressures appear to be most salient during transition periods, such as the freshman year in undergraduate education. Similar patterns of increased distress have been shown among first-year law and other graduate and professional students (see Chapter 8, this volume), which suggests that this is not merely a matter of age—it is also a matter of rapid change and new transitions.

Beginning college seems to be an especially challenging transition, however. The freshman year is often (i.e., especially for residential students) filled with "firsts," such as living away from home, advocating for oneself, and managing day-to-day obligations for the first time. Even severe concerns, like suicidality, have been found to be more frequent among freshmen than seniors (Brener, Hassan, & Barrios, 1999). Although it is quite costly to students and educational institutions alike, perhaps it is no surprise that approximately 25% of incoming freshmen fail to re-enroll at the same institution the next year (Gerald & Hussar, 2002). Emotional problems are one of the primary reasons for temporary discontinuance of college enrollment (Arria et al., 2013) or actual drop out (Eisenberg, Golberstein, & Hunt, 2009).

Experts suggest that first-year students succeed when they make progress toward developing not only academic and intellectual competence, but also emotional and social competence (Upcraft, Gardner, & Barefoot, 2005). It is important that freshman students receive proper assistance, as struggles that take root early in college may be likely to persist (Zivin, Eisenberg, Gollust, & Golberstein, 2009). Thus the transition to college offers an important target and opportunity for promoting psychological skills that can dramatically affect the lifelong mental health trajectories of these emerging adults (Salmela-Aro, Aunola, & Nurmi, 2008).

In this chapter we will: (a) highlight some of our own research suggesting that approaches targeting psychological flexibility (PF; described below) as a common core process are well matched to college freshmen; (b) describe, and summarize preliminary findings, of a study utilizing a classroom-based approach attempting to prevent and/or ameliorate mental health problems in college freshmen based on acceptance and commitment therapy (ACT; Hayes, Strosahl, & Wilson, 2012); and, (c) discuss challenges we have faced and lessons we have learned that can potentially help the field in the conduct of this type of research, prevention efforts in particular, in the future.

Adjustment to College Seminars Might Be an Ideal Venue to Teach Psychological Skills to College Freshmen

To help college freshmen adjust effectively to college, and thereby counteract the many stressors and avoid premature dropout from college, most universities offer some type of first year seminar (FYS) to freshman students (Padgett & Keup, 2011). A study by the Policy Center on the first year of college showed that 94% of accredited four-year colleges and universities in the United States offer a FYS to at least some students and over half offer a FYS to 90% or more of their first-year students (2002; www.firstyear.org).

FYSs vary a great deal in terms of content, duration, and whether or not they are mandatory to freshman students (Padgett & Keup, 2011). A common form of FYS is that of an "extended orientation" consisting of "an introduction to campus resources, time management, academic and career planning, learning strategies, and an introduction to student development issues" (Padgett & Keup, 2011, p. 2). Participation in FYS is generally associated with persistence into the second year in college, better academic outcomes, and other positive changes due to retention in college (as summarized in Cuseo, 2009, and Pascarella & Terenzini, 2005). Although FYSs have recently been shown to impact some cognitive variables (Padgett, Keup, & Pascarella, 2013) and coping with stress is a frequent topic in FYSs (Padgett & Keup, 2011), as far as we know, no randomized controlled trial to date has utilized a credit-earning class specifically to both prevent and ameliorate mental health problems among college freshmen. In principle, the delivery of psychological content via classes may make it more accessible, less stigmatizing (it's not therapy), less costly, and more easily disseminable.

An Approach That Is Empirically Validated and Transdiagnostic Might be Most Efficient

If psychological skills are taught to college students in order to prevent and ameliorate diverse forms of psychological suffering, the question remains: Which psychological treatment would be most appropriate for delivery in a classroom format for college freshmen? Typically the idea of addressing the specific content of the problem (e.g., substance abuse, depression) is appealing; however, as discussed by Block-Lerner and Cardaciotto in Chapter 1, college students are encountering *a number* of different issues. Some specific programs have been designed for college students in order to treat/prevent specific content such as substance abuse (Rimsza & Moses, 2005) or eating disorders (Phillips & Pratt, 2005). Even if such programs appear promising, when it comes to universal prevention, it would not be feasible to conduct a program for each possible problem, and comorbidity is common. Thus, prevention requires an approach that is adaptable to a range of problems and that could reach students who are distressed but also those who are not yet distressed. An obvious target for a transdiagnostic prevention approach is PF—the ability to be mindful of experiences in the present moment and to change, or persist in, behavior when doing so serves valued ends (Biglan, Hayes, & Pistorello, 2008).

There is a now substantial literature base indicating PF as a common protective factor across many psychological issues (Hayes, Luoma, Bond, Masuda, & Lillis, 2006), but it remained to be seen whether college freshmen's ability to be psychologically flexible would prospectively predict future campus-based behaviors, such as academic outcomes and health care utilization at the Student Health Center, and whether or not PF or inflexibility would serve as a determining transdiagnostic factor in this population. These fundamental questions were three initial lines of research pursued by our team.

Psychological Flexibility Predicts Early Graduation and Is a Common Core Process in Freshmen Psychological Issues and Healthcare Utilization

As part of a large, federally funded study to be described later, we assessed close to 2,400 entering freshmen's level of PF (while they were still in high-school) and followed their academic performance and enrollment in college for the next four years. Above and beyond the impact of standardized achievement tests such as the ACT/SAT, a 7-item measure of PF, the Acceptance and Action Questionnaire-II (AAQ-II; Bond et al., 2011), was predictive of graduation in four years or less. This finding is of significant interest for college administrators who need to attract, retain, and graduate students in order to fulfill their educational mission.

As part of the same project, a sub-sample of 972 first-year college student freshmen, average age of 18, completed self-report measures of PF and psychological distress as well as a structured diagnostic interview at baseline. PF was significantly lower across a range of current and lifetime depressive and anxiety disorders as well as lifetime history of eating disorders, relative to freshman students with no disorder, even after controlling for general psychological distress (Levin, MacLane, et al., 2014). A deficit in PF was more apparent among those having comorbid depressive, anxiety, and substance use disorders relative to those only having one of these diagnoses (Levin, MacLane, et al., 2014). These findings suggest that PF, or the lack thereof, as a mechanism of action, underlies several mental health problems among college freshmen and therefore interventions that effectively move it may be helpful to a range of presentations, including comorbid presentations that typically are thought of as more difficult to treat.

In another study (Hildebrandt, Hayes, Pistorello, Gallop, & Hamilton, unpublished manuscript), first-year freshmen who were currently living in a student residence hall ($N = 208$) took the AAQ (Hayes et al., 2004) to measure PF and a symptom inventory to measure psychological distress. Over the next four years, the interaction of PF and psychological distress significantly predicted visits to the university's Student Healthcare Center ($\beta = -0.817$, $t = -2.15$, $p = 0.032$). The main effect for PF also was significant ($\beta = 0.329$, $t = 2.83$, $p = 0.005$), in that the higher the psychological inflexibility in the freshman year, the higher the number of medical visits during college, while that for psychological distress was a trend ($\beta = 0.623$, $t = 1.87$, $p = 0.064$).

These findings suggest that PF is highly relevant to college student freshmen. That is true not only in terms of mental health issues, but also in terms of academic functioning and physical health. It is true both cross-sectionally and longitudinally.

What we do not have is clear evidence in the area of comprehensive interventions on how to change PF in college students. The closest set of data consists of an evaluation of the impact of an ACT self-help book on Japanese international students (Muto, Hayes, & Jeffcoat, 2011) in a small ($N = 70$) randomized trial. Results showed that reading the book improved general mental health at post and follow-up, and had positive effects for students who were moderately and above depressed or stressed, and for severely anxious students. Outcomes were mediated and moderated by PF. This is hopeful, but it does not yet show that college freshmen can be reached.

ACT as a First Year Experience Seminar

Based on these findings, we examined whether clinical acceptance and commitment training (ACT) technology would be acceptable and useful when presented as an FYS. This federally funded project[1] examined the impact of a 1-credit ACT seminar, composed of eight two-hour lessons designed to prevent and ameliorate mental health issues among college students. This class was compared to a didactic FYS class with content specifically selected based on its relevance to mental health issues in college: In addition to time management, making career choices, and learning about resources on campus, the class focused primarily on learning about depression, anxiety, substance abuse, and relationship problems among college students.

The ACT seminar attempted to increase PF in college freshmen by packaging typical ACT therapeutic content (Hayes et al., 2012) into a credit-earning class. Each class followed a PowerPoint presentation in order to enhance fidelity to the research protocol by different instructors.[2] Classes were small (9–15 students each), and were conducted by ACT-trained graduate students or postdoctoral fellows. To reduce financial obstacles, the credit for the class and the textbook across both conditions were paid for by grant funds.

The ACT class used as its textbook *Get Out of Your Mind and Into Your Life* (Hayes & Smith, 2005), which is a best-selling self-help workbook previously found helpful with international college students (Muto et al., 2011). The class was structured by covering 1–2 ACT processes each week, which roughly coincided with the workbook chapters (Hayes & Smith, 2005). The initial thought was to package a typical 2-day ACT workshop (16 hours) into a 1-credit class. Thus, the class included classic ACT elements, such as foundational conceptualizations (i.e., human suffering is ubiquitous and "normal"), metaphors (i.e., difficult thoughts, feelings, and images are like passengers on a bus we are driving—they will come along but need not dictate the direction of the bus), eyes closed exercises (i.e., instructing students to imagine each and every private event, like a thought or an emotion, as a leaf going down a flowing stream), and experiential exercises (i.e., having students pair up and each acting like the other's mind during a walk around campus or having students sit facing each other, being present while maintaining eye contact for a few minutes).

At the end of each class, homework was assigned, which typically included reading 1–2 chapters in the book and doing 1–2 exercises. Some examples of homework exercises include: practicing/listening to mindfulness exercises (which we named "noticing" exercises), writing about their "passengers," attending a university social event, making and keeping a commitment, and journaling about their reactions to a chapter. Homework was assigned and collected through WebCampus.[3] Additionally, each class started with homework review with students being asked to share whether or not they did the homework, what went well, and what didn't go well. The instructors looked for ways to reinforce even small steps toward ACT-consistent verbal reports and behavioral repertoire. Completion of homework, as well as attendance of classes and grades in two exams, contributed to the student's final grade.

Several principles were followed in order to adapt ACT into a classroom context with students who may or may not have been distressed, including the following:

1   using examples from non-clinical, as well as clinical, situations without inadvertently fragilizing the students;

2   assuming that the process within the class was just as important as the content;

3   orienting and re-orienting students as to the purpose of the class and some exercises, and asking permission before conducting more daring

experiential exercises (and making clear that students could decline participation if they so wished—few ever did);

4   relying as much as possible on engaging materials (e.g. youtube videos) with
content relevant to college as a venue for PF learning; and

5   allowing instructors some flexibility on which metaphors and interventions
were utilized as long as a specific process was targeted.

See Pistorello et al., 2013 for more details on this process.

Similarly, because the class included both students who were psychologically
distressed and those who weren't, and because we had as a primary goal prevention
of future problems, we contextualized the elements of the ACT class as something
that could be useful right away for some but perhaps in the future for others. In
classes 1–2, instructors stated something like, "This class is about what you can
do when things aren't working in your life, or when things get really hard, even if
that hasn't happened for you yet." Because of the diversity of experiences in the
classroom (not everyone was in distress, as is the case in clinical settings), instructors reinforced steps in the right direction and only gently challenged comments
that were not ACT-consistent, often inviting students to check on the workability of various behaviors in their lives in the future. For the last class (week 8),
to reinforce the preventive aspects of the class, instructors asked students to bring
something to share with the rest of the class that, in the future, could serve as a
reminder to them of what they had learned in this class.

Although the instructors of the ACT classes were clinically trained, it was made
clear to students that this was *not therapy* but rather an experiential class to help
the students adjust to college and life. However, the stance of the ACT instructors
matched the typical openness and vulnerability of an ACT therapist (Hayes et al.,
2012) in that the instructor, if feasible and advisable, participated in exercises and
used personal examples to model vulnerability and acceptance of difficult emotions, while highlighting the ubiquity of human suffering. For example, in class
8 students were asked to write down on a badge a word/judgment that they were
willing to let go of. The instructors participated in the exercise, and one instructor
wrote "imposter" on his own badge, noting that teaching often gave rise to that
self-judgment for him and what kept him teaching (not buying into that thought)
was focusing on the value of being helpful to students like themselves. Likewise,
the instructors attempted to be "present" and open, not "lecture" students but
instead promote engagement and discussion while allowing students "to be where
they are" without disapproval. As is typical of ACT, everything that showed up
in class discussions was viewed as "grist for the mill." Below are a couple of class
excerpts that demonstrate some elements of an ACT stance by instructors. In the
first extract, a student admits failing to do some homework.

Student: "I didn't do my homework this week. I completely blew it."

Instructor: [Bringing in values/choices] "So this week having fun was a little
more important? That's OK! Did you notice that you were making different
choices all along the way? I think what you had said you wanted last class was
balance, right? It's totally fine that you were out of balance this week. Did you

notice throughout that process that there were lots of little tiny choices along the way? Did you see that part?"

In this second excerpt a student finally gets around to discussing an awkward conversation.

> Student [talking about having a conversation with a professor he had been avoiding]: "It was an extremely awkward conversation."
>
> Instructor: "And you did it, despite that discomfort, that's great!"

The didactic class (or FYS as usual class) was in many ways more face valid in terms of what one might expect in an adjustment to college class. Students in the didactic class had a book that consisted of hand-picked chapters from available FYS materials. The book content always revolved specifically around college life, with college-based examples, pictures, issues, terminology, cartoons, and so on. (This was not the case with the textbook utilized in the ACT condition, which was written for individuals in some psychological pain.)

Method

College freshmen who had been admitted into a mid-sized Western state university were emailed prior to starting college and asked to complete a screening questionnaire in exchange for being entered into a raffle for iPods. Students were screened for levels of PF, via the AAQ-II, and to offset the potential that students very high on PF would be the first to volunteer to participate in the study, recruitment occurred in waves. Students lowest in PF/higher in avoidance tendencies were the first to be invited to take part in the class, whereas those highest in PF/lowest in avoidance were the last ones to be invited; recruitment proceeded until all available openings for the classes were filled. Between 2008 and 2010, approximately 2,300 freshmen (out of 7,200 emailed) completed the screening; 817 completed the initial assessment (85 dropped out before randomization). A total of 732 college freshmen were randomly assigned either to the ACT ($n = 365$) or the didactic ($n = 367$) conditions. Approximately 38% of the trial participants were male and 33% were from ethnic or racial minorities, with a mean age of 18 across the sample ($SD = 0.40$). The final sample resembled the campus population, with the exception that, as is typical in campus-based studies (e.g., Eisenberg, Golberstein, & Gollust, 2007), more female than male students participated.

Despite the recruitment strategy which favored participation by students lower in PF, the final mean level of PF obtained in this study was similar to other non-clinical college student samples and significantly higher than what has been observed in clinical samples (Bond et al., 2011), suggesting that the final sample is representative of college students in the general campus population. The average Beck Depression Inventory (BDI-II; Beck, Steer, & Brown, 1996) score was 8 ($SD = 6.96$), suggesting that, on average, participants suffered from minimal depression (the lowest level possible); 25% were diagnosable with a current mental health problem based on diagnostic interviews (a somewhat lower percentage than found in epidemiological interview studies—Blanco et al., 2008).

Results

Details of this study, and comprehensive outcome findings, are reported elsewhere (Pistorello et al., in preparation; Pistorello et al., 2014); however, below are findings regarding the acceptability and feasibility of conducting an ACT FYS class, as well as some preliminary primary outcome and process analyses findings.

Attendance

There were no differences by condition in terms of percentage of students who opted to drop out of the class and the overall number of classes attended. Approximately 8% of students dropped the class across both conditions (similar to other FYSs offered locally) and the average number of classes attended was 7 (out of 8) across both conditions.[4]

Satisfaction

A common standardized measure to assess students' satisfaction with the class, the *Student Evaluation of Educational Quality* (SEEQ; Marsh, 1982) was utilized. The SEEQ has been found to be reliable across a wide range of courses (Marsh, 1983). Ratings could range from 1 to 5, and classes from both conditions received high marks (in the 4 to 5 range on average), indicating high satisfaction. There were no differences across conditions in overall satisfaction, suggesting that the ACT class was as acceptable to college freshmen as an FYS specifically designed for this population. In terms of individual questions, ACT students were more likely than didactic students to indicate that the class was intellectually challenging and stimulating, that it had increased their interest in the subject area, that their instructors were enthusiastic, and that the class may have helped them deal with relationships in the future. In contrast, students in the didactic condition were more likely to report that they had learned and understood the subject material and that they expected the class to be helpful in dealing with alcohol and drug issues in the future (which makes sense considering that substance abuse was specifically addressed in the didactic seminar).

Importantly, the ACT class was found as acceptable to racial/ethnic minorities as the control condition.[5] This is an essential finding, considering how different (more personal/experiential) an ACT-based class is relative to more typical FYSs.

An informative finding emerged when psychological distress was entered as a moderator of satisfaction with the classes. When a median split was computed on the General Health Questionnaire (GHQ; Goldberg & Williams, 1988), it was found that students who were more distressed were more satisfied with the ACT class, whereas students who were less psychologically distressed preferred the didactic FYS. This suggests that, at least in terms of satisfaction, ACT classes may be better suited to students who are currently in some sort of mental distress.

Preliminary Primary Outcome Findings

Initial analyses do not show consistent differences in outcome in terms of most mental health issues between the two conditions (with follow-up assessments occurring up to three years after baseline). The primary focus of the grant, however, was on reducing suicidal risk. The outcome measures that focused on that area were the Suicidal Behavior Questionnaire (SBQ; Addis & Linehan, 1989), the Lifetime Suicide Attempt and Self-Injury Count (L-SASI) which is based on a more comprehensive version of a similar interview (Linehan, Comtois, Brown, Heard, & Wagner, 2006), and the Life Attitudes Schedule–Short Form (LAS-SF; Rohde, Lewinsohn, Seeley, & Langhinrichsen-Rohling, 1996). The LAS-SF is a 24-item self-report tool measuring suicide proneness (risk-taking and suicide-prone actions, thoughts, and feelings), and the only suicide-related measure that showed an intervention impact. The ACT class produced a significantly better reduction through follow-up in risk-taking and suicide-prone actions among college freshmen.

Preliminary Process Findings

Surprisingly, differences in some key processes have been small in magnitude. For example, although a significantly higher percentage of students in the ACT class showed reliable change in PF (as measured by changes in the AAQ-II administered before and after the seminar), this difference was small: 18% vs. 11% in the ACT versus didactic conditions, respectively.

The most consistent finding at the level of process has been that the ACT condition showed a pattern of moving intrinsic/positive motivations for valuing relationships and education much more so than the didactic condition. This was assessed through the Personal Values Questionnaire (PVQ; Ciarrochi, Blackledge, & Heaven, 2006), which requires participants to provide a brief narrative describing their values within each subscale domain (relationships and education). A series of 3 questions assessed intrinsic/positive motivations for this value on a 5-point scale ranging from 1 ("Not at all for this reason") to 5 ("Entirely for this reason"). Intrinsic/positive reasons include valuing education or relationships because they lend meaning to the students' lives or make their lives richer and more interesting. The findings of increased positive motivation toward education parallel those we have obtained with a brief web-based ACT prevention intervention with college freshmen (Levin, Pistorello, Seeley, & Hayes, 2014), and reinforce the idea that ACT may be especially useful in helping college students engage in values-based educational activities. There was also a trend toward a significant difference between conditions in terms of distress tolerance with students in the ACT class showing more distress tolerance, but there was no difference in terms of mindfulness or believability of thoughts.

Reasons for Taking the Class

One of the open-ended questions asked after the class was completed was what prompted students to take this class. Questions were coded by two different raters, who achieved good inter-rater reliability, and indicated that most students stated that they took the class for a combination of reasons but that 47% partly took the class because of the free credit and/or because they thought it'd be an easy class; 37% partly because they wanted help with college life, self-esteem, or mental health issues; 22% partly because of an intellectual interest or because they were Psychology majors; 18% because of the financial incentives for completing assessments (which went up to a $100 gift card for four hours of assessments in follow-up years 2 and 3); 10% to help the study/science; and others because it was a new experience, there was pressure from others (parents usually), and various other reasons. Although it is still not clear whether these motivational issues matter it places this study in a clearer context. In general, half of the students took the class at least in part for external or academic reasons—which is a notably different motivational set than for most other psychological intervention studies.

What Students Found Most Impactful About the ACT Class

At the end of the class, after the final test, students were asked to comment on what specific elements of the ACT class they found most impactful. By far the most often cited element was the "breathing/noticing exercises" (brief mindfulness exercises that were done at the beginning of class, discussed in the ACT text, or generally alluded to throughout the class/assigned as homework), with comments such as "Learning to notice things and to take a step back to watch my life" and "The noticing exercises, those allowed me to regroup and focus on what I could fix with the tools they gave us and helped me pay attention," with one student explaining potentially why this element stuck with them: "The noticing exercises impacted me the most because it is easy to do and remember every day."

Four additional elements very frequently mentioned were the leaves on a stream imagery exercise ("The metaphor of your thought flow being like a stream and each thought being like a leaf in the stream and that you should just notice it as a thought and let it keep floating by"), the bus metaphor ("Just because those passengers on your bus are pointing you toward that direction—that path that will lead you to sorrow,[sic] you can still keep going on your journey knowing that they are with you"), the Eyes On exercise ("The exercise where we had to sit really close to someone and just look in their eyes without talking. Then the instructor asked what does that person need to change to be perfect and I didn't have an answer like everyone else. I judge myself too harshly"), and Taking Your Mind for a Walk around Campus ("Walking around as each other's minds. It was fun").

Some ACT-related concepts were mentioned at a moderate frequency, such as willingness ("The willingness chapter. It made me realize that just because I don't want to do something doesn't mean I shouldn't do it. I need to be willing to do uncomfortable and annoying things sometimes"), defusion or the ability to not take private events literally ("The idea that my thoughts are just my thoughts and my mind thinks those thoughts"), the ubiquity of human suffering ("Knowing that human suffering is universal and that in my statistical sample, my problems were very much shared by the other students"), the experiential nature of the class ("The exercises that made me open up to others and perhaps get a little bit outside of my comfort zone"). Although less frequent, there were also comments about more complex concepts in ACT like self-as-context ("The part about the fact that there is a you right there behind your eyes that has always been there and always will. You will always be there; you can't lose it. Your mood may change or your body might change, but that part of you won't").

Given the preventive nature of the class, as part of the protocol we asked students to bring something (an object of some sort; it could be a poem or a favorite song even, or any other object) to share with their classmates on the last class that was meaningful to them and could later serve as a reminder of skills they had learned in this class. Several students mentioned how powerful this last class had been to them ("I liked the last exercise we did when we brought in something to take from this class to remember. It was the first time I truly thought about carrying something with me that had meaning").

Fewer than 3% of the comments to this question—about what was most impactful—were negative in nature ("To be honest, nothing really" and "I don't really know. I don't think this class was for me. Maybe I'm already adjusted to college life").

What Students Liked Least/Would Change About the ACT Class

By far the most frequently cited complaint, across both conditions, was that having the class last two hours at a time was too long ("Instead of making them once a week for two hours, maybe split it up because it just seemed long"). Several students suggested that the textbook (*Get Out of Your Mind and Into Your Life*) should be better integrated with the class ("I never read the book because it didn't seem to be required so maybe incorporating that") and more focused on college student life and/or less emphasis on being in pain ("A book that has the same ideas but with less bleakness").

Although one might fear that students would complain about the experiential/personal nature of an ACT class with college freshmen, there was just one comment about that ("It should be a larger class so that you're not always put on the spot to talk about your feelings every time a question is asked").

Conclusions, Challenges, and Lessons Learned

Psychological flexibility as a process applies to college students, but it is not yet clear how best to intervene on such processes in a general college student population using a universal prevention paradigm. Our research so far suggests both what to do and what not to do. In this section, we will first highlight some of the key findings and what they mean for dissemination of acceptance- and mindfulness-based methods in a FYS on college campuses. We will then discuss some of the challenges faced, lessons learned, and some suggestions for future directions.

The Class Is Acceptable, Especially for Distressed Students

We have learned that ACT, cast as an educational approach (acceptance and commitment *training*) but still recognizably related to methods used in clinical contexts, can be delivered as a credit-earning class to college freshmen, with high engagement, high satisfaction, and without any adverse events. When we first submitted the grant proposal to fund this project, reviewers were concerned that students would become too dysregulated and upset with the highly experiential nature of the class. That was not the case. As noted above, students tended to attend 7 out the 8 classes and the dropout rate in the ACT class was the same as in the didactic condition (which is similar to other FYSs). Satisfaction ratings with the class showed that students who were more psychologically distressed preferred ACT whereas the opposite was true for students who were less distressed. It is worth noting, however, that the ACT class in this study was taught by clinical psychology graduate students or postdoctoral fellows who had been trained in ACT. It is not clear if non-clinicians or clinicians with less ACT training can teach this approach as part of a class with as much acceptability by the students.

The ACT Seminar Developed Values-Based Motivation

This type of ACT class, more so than a typical FYS, helped college freshmen develop more intrinsic/positive motivations in both academic and relationship domains. This can be important in persuading campus administrators of the possible value of more psychologically oriented FYS classes with college freshmen. We do not know if much shorter ACT-based interventions would have a similar impact, but that seems possible. For example, Chase et al. (2013) found that a 15-minute online ACT values intervention led to a significant increase in GPAs over the next semester. A short online ACT intervention also increased positive educational values (Levin, Pistorello, et al., 2014). Students in our study complained that the length of each class was too long. It is quite possible that this may be a case of "less is more," particularly with this age group, and were we to redesign this intervention we would probably shorten its timeframe. In the age of YouTube videos and multitasking, we may need to utilize mindfulness-based interventions judiciously—probably in smaller doses.

The ACT Seminar Did not Move the Targeted Process Powerfully

Perhaps the most problematic finding from this study is that PF, the putative common core process targeted by ACT, did not move as much as expected, with only a 7% difference in percentage of students showing a reliable change across conditions. There are two possible explanations for this small effect. First, it may have been a measurement problem, as many studies show that to detect changes in PF it is best to adapt the AAQ to the specific presentation involved. For example, an AAQ reworded for diabetes (Gregg, Callaghan, Hayes, & Glenn-Lawson, 2007) or for work-setting (Bond, Lloyd, & Guenole, 2013), when applied to these different presentations, were more useful than the generic AAQ. This suggests that an AAQ reworded for college students and their specific campus issues needs to be developed and tested. For example, instead of "Worries get in the way of my success" the question could be reworded to say "Worries get in the way of my *academic* success."

A second explanation is that the technology needs to be further refined, although this issue is intertwined with other methodological aspects, such as what type of prevention work is being conducted and how students are recruited (see below for more on these topics). Our research clearly shows that the PF theoretical model applies to college freshmen given the findings of PF predicting graduation, healthcare utilization, and serving as a common factor among many diagnoses with this population. We also know that traditional ACT clinical technology will generally move PF measures in clinical populations, and that this movement often mediates outcomes (Hayes et al., 2006). So far, it appears that the ACT FYS class we developed needs to be modified to produce stronger process effects, or perhaps applied differently to students who are not distressed at all. One hypothesis, heretofore not empirically substantiated, is that having an FYS with *only* students in distress may generate a more powerful impact than observed in more heterogeneous classes, as the group process may have been hindered by the presence of students who were in no distress at all. Although a constant attempt was made to focus on non-clinical and even funny examples, more serious content was routinely brought up by some students. Another prevention strategy that perhaps could better reach students who are not distressed might be curriculum infusion, or the process of integrating mental health content into courses across the curriculum (e.g., Mitchell et al., 2012), as opposed to having a dedicated FYS class. Some such efforts have already been launched in the ACT world in the realm of psychology classes (see Pistorello et al., 2013 for two examples), but it would be useful to extend this reach across other disciplines as well, such as discussing the utility of mindfulness in a business class, or bringing up in a history class how a leader's inability to sit with discomfort could lead to disaster. This would involve developing materials for specific classes[6] that could be easily utilized and integrated by academic faculty, who would have to be recruited to learn more about these concepts. Although it may seem ambitious, at least in terms of mindfulness, our local campus has recently convened a large group of faculty members, across a number of disciplines, who are interested in learning about and teaching students mindfulness.

The Field Needs Better Measures for Prevention Trials

Most of the measures utilized targeted clinical concerns, and it is possible that these measures may not have been adequate to detect differences in a primarily non-clinical population. This hypothesis would fit with the fact that two of the measures that moved most were those regarding values motivation, which are applicable across a range of psychological functioning. In the future, measures that assess college students' mental health (including "flourishing"; Westerhof & Keyes, 2010), as well as mental illness, should be included in prevention trials or studies with college students in general.

Universal Versus Targeted Prevention: An Essential Distinction

This study was focused on suicide prevention and the intervention did have a superior impact on one of the three measures in this domain, but the approach used was universal prevention. There was no attempt to target students who were suicidal or who were engaging in risky behaviors. Meta-analyses on prevention studies show that universal prevention efforts yield much smaller effect sizes than interventions that specifically target individuals who are already showing some symptoms or who might be at risk of developing symptoms (cf. Muñoz, Beardslee, & Leykin, 2012). We conducted recruitment in waves, based on PF level, because we (rightfully, as it turns out), assumed that students who were high in PF would be more likely to be the "early birds" in signing up for the classes. The final sample recruited into the study was a very typical non-treatment-seeking student sample, with scores in PF and depression that placed the average participant in a "healthy normal" range. This is very different from other successful attempts at using ACT in a preventive manner that have tended to use targeted groups that are at risk of developing additional problems (e.g., Bohlmeijer, Fledderus, Rokx, & Pieterse, 2011).

How/When/Where Students Are Recruited Matters

We do know that recruitment matters. The higher satisfaction for distressed students suggests that perhaps an ACT FYS might be best utilized with students already reporting some distress. Some ACT treatment studies have shown an "incubation effect" where differences between conditions favoring ACT become evident only at follow-up (Luoma, Kohlenberg, Hayes, & Fletcher, 2012). Therefore, we expected that some of the effects would not show up at the end of the seminar, but might become noticeable at follow-up, and thus this study had extensive follow-up assessments, with the first two cohorts being assessed annually for three years and the last cohort for two years. In a few cases (e.g., the LAS-SF), it does appear that this pattern emerged, but in general it did not. The conundrum is that, on the one hand, recruiting students at the beginning of the fall, when they are excited and potentially less distressed than usual, may not be ideal if the presence of psychological pain may render students more willing to learn to be more psychologically flexible. On the other hand, delaying the start of prevention work until the spring semester may mean that freshmen may have already encountered problems so severe that this may result in their dropping out.

Although recruitment into the study advertised for a class on adjustment to college and life, some of the incentives for participation (free course credit, free textbook, and payment for assessments) may have inadvertently affected how participants approached the class. We purposely refrained from advertising the class as a way to deal with psychological problems because only one arm focused heavily on this, and we were afraid that, given the scope of the project (publicized campus-wide and during freshmen orientation), it might stigmatize those participating. We still think potential stigmatization of participants is a legitimate concern for campus-wide efforts; however, perhaps other methods of recruitment might be implementable that could allow FYS classes to be more targeted. For example, many campuses are using monitoring systems to identify at-risk college freshmen. Mental health is one area that could be assessed and perhaps only those students admitting to problems could be invited with an explicit message that this class would be about helping them cope with psychological issues, while other students would be provided other class content and messaging or incentives. Such an approach is not without its complexities though, as there might be issues of stigma and even of liability to consider. For example, case law following incidents such as the mass killing at Virginia Tech has demonstrated to colleges how vulnerable they are when they know a student is suicidal or homicidal.

Additionally, it may matter *where* students are recruited. Recruiting students who are already seeking counseling services would be quite different from recruiting non-treatment-seeking students. Individuals who have already made the decision to seek services are arguably at a different stage of change and may be much more amenable to interventions. Prevention studies with this population (and any other for that matter) need to carefully consider who is participating and why—this perhaps will allow the differences in outcome among different studies as well as the generalizability of studies to be better understood.

Our study was unique in its universal prevention approach and also the fact that neither ACT, nor mindfulness or acceptance, were mentioned in recruitment materials. Therefore, we did not select individuals interested in these topics—we sought students who were interested in "adjustment to college and life" as this applied to both active conditions. Studies that do not randomize or utilize a wait-list control condition often appear to mention specifics about the experimental approach in their recruitment, which may inadvertently select individuals specifically interested in a particular approach (mindfulness, for example), thus limiting the generalizability of the study.

Unlike other studies with college freshmen of which we are aware (e.g., Conley, Travers, & Bryant, 2013; Danitz & Orsillo, 2014), ours was the first to rely on both randomization and a credible active control condition. The two conditions were comparable at many levels: both relied on graduate students and postdoctoral fellows as instructors, they were conducted at the same time (students selected a time they wanted and *then* they were randomized to one of the conditions), both provided free credit and textbooks, both provided supervision/consultation to the instructors, and they offered the exact same class dosage. The control condition had a little more face validity for students, and the textbook was specifically designed for college freshmen seminars, whereas the ACT book was a generic self-help book. In the future, an ACT/mindfulness-oriented book developed specifically for college students might work better, as noted by some of the students in their evaluations.

It is important to learn how to increase the impact of ACT, and other acceptance and mindfulness-based methods, and to fit it to different kinds of college students in a prevention context. Our study showed a deficit in strength to move PF, whereas others have encountered other problems, including, for example, despite some promising findings, difficulty recruiting and maintaining students in the intervention (Danitz & Orsillo, 2014). College students are not monolithic, and a variety of methods and modes of delivery are going to be needed to make a difference. It was truly surprising to see how students varied in their perception of which ACT components made the biggest difference for them. There are two additional major avenues that might provide flexible ways of expanding an ACT approach with this population. One is the use of technology (Levin, Pistorello, et al., 2014), and the second is attempting to make more use of the social networks of students. For example, we have developed web-based guided self-help programs that can be used as part of the treatment efforts of college counseling centers (Levin, Pistorello, Hayes, Seeley, & Levin, 2015), and have trained college student peer mentors to identify and help distressed students on campus (Student Support Network or SSN; see Morse, 2013).

Conclusion

Transdiagnostic programs are the holy grail of psychological prevention in higher education settings. It is not yet known with certainty how best to produce gains that last and are broad ranging. The PF model appears to hold up cross-sectionally and longitudinally, providing a target of acceptance, mindfulness, and values for the development of important methods of change. Translating clinical technology to the classroom is clearly acceptable to college freshmen, and it increases their motivation toward positive/intrinsic academic and relational values, but it has produced relatively modest outcomes when utilized in a universal prevention context. More needs to be learned. That is the excitement of the scientific path.

Notes

1 This project was supported by Award Number R01MH083740 (PIs: S. C. Hayes and J. Pistorello) from the National Institute of Mental Health (NIMH). The content is solely the responsibility of the authors and does not necessarily represent the official views of the NIMH or the National Institutes of Health.

2 Class presentations and manual for instructors are available upon request from pistorel@ unr.edu.

3 WebCampus is a University-supported course management system which allows instructors to post course materials, grades, discussions, and more in a secure environment for students to access via the web.

4 Interestingly, the first year of the study, when the class was offered as Pass/Fail, the dropout rate was around 7% and only half of the students attended all 8 classes. For the second and third cohorts, based on instructors' feedback, we changed the grading method so that students received a letter grade for the class (instead of just Pass/Fail) and at that point,

the dropout rate increased to 10% but three-quarters of the students started attending every class. This pattern occurred for both conditions.

5 Across both conditions, students who self-identified as first generation and/or ethnic/ racial minorities reported higher satisfaction ratings and perceived usefulness of the FYS classes than non-minority/White students.

6 See http://gordiecenter.studenthealth.virginia.edu/faculty/curriculum-infusion for an example with substance abuse.

References

Addis, M., & Linehan, M. M. (1989, November). Predicting suicidal behavior: Psychometric properties of the Suicidal Behaviors Questionnaire. Poster presented at the Annual Meeting of the Association for the Advancement Behavior Therapy, Washington, D.C.

Arria, A. M., Caldeira, K. M., Vincent, K. B., Winick, E. R., Baron, R. A., & O'Grady, K. E. (2013). Discontinuous college enrollment: Associations with substance use and mental health. *Psychiatric Services, 64*(2), 165–172. doi:10.1176/appi.ps.201200106

Beck, A. T., Steer, R. A., & Brown, G. K. (1996). *Manual for Beck Depression Inventory II (BDI-II)*. San Antonio, TX: Psychology Corporation Harcourt Brace & Company.

Biglan, A., Hayes, S. C., & Pistorello, J. (2008). Acceptance and commitment: Implications for prevention science. *Prevention Science, 9*, 139–152. doi:10.1007/s11121-008-0099-4

Blanco, C., Okuda, M., Wright, C., Hasin, D. S., Grant, B. F., Liu, S.-M., & Olfson, M. (2008). Mental health of college students and their non-college-attending peers: Results from the national epidemiologic study on alcohol related conditions. *Archives of General Psychiatry, 65*, 1429–1437. doi:10.1001/archpsyc.65.12.1429

Bohlmeijer, E. T., Fledderus, M., Rokx, T. A., & Pieterse, M. E. (2011). Efficacy of an early intervention based on acceptance and commitment therapy for adults with depressive symptomatology: Evaluation in a randomized controlled trial. *Behaviour Research and Therapy, 49*, 62–67. doi:10.1016/j.brat.2010.10.003

Bond, F. W., Hayes, S. C., Baer, R. A., Carpenter, K. C., Guenole, N., Orcutt, H. K., . . . Zettle, R. D. (2011). Preliminary psychometric properties of the Acceptance and Action Questionnaire – II: A revised measure of psychological flexibility and acceptance. *Behavior Therapy, 42*, 676–688. doi:10.1016/j.beth.2011.03.007

Bond, F. W., Lloyd, J., & Guenole, N. (2013). The work-related acceptance and action questionnaire: Initial psychometric findings and their implications for measuring psychological flexibility in specific contexts. *Journal of Occupational and Organizational Psychology, 86*, 331–347. doi:10.1111/joop.12001

Brener, N. D., Hassan, S. S., & Barrios, L. C. (1999). Suicidal ideation among college students in the United States. *Journal of Consulting and Clinical Psychology, 67*, 1004–1008. doi:10.1037/0022-006X.67.6.1004

Chase, J. A., Houmanfar, R., Hayes, S. C., Ward, T. A., Vilardaga, J. P., & Follette, V. M. (2013). Values are not just goals: Online ACT-based values training adds to goal-setting in improving undergraduate college student performance. *Journal of Contextual Behavioral Science, 2*, 79–84. doi:10.1016/j.jcbs.2013.08.002

Ciarrochi, J., Blackledge, J. T., & Heaven, P. Initial validation of the Social Values Survey and Personal Values Questionnaire. Presented at the Second World Conference on ACT, RFT, and Contextual Behavioral Science; London, UK; July 2006.

Conley, C. S., Travers, L. V., & Bryant, F. B. (2013). Promoting psychosocial adjustment and stress management in first-year college students: The benefits of engagement in a psychosocial wellness seminar. *Journal of American College Health, 61*(2), 75–86. doi: 10.1080/07448481.2012.754757

Cuseo, J. B. (2009). The empirical case for the first-year seminar: Course impact on student retention and academic achievement. *E-Source for College Student Transitions, 6*(6), 5–7. Retrieved from http://webs.wichita.edu/depttools/depttoolsmemberfiles/OFDSS/101%20FYS%20Research/FYS-empirical-evidence-10.pdf

Danitz, S., & Orsillo, S. (2014). The mindful way through the semester: An investigation of the effectiveness of an Acceptance-Based Behavioral Therapy program on psychological wellness of first year students. *Behavior Modification, 38,* 549–566. doi:10.1177/0145445513520218

Eagan, K., Stolzenberg, E. B., Ramirez, J. J., Aragon, M. C., Suchard, M. R., & Hurtado, S. (2014). *The American freshman: National norms Fall 2014.* Los Angeles: Higher Education Research Institute, UCLA.

Eisenberg, D., Golberstein, E., & Gollust, S. E. (2007). Help-seeking and access to mental health care in a university student population. *Medical Care, 45,* 594–601.

Eisenberg, D., Golberstein, E., & Hunt, J. B. (2009). Mental health and academic success in college. *B. E. Journal of Economic Analysis and Policy, 9,* 40. doi:10.2202/1935-1682.2191

Gerald, D. E., & Hussar, W. J. (2002). *Projections of education statistics to 2012.* Washington, DC: National Center for Education Statistics.

Goldberg, D. P., & Williams, P. (1988). *The user's guide to the General Health Questionnaire.* Windsor, Berks: NFER–Nelson.

Gregg, J. A., Callaghan, G. M., Hayes, S. C., & Glenn-Lawson, J. L. (2007). Improving diabetes self-management through acceptance, mindfulness, and values: A randomized controlled trial. *Journal of Consulting and Clinical Psychology, 75*(2), 336–343. doi:10.1037/0022-006X.75.2.336

Hayes, S. C., & Smith, S. (2005). *Get out of your mind and into your life: The new acceptance and commitment therapy.* Oakland, CA: New Harbinger.

Hayes, S. C., Strosahl, K. D., Wilson, K. G., Bissett, R. T., Pistorello, J., Toarmino, D., . . . McCurry, S. M. (2004). Measuring experiential avoidance: A preliminary test of a working model. *The Psychological Record, 54,* 553–578.

Hayes, S. C., Strosahl, K., & Wilson, K. G. (2012). *Acceptance and commitment therapy: The process and practice of mindful change* (2nd ed.). New York, NY: Guilford Press.

Hayes, S. C., Luoma, J. B., Bond, F. W., Masuda, A., & Lillis, J. (2006). Acceptance and commitment therapy: Model, processes and outcomes. *Behavior Research and Therapy, 44,* 1–25. doi:10.1016/j.brat.2005.06.006

Hildebrandt, M., Hayes, S., Pistorello, J., Gallop, B., & Hamilton, J. (2012). *Predicting healthcare utilization among college students: Examining the role of psychological flexibility.* Unpublished manuscript.

Kadison, R., & DiGeronimo, T. F. (2004). *College of the overwhelmed: The campus mental health crisis and what to do about it.* San Francisco, CA: Jossey-Bass.

Levin, M. E., MacLane, C., Daflos, S., Seeley, J., Hayes, S. C., Biglan, A., & Pistorello, J. (2014). Examining psychological inflexibility as a transdiagnostic risk factor for Axis I disorders among first year college students. *Journal of Contextual Behavioral Science, 3,* 155–163. doi:10.1016/j.jcbs.2014.06.003

Levin, M. E., Pistorello, J., Hayes, S. C., Seeley, J. R., & Levin, C. (2015). Feasibility of an acceptance and commitment therapy adjunctive Web-based program for counseling centers. *Journal of Counseling Psychology, 62,* 529–536. doi:10.1037/cou0000083

Levin, M. E., Pistorello, J., Seeley, J., & Hayes, S. C. (2014). Feasibility of a prototype web-based acceptance and commitment therapy prevention program for college students. *Journal of American College Health, 62,* 20–30. doi:10.1080/07448481.2013.843533

Linehan, M. M., Comtois, K. A., Brown, M. Z., Heard, H. L., & Wagner, A. (2006). Suicide Attempt Self-Injury Interview (SASII): Development, reliability, and validity of a scale to assess suicide attempts and intentional self-injury. *Psychological Assessment, 18,* 303–312. doi:10.1037/1040-3590.18.3.303

Luoma, J. B., Kohlenberg, B. S., Hayes, S. C., & Fletcher, L. (2012). Slow and steady wins the race: A randomized clinical trial of acceptance and commitment therapy targeting shame in substance use disorders. *Journal of Consulting and Clinical Psychology, 80,* 43–53. doi:10.1037/a0026070

Marsh, H. W. (1982). SEEQ: A reliable, valid, and useful instrument for collecting students' evaluations of university teaching. *British Journal of Educational Psychology, 52,* 77–95.

Marsh, H. W. (1983). Multidimensional ratings of teaching effectiveness by students from different academic settings and their relation to student/course/instructor characteristics. *Journal of Educational Psychology, 75,* 150–166.

Mitchell, S., Darrow, S., Haggerty, M., Neill, T., Carvalho, A., & Uschold, C. (2012). Curriculum infusion as college student mental health promotion strategy, *Journal of College Student Psychotherapy, 26,* 22–38. doi:10.1080/87568225.2012.633038

Morse, C. (2013). Teaching mindfulness and acceptance within college communities to enhance peer support. In J. Pistorello (Ed.), *Mindfulness and acceptance for counseling college students: Theory and practical applications for intervention, prevention, and outreach* (pp. 203–222). Oakland, CA: New Harbinger.

Muñoz, R. F., Beardslee, W. R., & Leykin, Y. (2012). Major depression can be prevented. *American Psychologist, 67,* 285–295. doi:10.1037/a0027666

Muto, T., Hayes, S. C., & Jeffcoat, T. (2011). The effectiveness of acceptance and commitment therapy bibliotherapy for enhancing the psychological health of Japanese college students living abroad. *Behavior Therapy, 42,* 323–335. doi:10.1016/j.beth.2010.08.009

Padgett, R. D., & Keup, J. (2011). *2009 National Survey of First Year Seminars: Ongoing efforts to support students in transition (Research Reports on College Transitions No. 2).* Columbia, SC: University of South Carolina, National Resource Center for the First-Year Experience and Students in Transition.

Padgett, R. D., Keup, J. R., & Pascarella, E. T. (2013). The impact of first-year seminars on college students' life-long learning orientations. *Journal of Student Affairs Research and Practice, 50,* 133–151. doi:10.1515/jsarp-2013-0011

Pascarella, E. T., & Terenzini, P. T. (2005). *How college affects students: A third decade of research.* San Francisco, CA: Jossey-Bass.

Phillips, E., & Pratt, H. (2005). Eating disorders in college. *Pediatric Clinics of North America, 52,* 85–96.

Pistorello, J., Hayes, S. C., Lillis, J., Long, D., Christodoulou, V., LeJeune, J., . . . Yadavaia, J. (2013). Acceptance and Commitment Therapy (ACT) in classroom settings. In J. Pistorello (Ed.), *Mindfulness and acceptance for counseling college students: Theory and practical applications for intervention, prevention, and outreach* (pp. 223–250). Oakland, CA: New Harbinger.

Pistorello, J., Hayes, S., Seeley, J., Lillis, J., Villatte, J., Long, D., . . . Locklear, R. (2015). *ACT as a First Year Seminar (FYS): Satisfaction and perceived usefulness.* Manuscript in preparation.

Rimsza, M., & Moses, K. (2005). Substance abuse on the college campus. *Pediatric Clinics of North America, 52*(1), 307–319. doi:10.1016/j.pcl.2004.10.008

Rohde, P., Lewinsohn, P. M., Seeley, J. and Langhinrichsen-Rohling, J. (1996). The Life Attitudes Schedule Short Form: An abbreviated measure of life-enhancing and life-threatening behaviors in adolescents. *Suicide and Life-Threatening Behavior, 26,* 272–281.

Salmela-Aro K., Aunola K., Nurmi J. E. (2008). Trajectories of depressive symptoms during emerging adulthood: Antecedents and consequences. *European Journal of Developmental Psychology, 5,* 439–465. doi:10.1080/17405620600867014

Upcraft, M. L., Gardner, J. N., Barefoot, B. O., (Eds.) (2005). *Challenging and supporting the first-year student: A handbook for improving the first year of college.* San Francisco: John Wiley & Sons, Inc.

Westerhof, G. J., & Keyes, C. L. M. (2010). Mental illness and mental health: The two continua model across the lifespan. *Journal of Adult Development, 17,* 110–119. doi:10.1007/s10804-009-9082-y

Zivin, K., Eisenberg, D., Gollust, S. E., Golberstein, E. (2009). Persistence of mental health problems and needs in a college student population. *Journal of Affective Disorders, 117,* 180–185. doi:10.1016/j.jad.2009.01.001

7 Acceptance and Commitment Training for Academic Risk

Emily K. Sandoz and R. Ashlyne Mullen

Introduction

The purpose of a university or college is to educate students to a particular standard, culminating in the awarding of a degree at graduation. Yet 41% of those who enroll in college do not leave that institution with a degree within six years (US Department of Education, 2015), and many of those do not leave with a degree at all. A majority of these students are identifiable as "at-risk" for academic failure and withdrawal early in their academic careers (O'Banion, 1997; Thompson & Green, 2002). It seems that for many students, from the moment they arrive on campus, the odds support them leaving without a degree.

Leaving college without a degree greatly limits an individual's chance of success. About 60% of jobs in the United States require a college degree, and this number will only increase over the next decade (Carnevale, Smith, & Strohl, 2010). Among those who have jobs, people with 4-year degrees make 76% more on average than those with only a high-school degree (Julian, 2012). Put another way, a college graduate will make over one million dollars more than someone with only a high-school degree (Julian, 2012). Further, individuals with some college may be in a more vulnerable position than those with none, as they are left with debt from educational expenses but only a minimally paying job.

One approach to improving retention rates is to increase academic criteria for selection to prevent entry of students who are at risk for failure and/or withdrawal. This is not financially feasible for most universities, and prevents the kind of upward mobility that most universities are proud to facilitate (Seidman, 2012). Over the past decade, instead of increasing admissions standards to eliminate at-risk students, universities have made great efforts to address their needs for academic persistence (Choy & Bobbitt, 2000; Noel-Levitz, 2007). For example, many universities employ first-year seminars (e.g., Hunter & Linder, 2005; Tampke & Durodoye, 2013) and academic counseling (e.g., Sharkin, 2004). These efforts have met with some success (Sharkin, 2004; Turner & Berry, 2000). Retention rates remain low, however, suggesting that there is much room for improvement in interventions for at-risk students (Seidman, 2005; Tinto, 2012). The psychological flexibility (PF) model of psychological functioning may offer an alternative approach to buffering risk by focusing on the common struggles of the at-risk student.

This chapter provides an overview of the literature on at-risk students, and offers a contextual behavioral science (CBS) perspective on academic risk and persistence. We will describe what factors put a student at risk for academic failure and withdrawal and how these factors might be understood in terms of PF. Finally, we will describe three programs in development at the University of Louisiana at Lafayette (UL) that integrate flexibility-based interventions, with an emphasis on feasibility, preliminary outcomes, and challenges faced.

At-Risk College Students

In general, universities are successful at identifying students as "at-risk" for academic failure and withdrawal early in their academic careers (O'Banion, 1997; Thompson & Green, 2002). Many risk factors are identifiable upon admission (Lotkowski, Robbins, & Noeth, 2004)—for example, students who: come from low-income households (ACSFA, 2010; Lotkowski et al., 2004; Tinto & Pusser, 2006); are first generation college students (Choy, 2002); are of minority backgrounds (Fenske, Porter, & DuBrock, 2000; Tinto, 2003); or have a low high-school GPA and/or who have low college aptitude scores (Lotkowski et al., 2004). These types of students are all more likely to leave college without a degree.

These risk factors seem to interfere with students developing during their first year the behavioral repertoires that are necessary for academic success. For example, students likely to withdraw tend to have low attendance rates (Geltner, 2001), struggle with adequate academic performance (Ishitani & DesJardins, 2002), and/or work excessive hours (Light, 1996). Tinto (1993) proposes that at-risk college students fail to effectively navigate the challenges of college life in three domains: development of appropriate academic behaviors, resolution of and commitment to goals, and incorporation into the fabric of university life.

Tinto's model of student departure (1993) further suggests that these challenges can be met more readily through students' academic and social integration into the university community. Academic integration might involve behaviors such as attending class regularly, participating in classes and completing coursework, meeting with professors and advisors, or joining academically-focused student organizations. Social integration might involve behaviors such as communicating with classmates out of class, joining athletic, recreational, or philanthropic student organizations, or attending athletic or other social university events.

Intervening With At-Risk College Students

In Tinto's model, high levels of integration are proposed to support at-risk students' navigation of college challenges. For example, integration affords students who enter college with academic deficits with opportunities to receive direct feedback from instructors, observe more effective models, identify supplementary academic resources, and seek academic assistance. Similarly, integration provides first generation and low-income students who enter college with minimal exposure to university policies, procedures, resources, and areas of study with opportunities for socialization by peer models and faculty mentors.

Four common interventions that aim to support academic persistence by facilitating integration are service learning programs, learning communities, mentoring programs, and first-year seminars (Bean & Eaton, 2001/2002). However, at-risk students present special challenges for academic support interventions (Hollingsworth, Dunkle, & Douce, 2009), such that those in the most need are often those least likely to take advantage of such interventions. Many of the behaviors that are interfering with academic success make at-risk students difficult to access. For example, students struggling to attend class or complete assignments are no better at attending meetings (e.g., with mentors, service directors, or learning teams) or responding to emails. A recent review suggested that, at best, current retention interventions seem to result in small, short-term benefits for at-risk students (Valentine et al., 2011).

It may be that struggles with integration, persistence, and accessing interventions to enhance persistence are attributable, at least in part, to psychological barriers. Many of the same students who are at risk for academic failure are likewise at risk for psychological struggles. For example, students of low socioeconomic status are at increased risk for psychological problems (Eisenberg, Gollust, Golberstein, & Hefner, 2007). In addition, psychological struggles may interact with other student characteristics to disrupt persistence. A recent survey by Gruttadaro and Crudo (2012) revealed that 64% of students who withdrew from college in the past five years attributed withdrawal to psychological difficulties. However, these struggles are addressed only indirectly in the majority of persistence interventions (Bean & Eaton, 2001/2002).

For universities to appropriately intervene on student persistence, it may be necessary to consider psychological mechanisms of and barriers to persistence. In their psychological model of student persistence, Bean and Eaton (2000) suggest that students achieve social and academic integration when they are able to stop avoiding the emotional challenges of college adjustment and learn to cope appropriately. Among college students, avoidant coping predicts, above and beyond stressors, psychological outcomes such as depression (Dyson & Renk, 2006) and academic outcomes such as failure (DeBerard, Spielmans, & Julka, 2004). It may be that successfully promoting persistence among at-risk students will require replacing avoidance with more appropriate skills for coping with the dynamic situational and emotional challenges that college presents. In other words, it may be that successful integration, and subsequent academic persistence, requires PF.

Psychological Flexibility

The at-risk college student often faces typical college challenges somewhat handicapped by his or her life circumstances. He or she must navigate not only the challenges themselves, but also fear and distress associated with those challenges. For at-risk students, lacking appropriate academic skills and/or socialization, the development of appropriate academic behaviors, resolution of and commitment to goals, and incorporation into the fabric of university life likely involves feeling inadequate, different, and afraid of failure. Unfortunately, at-risk students may feel most inadequate, different, and afraid in the very contexts designed to promote integration. For example, discussing college policies in a first-year seminar may only serve to highlight how naive the first generation college student feels to such. The student with academic struggles may feel most different and alone when studying with peers in a learning community. In an effort to manage these difficult experiences, at-risk college students may find themselves avoiding class, meetings, emails, and any other situations that remind them of just how challenging being successful is going to be.

The PF model suggests an alternative way of coping. Psychological flexibility has been described as a fundamental aspect of psychological well-being (Kashdan & Rottenberg, 2010), with the model suggesting that dysfunction emerges when people avoid painful experiences in a way that costs value and meaning in their lives (Hayes, Luoma, Bond, Masuda, & Lillis, 2006). PF involves openness to one's own experiences, without defense, and as a fully conscious human being, while engaging in meaningful, committed action (Hayes, Strosahl, & Wilson, 2011). For an at-risk college student, being psychologically flexible might mean being willing to feel inadequate, different, and afraid in service of the purpose he or she chooses for being in college. Instead of becoming increasingly avoidant until finally withdrawing, the psychologically flexible at-risk student could likely access the resources available, allowing for development of appropriate academic behaviors, resolution of and commitment to goals, and incorporation into the fabric of university life.

Acceptance and commitment training (ACT) is based on an empirically-supported psychotherapeutic approach (acceptance and commitment *therapy;* Hayes et al., 2012) that fosters PF to promote increased effectiveness, satisfaction, and meaning in living. ACT training seems to be effective in improving academically relevant behaviors. For example, ACT training with anxious students struggling academically resulted in more hours studying, improved class attendance, and other academic behaviors (Tirado, Ortega, Heilborn Diaz, & Fernández Martín, 2005). A small randomized controlled trial of ACT and cognitive therapy (CT) for test anxiety revealed better exam grades for students in the ACT workshop than in the CT workshop (Brown et al., 2011). Finally, an ACT-based procrastination workshop (i.e., a workshop aiming to develop ACT skills in the service of taking a more proactive approach toward work instead of letting tasks wait until the last minute) with college students resulted in an increase in self-reported PF and a decrease in self-reported procrastination (Scent & Boes, 2014).

Applied to student persistence, ACT may provide an opportunity for at-risk college students to establish their own sense of purpose for being in college and to practice being vulnerable to difficult experiences (e.g., feeling inadequate, different, and afraid of failure) when it serves that purpose. To date, only one study (Sandoz, Kellum, & Wilson, 2014) has directly evaluated ACT training for at-risk college students. Fourteen poorly performing students were referred from an academic support program for high-merit, high-risk students. Group-based experiential ACT training was provided over two months, first weekly, then once every two weeks. Training focused on first contacting academically relevant values and then on building PF skills. Participants exhibited significant improvements in GPA during the semester following the intervention, with 64% of the participants making the required GPA (2.25) to continue to participate in the program from which they were referred. In addition, 57% of the participants went on to earn a degree within six years and one of fourteen to earn a Master's degree. These results compare favorably with other retention interventions deemed "successful" in a national report on student retention (Noel-Levitz, 2007) while still leaving room for improvement.

Preliminary data suggest that ACT is likely to be effective at promoting academic persistence and performance among at-risk college students (Sandoz et al., 2014). ACT has been successfully adapted to a number of formats (Hayes, Luoma, Bond, Masuda, & Lillis, 2006), and could be easily incorporated into a number of typical interventions to increase the PF of at-risk students. Two pilot programs being conducted at the University of Louisiana (UL) at Lafayette which integrate ACT into existing interventions with at-risk students are described in what follows.

ACT-Based Procrastination Workshop

We examined the impact of a two-hour ACT workshop on at-risk college students' self-reported procrastination. At-risk participants were drawn from two different populations: sophomore students on academic probation within the university's Academic Success Center (ASC) for not having met requirements for continued enrollment or funding ($n = 20$), and freshman students who had college entrance exam scores below the university's admission criteria—that is, ACT college entrance exam score below 23 ($n = 6$). Participation was voluntary. Potential participants were contacted by the ASC via email with a description of the study, an invitation to attend an initial meeting, and a link to register online.

Potential participants attended an initial meeting during which we first described the study along with related risks and benefits. Those who consented to serve as participants then completed a packet of questionnaires assessing procrastination (the Irrational Procrastination Scale; IPS; Steel, 2010) and components of PF (the Acceptance and Action Questionnaire-II [AAQ-II; Bond et al., 2011], Cognitive Fusion Questionnaire [CFQ; Gillanders et al., 2014], Committed Action Questionnaire [CAQ; McCracken, 2013], and Valuing Questionnaire-8 [VQ-8; Smout & Davies, 2011]). Participants then selected from multiple dates and times which workshop they would attend.

During the next four days, participants engaged in ecological momentary assessment (EMA), responding to five text messages every day for four days at their preferred times between 10:00 AM and 10:00 PM. Each day, the first four text messages linked participants to a flexibility sampling survey (two questions pulled from each of the AAQ-II, CFQ, CAQ, and VQ-8), and the message sent at the end of the day linked participants to a procrastination sampling survey (nine questions from the IPS). All text messages were automated through a mass messaging system, TXT180, in which information was secure and confidential. Three days later, on the subsequent Monday, participants attended the ACT workshop, followed by another four days of EMA assessments. Once the three phases were complete, students received an email that provided a link for them to respond to the full questionnaire battery they had completed upon volunteering (AAQ-II, CFQ, CAQ, VQ-8, and IPS).

Of the 26 participants, 54% were male ($n = 14$), 42% identified as White ($n = 11$), 42% identified as Black, 4% identified as Asian, and 12% identified as Other. Their ages ranged from 18 to 32 ($M = 20.71$, $SD = 2.85$). Forty-two percent ($n = 11$) of participants' incoming high-school GPA was between 2.5 and 2.9, 27% between 3.0 and 3.4 ($n = 7$), 19% between 3.5 and 4.0 ($n = 5$), 8% less than 2.0 ($n = 2$), and 4% between 2.0 and 2.4 ($n = 1$). Sixty-two percent ($n = 16$) were admitted with an incoming college exam (ACT) score between 20 and 23, 19% obtained a score between 16 and 19 ($n = 5$), 8% with a score between 24 and 27 ($n = 2$), and 8% with a score between 28 and 32 ($n = 2$). All of the demographic information was self-reported. One participant did not report his/her score.

The ACT intervention was a two-hour workshop delivered by an ACT-trained master's-level psychology student and supervised by a licensed, doctoral-level psychologist with ACT expertise. The workshop included both didactic and experiential components, and discussion was encouraged throughout.

The workshop began with values work. The workshop leader asked the students to think about why they were in school and recorded responses on the board. Then the leader introduced the distinction between actions motivated by values and those motivated by cognitive fusion (i.e., rigid cognitive patterns that tend to dominate attention and behavior). Next, students were asked to consider what life would be like if they could choose why they were in school and work to serve that chosen value. Responses were shared and contrasted with current coping strategies. The leader then related these strategies to four aspects of psychological inflexibility: (1) difficulty being present (i.e., "we don't pay enough attention to notice opportunities for valued living"), (2) problems with fusion (i.e., "our minds tell us it won't/can't work out"), (3) experiential avoidance (EA; i.e., "pursuing values is hard and often painful"), (4) struggles with limiting self-concept (i.e., "we don't love or trust ourselves enough to handle the things we want").

Next, the leader provided opportunities to practice PF (being present, experiential acceptance, cognitive defusion, and self-as-context). For each component of flexibility, the workshop leader introduced the concept, invited a group discussion including examples and feedback, led experiential work to foster practicing flexibility, and provided an opportunity for reflection.

- Being present: The workshop leader described difficulties with being present, and led students through two experiential exercises: mindful eating and imagined task completion (Boone, 2013). During the exercises, students were encouraged to notice their thoughts, feelings, sensations, and memories in the moment. The exercises were followed by a brief writing exercise, where students wrote about what they noticed.

- Cognitive defusion: The workshop leader described cognitive fusion, and guided students in an experiential exercise. Specifically, students were asked to notice the thoughts they feel interfere with their progress and share one of these thoughts with a partner. The partner recorded the thought on a sticky note, and stuck it to the student. Once all students were wearing notes, they returned to the group and were given an opportunity to notice and relate to what other students' notes said. Then, the group practiced contacting values even with these thoughts present.

- Experiential acceptance: The workshop leader introduced EA using the avoidance and control worksheet (Boone, 2013), which facilitates reflection on long- and short-term consequences of avoidance. Avoidance was contrasted with acceptance, which was introduced using a video, *Struggling with Internal Hijackers* (mindifriend, 2012). The group then discussed what experiences they would be challenged to accept in pursuing their values.

- Self-as-context: The workshop leader introduced how self-concepts or roles can limit academic and values progress. The leader then led an experiential exercise using sentence completion with "I am" and "I am not" phrases to generate self-related content. Then students practiced self-as-context by crossing that content out little by little, until all that remained was "I am" and "I am not" (Sandoz, Wilson, & DuFrene, 2011). The group discussed the importance of a full, flexible experience of self while choosing the person they want to be.

The final part of the workshop focused on commitment to specific values-consistent actions. The students were asked to consider the values they discussed earlier, and identify SMART (specific, measurable, attainable, realistic, and time-oriented) goals that are in service of their chosen values.

The impact of the workshop was examined in terms of changes in flexibility and procrastination. This summary will focus on questionnaire data, as our sample size limited the power below what we would need to analyze EMA data using multilevel modeling.

Dependent samples t-tests were conducted to explore differences between pre-intervention and post-intervention scores on flexibility and procrastination assessments. Responses were obtained prior to the intervention by the researcher and following the intervention through an online survey. IPS means decreased following the intervention, indicating that procrastination decreased following the workshop; however, the p-levels were only nearing significance $t(25) = -1.89$, $p = 0.06$. There were no significant differences between means on pre- and post-workshop measures of any component of PF.

We were also interested in relations among flexibility and procrastination variables. Correlational analyses were conducted to explore bivariate relationships among PF and procrastination variables. Pre-workshop and post-workshop data showed that higher levels of procrastination were associated with higher levels of avoidance, fusion, and values obstruction, and decreased levels of values progress and committed action.

Following the workshop, students were asked about what was most helpful, their general reaction, and whether this was something they felt they could use in the future. Reception of the workshop overall was positive. For example, one participant reported, "The procrastination workshop helped a lot! It taught me to not let my feelings about a particular class guide me. If I had a chance, I would attend another. Thanks for the opportunity." Students reported the mindfulness and defusion exercises were the most helpful parts of the workshop. Many students also mentioned their surprise to how universal their problems were. One student said it was "surprising to see others have similar problems that I do." Students did not provide any negative feedback.

We were interested in whether an ACT-based workshop would decrease procrastination in at-risk students, and what role, if any, PF might play. Although the preliminary analyses were underpowered, the results tentatively suggest that procrastination is decreasing following the workshop. This is consistent with previous studies with typical college students (Scent & Boes, 2014). Further, EA, cognitive fusion, values progress, and committed action predicted procrastination levels before and after the workshop. Finally, the workshop was well-received by those who participated. This study provides preliminary evidence that an ACT-based workshop decreases problematic academic habits such as procrastination.

ACT-Based Interview and Self-Monitoring in Academic Counseling

We examined the impact of a brief ACT-based interview and self-monitoring intervention with students on academic probation. Thirty freshman students who had obtained a GPA below 2.0 were randomly selected for enhanced academic counseling. These students were sent an email from an ACT-trained academic counselor during the first few weeks of the Spring 2014 semester. The email invited students to participate in an experimental program to help them with academic success. Those who chose to participate were allowed to retain access to their registrar account, which was otherwise blocked until completion of academic counseling. Students who wanted to participate completed a self-assessment regarding their attendance, work hours, learning style, test-taking skills, and study environments, and responded to schedule at least two appointments with their academic counselor. Seventeen (57%) students responded to the email. One student had to be excluded due to a late response, leaving a total of 16 students to participate in the enhanced academic counseling.

The enhanced academic counseling focused on acceptance and values-driven behavior as they relate to academic effectiveness, and first employed a 45-minute ACT-based interview session. All interviews were conducted by an ACT-trained master's-level psychology graduate student working as an academic counselor. Upon arriving for the session, the student filled out the AAQ-2 and VQ-8 questionnaires to assess both their PF and values-based behavior. The interview began with a discussion of their self-assessment, focusing on the specific factors that seem to hinder their academic performance. Then the counselor conducted a semi-structured, experiential interview adapted from the Values Bull's Eye assessment (Lundgren, Luoma, Dahl, Strosahl, & Melin, 2012; Murrell, Coyne, & Wilson, 2004).

First, the counselor guided a brief, values-focused experiential exercise. The student imagined his 50th birthday party, where all of his loved ones were present and giving toasts acknowledging the student. The student was to imagine what his loved ones would say in these toasts if he had lived totally consistently with his values for the years prior, from the present until the time he were 50.

Second, the student clarified specifics related to his values, from four domains: work/academics, leisure, relationships, and health/personal growth. For each area, the student was asked to discuss specific desires, goals, and expectations. Then the counselor described the relationships between goals and values, and the student recorded a personal value for each area of living.

Third, the student was presented with an image of a dartboard, and the counselor described the center of the dartboard (the "bull's eye") as representing the student engaging perfectly well each of the four values he described and each of the four quadrants representing a different valued domain. Then the student marked on the dartboard how consistently he felt his behavior was to what he valued. The closer the X was to the center of the bull's eye, the more consistently the student felt he was living with that value.

Fourth, the student identified specific obstacles preventing him from moving closer to the center of the dartboard (i.e., "my life is just as I want it to be"). When identifying obstacles, students were encouraged to consider thoughts, feelings, and emotions that may contribute to their academic performance (e.g., "I'm a failure," or "I'm not smart enough," or "my parents will be ashamed of me"). The counselor guided a brief experiential exercise, built around the Tug-of-War-with-a-Monster metaphor (Hayes et al., 2012), in which the student practiced accepting and distancing himself from problematic thoughts rather than letting them dominate his experience. Students were encouraged to practice strategies such as these to facilitate engagement in their lives.

Finally, the counselor asked the student to commit to four specific goals in the service of each of the four values he had previously identified. For example, one student wrote "get at least eight hours of sleep" for his commitment that corresponds with his value of "living a long and healthy life." The counselor introduced self-monitoring as a way of increasing values-consistent engagement in their lives by increasing presence and self-awareness. Students were given an academic bull's eye self-monitoring form (see pp. 205–206) to track how present and engaged they were in each class (developed in conjunction with the Mississippi Center for Contextual Psychology). The form included an adapted bull's eye form, including a dartboard for each school day on which students were instructed to write numbers on the dartboard representing their engagement in valued action for each course they attended that day. Students were asked to return the completed academic bull's eye to the subsequent meetings.

Students were only required to attend two meetings in order to retain access to their registrar account, but were encouraged to attend multiple meetings throughout the semester. Prior to each meeting, the student completed the AAQ-2, VQ8, and bull's eye, and was then asked to what extent they maintained their value-based goals (on a scale of 1 to 7). During the twenty-minute session, the student and counselor reviewed values, values-based action, and commitments made during the previous session. Unwanted thoughts, feelings, and emotions that arose while making these valued-based steps during the week were discussed. On average, students attended 2.9 sessions.

For each session, students completed the AAQ-2, VQ8, and bull's eye (i.e., BULLI). Following the initial session, students were also asked, "To what extent did you maintain or keep your valued goal?" Dependent samples t-tests were conducted to examine potential changes in PF (AAQ-2, values progress and obstruction [VQ8]) and overall values consistency (BULLI) from the first to the last session. Results indicated that there were significant changes in bull's eye ratings in the work/education $t(15) = -7.73$, $p = 0.001$, leisure $t(15) = -2.23$, $p = 0.04$, and health $t(15) = -3.29$, $p = 0.005$ domains. BULLI scores decreased following the intervention, suggesting that students were living more consistently with their chosen value in work/education, leisure, and health areas. There were also significant changes in values obstruction scores $t(15) = -2.26$, $p = 0.04$. Values obstruction scores decreased following the intervention, suggesting a decrease in disruption of valued living following the values intervention. There were no significant differences in values progress scores, $t(15) = 0.79$, $p = 0.44$ or AAQ-2 scores $t(15) = -0.77$, $p = 0.46$.

We also were interested in whether the workshop had an effect on the student's GPA. Results found that 11 students (69%) had a positive increase in their semester GPA, with 9 obtaining above a 2.0 (56%). One student withdrew from the university. The primary goal of the intervention was for the students to make above a 2.0 GPA so that they would not end up on academic suspension.

In sum, students provided positive feedback regarding their academic counseling experience. Students described the bull's eye exercise as most helpful. One described, in particular, that quantifying his values consistency "put things into perspective." Several students also mentioned the 50th birthday exercise as influential. Many students seemed to find self-monitoring using the academic bull's eye as least helpful, requiring too much work. In keeping with these complaints, compliance with the self-monitoring task was limited.

We were interested in exploring the potential benefits of incorporating ACT-based interviewing into academic counseling with the at-risk population. Not only were there increases in values-consistent behavior, but more than half of the students' GPAs increased. It may be that interventions that focus on values-based behavior within academics could enhance and impact the student's academic standing and quality of life.

Challenges Faced and Lessons Learned

Both programs being piloted by UL Lafayette provide preliminary support for ACT for academic risk, with results comparable or surpassing many existing retention efforts (Noel-Levitz, 2007). These programs also highlighted a number of challenges in communicating with, accessing, and appropriately timing inter-ventions with at-risk college students.

Communication

One challenge we faced during recruitment, active participation, and follow-up was communication. Consistent with their limited engagement in academic life, many of the at-risk students we targeted did not check their university email regu-larly, resulting in late replies, and often missed deadlines or meetings. In recruiting for future interventions, we plan to explore other methods of contacting students such as by text message. Our participants were open to using text messages for the EMA portions of our studies, and we anticipate that they may be similarly recep-tive to brief notices from the ASC about services available.

The at-risk students we targeted also were not eager to be reminded of their risk status via our communications. Probation students often receive notices of their probation status and the imminent negative consequences of this status. Many were in the habit of ignoring such emails, meaning that a number of students who received our emails did not actually read them. Starting with the subject line, and throughout the body of the email, we tried to focus our communications on the specific potential benefits of the services we were offering and on incentives (e.g., retaining access to their registrar account) for allowing us to track their progress for research.

Finally, many of the at-risk students we targeted had not experienced much support for their academic strivings. Many of the students reported having poor relationships with their academic advisors and teachers, saying they had never experienced someone from the university being specifically interested or invested in their success. These students seemed to receive our offers for help with uncer-tainty and even suspicion. With this in mind, we avoided mass emailing students, and instead, attempted to address students individually, by using their names, speaking specifically to their situation, and inviting questions or comments.

Access

Another challenge we faced with both group and individual meetings was sched-uling to ensure access to the students we were hoping to serve. As is the case at many universities (Light, 1996), the majority of the at-risk students we tar-geted for intervention worked between 20 and 40 hours a week. In addition, many were taking a heavy course load in an effort to boost their GPAs. Some students had arranged their course schedule around their work schedule, leaving virtually no time unscheduled. Many students who were eligible for the interventions we offered did not even express initial interest, knowing their schedules left no time for face-to-face meetings.

Consistent with recent studies suggesting that ACT can be successfully admin-istered online with college students (Chase, 2010; Chase et al., 2013), we have begun piloting an online intervention that might allow for more convenient access by at-risk college students. It has been challenging to keep students interested and engaged in the online modules, but those who have successfully completed them report improvements in quality of life. We also plan to explore the utility of ACT-based smart phone apps that would allow for not only in-the-moment tracking of behavior, but also in-the-moment interventions. For example, the next steps of the enhanced academic counseling project at UL Lafayette involve EMA and intervention to facilitate self-monitoring along with brief ACT interventions (e.g., reminders for "mindful moments" or instructions for identifying the "next meaningful step;" see Danitz and Orsillo, (2014) for use of this type of approach as a follow-up to a brief intervention).

Another approach to accessing at-risk students might be to integrate ACT-based work into an existing course that is part of the required curriculum. Another program we piloted involved creating a specific section of a freshman seminar course that was made up only of first generation students, and included weekly journaling modules focused on different aspects of PF. The students were quite receptive to this program, and reported feeling more engaged and at home in the university environment.

Timing

Another challenge we faced in working with at-risk students was the importance of timing. Both of the interventions we described involved primarily students who were at-risk for academic failure and withdrawal as a result of poor performance. These students had but a single semester to improve their performance to be removed from academic probation. At the beginning of the semester, many of the students we targeted seemed uninterested. Some, it seemed, had plans for improving their performance, and seemed unconvinced that they needed help. Others, it seemed, did not have a plan, but seemed to just be biding time before their imminent failure. We noted a curvilinear pattern where students were most likely to respond to our efforts just before the middle of the semester, when performance problems were apparent, but not irreconcilable. Another pilot involves an expanded ACT-based academic counseling program that would involve meeting with probation students at the beginning of the semester, then continue throughout the semester, such that the relationship is established by the time students begin to struggle.

Assessment

One challenge that is particularly relevant to research and thus continued scientific progress in this area is the selection of appropriate assessments. Assessments should ideally be varied, simple, and easy to administer often. Obviously reducing risk by improving academic performance (i.e., GPA) is the ultimate outcome we target with at-risk students. However, GPAs are difficult to compare across semesters and groups, and provide little information about what, if anything, is actually changing. In addition, interventions with at-risk students ideally track longitudinal outcomes so that the dynamic relationship between the intervention and risk-relevant behaviors can be examined. Unfortunately, GPA calculations during the semester are unreliable and often unfeasible. Thus, we suggest supplementing GPA data with additional assessments. In selecting outcome variables, researchers should identify problematic behaviors that contribute to poor GPA (e.g., attendance problems, procrastination, poor study habits). In selecting a format for assessment, we suggest using behavioral measures whenever possible, and supplementing them with self-monitoring approaches, as this increases students' awareness of the contingencies supporting problematic and effective behaviors. The measures should also be feasible to administer relatively quickly. It is not always easy to predict the kinds of assessment that will be preferred by students. In the programs we have reviewed here, students were quite challenged to complete the adapted bull's eye on a daily basis, but seemed to almost enjoy answering EMA probes by text message.

Experimental Rigor

Finally, the conclusions that can be drawn from the pilot work described here are greatly limited by weaknesses in their design. With pilot research providing the foundation for continued work in this area, future researchers are challenged to investigate the contributions of ACT interventions with at-risk college students in experimental designs with improved rigor. This comes with specific challenges that our work fell short of addressing through our use of small sample group designs. For example, most of the research relevant to retention intervention is effectiveness research (i.e., sacrificing internal validity for external validity). This is understandable. ACT interventions designed to support at-risk students will make little impact if they are not demonstrated to be effective with at-risk students, feasible with support staff and other readily available resources, and sensitive to practical contingencies that universities face around retention requirements. With this in mind, however, we recommend not only rigor but diversity in research designs. Ideally, research on ACT for at-risk students will include not only large, randomized controlled efficacy studies where feasible, but also single case designs, which emphasize experimental control at the level of individual outcomes.

Conclusion

The PF model suggests that at-risk college students may be most apt to succeed when they are willing to feel inadequate, different, and afraid in service of the purpose he or she had chosen for being in college. To date, only one study has directly examined the impact of ACT, which directly targets PF, on the academic performance and persistence of at-risk college students (Sandoz et al., 2014). Both programs being piloted by UL Lafayette provide preliminary support for ACT for academic risk, suggesting that ACT can be used with an at-risk population to reduce problematic academic behaviors (e.g., procrastination), increase values-based behavior (e.g., seeking tutoring when needed), and increase academic performance (e.g., as indicated by GPA).

References

Advisory Committee on Student Financial Assistance (ACSFA). (2010). *The rising price of inequality: How inadequate aid limits college access and persistence.* Retrieved from www.ed.gov/acsfa

Bean, J., & Eaton, S. B. (2000). A psychological model of college student retention. In J. M. Braxton (Ed.), *Reworking the departure puzzle: New theory and research on college student retention* (pp. 48–61). Nashville, TN: University of Vanderbilt Press.

Bean, J., & Eaton, S. B. (2001/2002). The psychology underlying successful retention practices. *Journal of College Student Retention, 3,* 73–89. doi:10.2190/6R55-4B30-28XG-L8U0

Bond, F. W., Hayes, S. C., Baer, R. A., Carpenter, K. C., Guenole, N., Orcutt, H. K., . . . Zettle, R. D. (2011). Preliminary psychometric properties of the Acceptance and Action Questionnaire – II: A revised measure of psychological flexibility and acceptance. *Behavior Therapy, 42,* 676–688. doi:10.1016/j.beth.2011.03.007

Boone, S. B. (2013). Acceptance and commitment therapy (ACT): Processes and application. In J. Pistorello (Ed.), *Mindfulness and acceptance for counseling college students: Theory and practical applications for intervention, prevention, and outreach* (pp. 47–72). Oakland, CA: New Harbinger.

Brown, L., Forman, E., Herbert, J., Hoffman, K., Yuen, E., & Goetter, E. (2011). A randomized controlled trial of acceptance-based behavior therapy and cognitive therapy for test anxiety: A pilot study. *Behavior Modification, 35,* 31–53. doi:10.1177/01454 45510390930

Carnevale, A. P., Smith, N., & Strohl, J. (2010). *Help wanted: Projections of jobs and education requirements through 2018.* Washington, DC: Georgetown University, Center on Education and the Workforce. Retrieved from http://cew.georgetown.edu/jobs2018

Chase, J. A. (2010). The additive effects of values clarification training to an online goal-setting procedure on measures of student retention and performance. *Dissertation Abstracts International: Section B: The Sciences and Engineering, 71*(6-B), 3921.

Chase, J. A., Houmanfar, R., Hayes, S. C., Ward, T. A., Vilardaga, J. P., & Follette, V. M. (2013). Values are not just goals: Online ACT-based values training adds to goal setting in improving undergraduate college student performance. *Journal of Contextual Behavioral Science, 2,* 79–84. doi:10.1016/j.jcbs.2013.08.002

Choy, S. P. (2002). *Access and persistence: Findings from 10 years of longitudinal research on students.* Washington, DC: American Council on Education, Center for Policy Analysis.

Choy, S. P., & Bobbitt, L. (2000). Low-income students: Who they are and how they pay. *Opportunity Outlook, 11,* 9–11.

Danitz, S. B., & Orsillo, S. M. (2014). The mindful way through the semester: An investigation of the effectiveness of an acceptance-based behavioral therapy program on psychological wellness in first-year students. *Behavior Modification, 38,* 549–566. doi:10.1177/0145445513520218

DeBerard, M. S., Spielmans, G. I., & Julka, D. C. (2004). Predictors of academic achievement and retention among college freshmen: A longitudinal study. *College Student Journal, 38,* 66–80.

Dyson, R., & Renk, K. (2006). Freshmen adaptation to university life: Depressive symptoms, stress, and coping. *Journal of Clinical Psychology, 62,* 1231–1244. doi:10.1002/jclp.20295

Eisenberg, D., Gollust, S. E., Golberstein, E., & Hefner, J. L. (2007). Prevalence and correlates of depression, anxiety, and suicidality among university students. *American Journal of Orthopsychiatry, 77,* 534–542. doi:10.1037/0002-9432.77.4.534

Fenske, R. H., Porter, J. D., & DuBrock, C. P. (2000). Tracking financial aid and persistence of women, minority, and needy students in science, engineering, and mathematics. *Research in Higher Education, 41,* 67–94.

Geltner, P. (2001). *The characteristics of early alert students.* Santa Monica, CA: Santa Monica College.

Gillanders, D. T., Bolderston, H., Bond, F. W., Dempster, M., Flaxman, P. E., Campbell, L., . . . Remington, B. (2014). The development and initial validation of the cognitive fusion questionnaire. *Behavior Therapy, 45*, 83–101. doi:10.1016/j.beth.2013.09.001

Gruttadaro, D., & Crudo, D. (2012). *College students speak: A survey report on mental health.* Arlington, VA: National Alliance on Mental Illness (NAMI). Retrieved from www.nami.org/collegereport.

Hayes, S. C., Luoma, J., Bond, F., Masuda, A., & Lillis, J. (2006). Acceptance and Commitment Therapy: Model, processes, and outcomes. *Behaviour Research and Therapy, 44*, 1–25. doi:10.1016/j.brat.2005.06.006

Hayes, S. C., Strosahl, K. D., & Wilson, K. G. (2012). *Acceptance and commitment therapy: The process and practice of mindful change* (2nd ed.). New York, NY: Guilford Press.

Hollingsworth, K. R., Dunkle, J. H., & Douce, L. (2009). The high-risk (disturbed and disturbing) college student. *New Directions for Student Services, 128*, 37–54. doi:10. 1002/ss.340

Hunter, M. S., & Linder, C. W. (2005). First-year seminars. In M. L. Upcraft, J. N. Gardner, & B. O. Barefoot (Eds.), *Challenging and supporting the first-year Student: A handbook for improving the first year of college* (pp. 275–291). San Francisco, CA: Jossey-Bass.

Ishitani, T. T., & DesJardins, D. L. (2002, June). *A longitudinal investigation of dropout from college in the United States.* Paper presented at symposium conducted at the AIR 42nd Annual Forum, Toronto, Canada. Retrieved from http://irt2.indstate.edu/home/stats/briefs/2002/AIRForumPaper.pdf

Julian, T. (2012). *Work-life earnings by field of degree and occupation for people with a bachelor's degree: 2011.* Washington, DC: U.S. Department of Commerce. Retrieved from www.census.gov/prod/2012pubs/acsbr11-04.pdf

Kashdan, T. B., & Rottenberg, J. (2010). Psychological flexibility as a fundamental aspect of health. *Clinical Psychological Review, 30*, 865–878. doi:10.1016/j.cpr.2010.03.001

Light, A. (1996). Hazard model estimates of the decision to re-enroll in school. *Labour Economics, 2*, 381–406. doi:10.1016/0927-5371(95)80042-V

Lotkowski, V. A., Robbins, S. B., & Noeth, R. J. (2004). *The role of academic and non-academic factors in improving college retention.* ACT policy report. Iowa City, IA: American College Testing. Retrieved from www.act.org/research/policymakers/pdf/college_retention.pdf

Lundgren, T., Luoma, J. B., Dahl, J., Strosahl, K., & Melin, L. (2012). The bull's-eye values survey: A psychometric evaluation. *Cognitive and Behavioral Practice, 19*(4), 518–526. doi:10.1016/j.cbpra.2012.01.004

McCracken, L. M. (2013). Committed action: An application of the psychological flexibility model to activity patterns in chronic pain. *The Journal of Pain, 14*, 828–835. doi:10.1016/j.jpain.2013.02.009

mindifriend. (2012, July 25). *Struggling with internal hijackers?* [video file]. Retrieved from https://www.youtube.com/watch?v=NdaCEO4WtDU

Murrell, A. R., Coyne, L. W., & Wilson, K. G. (2004). ACT with children, adolescents, and their parents. In S. C. Hayes, K. D. Strosahl, & K. G. Wilson (Eds.), *A practical guide to acceptance and commitment therapy* (pp. 249–273). New York, NY: Springer.

Noel-Levitz. (2007). *National research report: Student retention practices at four-year institutions.* Braintree, MA: Noel-Levitz.

O'Banion, T. (1997). *A learning college for the 21st century.* Phoenix, AZ: Oryx Press.

Sandoz, E. K., Kellum, K., & Wilson, K. G. (2014). *Feasibility and preliminary effectiveness of acceptance and commitment training for academic success of at-risk college students from low income families.* Manuscript under review.

Sandoz, E. K., Wilson, K. G., & DuFrene, T. (2011). *The mindfulness and acceptance workbook for bulimia: A guide to breaking free from bulimia using acceptance and commitment therapy.* Oakland, CA: New Harbinger.

Scent, C. L., & Boes, S. R. (2014). Acceptance and commitment training: A brief intervention to reduce procrastination among college students. *Journal of College Student Psychotherapy, 28,* 144–156. doi:10.1080/87568225.2014.883887

Seidman, A. (2005). Introduction. In A. Seidman (Ed.), *College student retention* (pp. xi–xiv). Westport, CT: Praeger Publishers.

Seidman, A. (2012). *College student retention: Formula for student success.* Lanham, MD: Rowman & Littlefield Publishers.

Sharkin, B. S. (2004). College counseling and student retention: Research findings and the implications for counseling centers. *Journal of College Counseling, 7,* 99–108. doi:10.1002/j.2161-1882.2004.tb00241.x

Smout, M., & Davies, M. (2011, July). Development of the Valuing Questionnaire. In M. Smout (Chair), *Innovations in the assessment and application of values.* Symposium presented at the Association of Contextual Behavioral Science, Parma, Italy.

Steel, P. (2010). Arousal, avoidant and decisional procrastinators: Do they exist? *Personality and Individual Differences, 48,* 926–934. doi:10.1016/j.paid.2010.02.025

Tampke, D. R., & Durodoye, R. (2013). Improving academic success for undecided students: A first-year seminar/learning community approach. *Learning Communities Research and Practice, 1*(2), Article 3. Available at: http://washingtoncenter.evergreen.edu/lcrpjournal/vol1/iss2/3

Thompson, B. R., & Green, P. R. (2002). Classroom strategies for identifying and helping college students at risk for academic failure. *College Student Journal, 36,* 398.

Tinto, V. (1993). *Leaving college: Rethinking the causes and cures of student attrition* (2nd ed.). Chicago, IL: University of Chicago Press.

Tinto, V. (2003). Establishing conditions for student success. In L. Thomas, M. Cooper, & J. Quinn (Eds.), *Improving completion rates among disadvantaged students* (pp. 1–10). Stoke on Trent, Staffordshire, UK: Trentham Books Limited.

Tinto, V. (2012). *Completing college: Rethinking institutional action.* Chicago, IL: University of Chicago Press.

Tinto, V., & Pusser, B. (2006). *Moving from theory to action: Building a model of institutional action for student success.* Washington, DC: National Postsecondary Education Cooperative.

Tirado, J., Ortega, S., Heilborn Diaz, V. A., & Fernández Martín, F. D. (2005). Terapia breve en estudiantes universitarios con problemas de rendimiento académico y ansiedad: Eficacia del modelo 'La Cartuja'. *International Journal of Clinical and Health Psychology, 5,* 589–608. doi:http://hdl.handle.net/10481/32650

Turner, A. L., & Berry, T. R. (2000). Counseling center contributions to student retention and graduation: A longitudinal assessment. *Journal of College Student Development, 41,* 627–636.

U.S. Department of Education. (2015). *Institutional Retention and Graduation Rates for Undergraduate Students.* Retrieved from http://nces.ed.gov/programs/coe/indicator_cva.asp

Valentine, J. C., Hirschy, A. S., Bremer, C. D., Novillo, W., Castellano, M., & Banister, A. (2011). Keeping at-risk students in school: A systematic review of college retention programs. *Educational Evaluation and Policy Analysis, 33,* 214–234. doi:10.3102/0162373711398126

8   Acceptance-Based Behavioral Training for Pre-Professional Students

Sara B. Danitz, Susan M. Orsillo, Agnes K. Lenda, Kendahl M. Shortway, and Jennifer Block-Lerner

Introduction

Graduate programs aimed at educating and preparing students to become professionals in the areas of law, medicine, and allied health offer unique challenges and opportunities. The clear benefit of professional programs is that they allow students to integrate classroom learning with highly supervised "on the job" training. However, this form of graduate education is also often quite costly, in terms of both financial and time commitments. Students in professional programs typically juggle demanding coursework along with externships or fieldwork while also managing various other professional and personal responsibilities, in a competitive and high-pressured academic culture. They may struggle to be present with the clients or patients they treat or otherwise work with in their trainee roles, in part because of the demands associated with trying to recall the readings and classroom learning relevant to each case. Not surprisingly, students in professional graduate programs are at heightened risk for developing depression, stress, and reduced quality of life (e.g., Dyrbye et al., 2011; Walter et el., 2013). Further, the risk for such outcomes is magnified within program cultures that imply that such distress should be concealed (e.g., Walter et al., 2013).

On the other hand, the challenges of professional graduate education can offer students an opportunity to establish and hone life skills that can truly shape their professional and personal development. If students are able to cultivate life skills that help them manage the difficult emotions that arise during graduate school and pursue personally meaningful activities in the face of multiple demands, it can both enhance their ability to manage academic stress and positively impact those clients, patients, consumers, and colleagues they interact with throughout their careers. This chapter provides an overview of the developing literature on the potential role mindfulness and related practices can play in professional graduate education. These approaches increasingly have been utilized with demonstrated intrapersonal and interpersonal benefits across a multitude of settings, including with graduate students and healthcare professional trainees of various disciplines. After providing a brief review of the literature, we will highlight our own work thus far with students enrolled in law school and occupational therapy master's programs, and discuss our plans for using these approaches to enhance interprofessional practice, or the deliberate collaboration among health professionals with the common goal of providing patient-centered care (Bridges, Davidson, Odegard, Maki, & Tomkowiak, 2011).[1] We conclude by discussing challenges we have faced and lessons we have learned in the service of informing future directions.

Mindfulness and related practices potentially offer a number of benefits to professional students. First, they facilitate increased self-awareness and attention (Walsh & Shapiro, 2006), which can be beneficial on both professional and personal levels. Self-awareness fosters the identification of strengths and areas for improvement and development, skills that are critical to the developing professional, while also enhancing communication and improving client-helper relationships (Jack & Smith, 2007). Further, mindfulness and related practices have the potential to minimize fatigue and burnout (Escuriex & Labbé, 2011; Felton, Coates, & Christopher, 2013; McGarrigle & Walsh, 2011), and increase engagement in self-care and stress management (Dobkin & Hutchinson, 2013; Khoury et al., 2013). Additionally, remaining in touch with one's values, particularly those values that lead the student to his or her professional training path and those that direct the qualities and behaviors the student hopes to bring to his or her career can provide motivation and meaning to students struggling with the demands of training.

Over the past decade, mindfulness and related practices have been increasingly applied within a variety of professional graduate programs. A recent review of the literature identified fourteen schools that teach mindfulness to medical and dental students and residents (Dobkin & Hutchinson, 2013). Program formats range from lectures, to 1-day workshops, to 8–10 week programs. Dobkin and Hutchinson (2013) identified two medical schools (University of Rochester School of Medicine and Dentistry; Monash University Medical School in Australia) that have integrated mindfulness into their core curricula. At University of Rochester, all third-year medical students are required to take five 90-minute courses that include themes such as noticing and awareness, communication, reactivity, burnout and self-care, healing and suffering, and professionalism (Dobkin & Hutchinson, 2013). At Monash University, researchers have found that undergraduate level medical students receiving the "Health Enhancement Programme" (HEP), which integrates mindfulness-based stress management and lifestyle programs, reported significant improvements in quality of life and reductions in psychological distress (Hassed, de Lisle, Sullivan, & Pier, 2009). Curriculum-based interventions may be especially suited for student populations, given barriers to seeking services including very limited time and limited awareness of their potential value (Eisenberg, Speer, & Hunt, 2012).

Other medical school programs have offered mindfulness-based courses as electives. These mindfulness-based programs have effectively reduced psychological distress (e.g., Finkelstein, Brownstein, Scott, & Lan, 2007; Rosenzweig, Reibel, Greeson, Brainard & Hojat, 2003) and have increased levels of empathy (Shapiro, Schwartz, & Bonner, 1998). In a recent randomized control trial with medical students in their final two years of earning their degree, Warnecke, Quinn, Ogden, Towle, and Nelson (2011) found that the students who received Mindfulness-Based Stress Reduction (MBSR; Kabat-Zinn, 2005) had significantly lower levels of stress and anxiety, which were maintained at 8-week follow-up. These voluntary formats may be beneficial since students opt into these courses, which may result in more engaged learning. Overall, findings across studies involving medical and dental students demonstrate the benefits of mindfulness-based programs in enhancing mindfulness and self-compassion, and reducing stress (Dobkin & Hutchinson, 2013).

Programs aimed at enhancing students' mindfulness have also been applied to other professional students, including those in nursing programs (e.g., Beddoe & Murphy, 2004), law school (e.g., Danitz & Orsillo, 2014), and occupational therapy programs (e.g., Reid, 2013; Stew, 2011). Baccalaureate nursing students who participated in a voluntary 8-week MBSR course demonstrated a significant reduction in anxiety (Beddoe & Murphy, 2004). Online curriculum approaches have also been introduced; an online 8-week mindfulness program for occupational therapy graduate students resulted in a significant increase in mindfulness levels (Reid, 2013). Such novel means of service delivery may be part of a portfolio of interventions (Kazdin & Blasé, 2011) that foster wellness in student populations. The following sections will describe our own work within different professional programs and settings.

An Acceptance-Based Behavioral Workshop for First-Year Law Students

We (Danitz & Orsillo, 2014) examined the impact of a 1-session acceptance-based behavioral workshop, "The Mindful Way through the Semester," for first-year law students enrolled in a private university in Boston, Massachusetts.[2] The first year of law school has long been documented as a time of heightened stress for students (McIntosh, Keywell, Reifman, & Ellsworth, 1994; Schick, 1996) that can increase their risk for anxiety and depression (Dammeyer & Nunez, 1999; Shanfield & Benjamin, 1985). Thus, our goal was to develop and test the efficacy of an accessible, cost-effective, and time-efficient program aimed at easing the transition to law school.

During the first two weeks of the fall semester, all first-year law students ($N = 535$) received an email from the Associate Dean of Students of the law school with a description of the study including information about an incentive for participating (i.e., an Amazon gift card for study completers) and a link to enroll online through Survey Monkey. Enrollment in the study was voluntary, and we also recruited with descriptive flyers hung around the law school. To reduce the likelihood of dropout, we pre-selected the workshop dates, chosen in collaboration with the Associate Dean of Students, so that only those students who were available for the workshops would participate.

Participants completed questionnaires via Survey Monkey at baseline (at the beginning of the semester before receiving the workshop) and at 3-month follow-up. In order to get a sense of the impact of the program on psychological functioning, we assessed depression, anxiety and stress using the Depression Anxiety Stress Scales-21 (DASS-21; Lovibond & Lovibond, 1995). We also measured the potential effect of the program on mindfulness via the Philadelphia Mindfulness Scale (PHLMS; Cardaciotto, Herbert, Forman, Moitra, & Farrow, 2008), and academic/educational values using a subscale from the Valued Living Questionnaire (VLQ; Wilson, Sandoz, Kitchens, & Roberts, 2010).

Interestingly, only 34 (6.4%) of students indicated an interest in the study by completing the baseline questionnaires. Half of these students were then randomly assigned to the workshop condition ($n = 17$) while the other 17 were placed in a waiting list condition (they were offered the opportunity to participate in the workshop during the spring semester). Just over half of those students assigned to the workshop ($n = 9$) attended it and all attendees also completed the 3-month follow-up questionnaires. About three-quarters ($n = 12$) of the students assigned to the control condition filled out the 3-month follow-up questionnaires. Despite their interest in the fall, when contacted at the beginning of the spring semester none of the participants in the wait-list control condition opted to attend a workshop. In sum, we had 21 study completers, 66.7% of whom were female, 71.4% identified as White, and 14.3% identified as Hispanic/Latino. Their ages ranged from 21 to 39 ($M = 25.05$, $SD = 4.86$).

The workshop was a 90-minute program delivered by two doctoral-level graduate students in clinical psychology. One workshop consisted of three students, and the other had six student participants. Our workshop was informed by our (Sue Orsillo) work using an acceptance-based behavioral therapy (ABBT) to treat anxiety (Roemer & Orsillo, 2009)—a program that integrates concepts from acceptance and commitment therapy (ACT; Hayes, Strosahl, & Wilson, 1999; 2012) and mindfulness-based cognitive therapy (MBCT; Segal, Williams, & Teasdale, 2002; 2012) with traditional cognitive-behavioral therapy (CBT). The program was primarily didactic with some guided discussion and an experiential component. We began the workshop with a discussion of first-year stressors and common coping strategies. Control and avoidance were discussed as popular, yet potentially problematic, strategies. Specifically, we highlighted the ways in which these strategies can paradoxically increase distress, reduce self-awareness, amplify self-judgment, and interfere with one's ability to engage in activities that personally matter. We then introduced mindfulness, acceptance, and values articulation as alternative coping strategies that have the potential to reduce suffering, facilitate self-awareness, and increase engagement in valued actions. To experientially demonstrate these concepts, we guided participants through two mindfulness exercises: "Mindfulness of Breath" (Orsillo & Roemer, 2011) and "Inviting a Difficulty in" (adapted from Williams, Teasdale, Segal, & Kabat-Zinn, 2007; see Appendix C for a copy of the script), and we debriefed with them about their experiences afterwards. We also invited students to engage in a 10-minute values articulation exercise about academics (adapted from Orsillo & Roemer, 2011; see Appendix D for a copy of the prompt). The exercise involved writing about the type of student one would like to be, the types of relationships and communication one would like to have with peers and professors, and the challenges one would like to take on in law school. Participants were encouraged to keep their values writing so that they could revisit and reflect on it following the workshop, and we provided them with a website where they could listen to mindfulness recordings and engage in their own practice.

At equal intervals over the remainder of the semester, we sent students three email or text message tips (depending on what the participant opted into) to remind them about the strategies they learned in the workshop. The tips encouraged the participants to engage in mindfulness practice and to review their values writing and reflect on how consistently they were living with their values, throughout their time as students. A few weeks before the end of the semester, participants in both the workshop and wait-list control conditions filled out 3-month follow-up questionnaires.

To measure the impact of the program we conducted a series of analyses of covariance (ANCOVAs) on our outcome variables, with baseline scores entered as covariates for each follow-up score. There was a significant difference between the two groups at the end of their first semester of law school, $F(1, 18) = 6.8$, $p = 0.018$, with a moderate-to-large effect size ($d = 0.70$), such that students who received the workshop reported significantly less depression than those in the control condition. Similarly, students in the workshop condition reported significantly less stress at the end of the semester, $F(1, 18) = 8.4$, $p = 0.01$, with a large effect size ($d = 0.94$). In contrast, the groups did not significantly differ at the end of the semester in their self-reported anxiety, $F(1, 18) = 2.9$, $p = 0.10$, although the marginal means (adjusted to account for baseline scores) were in the expected direction (M [workshop] = 7.72; M [control] = 10.88) and there was a small effect size, $d = 0.32$.

We were also interested in examining whether or not the workshop enhanced the extent to which law students reported valuing their academic pursuits. An ANCOVA was conducted on the education subscale of the VLQ at the end of the semester, with baseline score as a covariate. As predicted, after adjusting for baseline scores, the two groups significantly differed in their endorsement of academic values, $F(1, 18) = 7.7$, $p = 0.01$, with a large effect size, $d = 1.16$, with students in the workshop condition more strongly affirming and engaging in actions consistent with their academic values. Despite the inclusion of mindfulness exercises in the workshop, we did not find that the two groups significantly differed in their self-report of mindfulness at the end of the semester. After adjusting for baseline scores, there were no significant differences between the groups on the awareness subscale of the PHLMS, $F(1, 17) = 0.27$, $p = 0.61$, $d = 0.17$, or the acceptance subscale of the PHLMS $F(1, 18) = 2.8$, $p = 0.11$, $d = 0.50$, although for the acceptance subscale the marginal means (adjusted for baseline scores) were in the predicted direction (M [workshop] = 30.80; M [control] = 27.15) and there was a moderate effect size.

At follow-up, most (56%) of the participants reported using the mindfulness exercises that they learned during the program just "a few times total," which may help to explain the modest change in mindfulness skills noted above. However, all nine participants endorsed that they planned to use the skills and exercises from the workshop in the future. Their reasons included, "Because they were helpful and provided a different mechanism to cope with emotions and stress," and

"I think proper breathing and relaxation will help me stay more focused in law school," and, "The values articulation was useful and perhaps something I would consider using at different points in the future."

We also asked students about which elements of the workshop they found most and least helpful. Sixty-seven percent of the students in the workshop condition reported that they found the "Mindfulness of Breath" exercise to be the most useful skill they acquired. For example, students commented, "I was able to use it anywhere given a few moments to compose my thoughts," and "It helped me regain focus afterwards and not be so stressed." For the two students who identified that the values articulation exercise was the most useful component of the workshop, one stated, "It helped me reinstate my goals and realize my purpose to continue working hard," and the other remarked, "It caused me to become more acutely aware of my goals." In contrast, another student found the values articulation exercise to be the least useful component of the workshop, noting, "I write so much in school that I did not have much interest in writing the values." Interestingly, when asked about the things that the participants did not enjoy or find helpful from the intervention, most participants (56%) responded with "N/A" or "I wasn't turned off by anything in the workshop."

Our preliminary work in this area suggests that law students can achieve considerable benefits from participating in a brief acceptance-based behavioral program. Unfortunately, the greatest challenge appears to be recruiting students into the workshop. It may be that integrating programs directly into the curriculum and/or offering online versions could enhance reach and impact. Clearly, further work in this area is indicated.

Curriculum-Based Mindfulness- and Acceptance-Based Behavioral Workshops for Master's Level Occupational Therapy Students

The aims of our (Jennifer Block-Lerner, Agnes Lenda, Kendahl Shortway) two studies were to implement brief mindfulness- and acceptance-based behavioral interventions in a highly-selective MA-level occupational therapy (OT) program to determine need for, experience with, and interest in additional related practices and resources, as well as to preliminarily examine correlates of receptivity (Barrasso et al., 2014). In Study 1, a 2-session workshop (sessions approximately 60 minutes each, 1 week apart) was implemented with first-year students during their second (i.e., Spring) semester. The workshop was conducted in three separate class sections with approximately 12 students in each. In response to feedback from students in Study 1 to OT program faculty (gleaned via the department's own internal survey) expressing a desire to have been exposed to such skill-development practices earlier, Study 2 entailed a 1-session workshop (approximately 120 minutes) conducted during program orientation for first-year students (the Fall semester of the following academic year).

The workshop protocol (Block-Lerner, Barrasso, & Kowarz, 2013), delivered by a faculty member and 1–2 advanced doctoral students, consists of didactic and experiential components focusing on mindfulness (e.g., discussion of mindlessness in daily life, a mindful eating exercise), values clarification (e.g., presentation of the "Big Rocks" story [Covey, Merrill, & Merrill, 1994], the bulls-eye exercise [Lundgren, Luoma, Dahl, Strosahl, & Melin, 2012]), and experiential acceptance (e.g., practicing different ways of "holding" one's thoughts and sensations related to a challenge in one's life).[3] At the end of the workshop, all participants were provided with a list of books, websites, smartphone applications, and other resources should they be interested in learning more about the approach or related practices. More details about the protocol are provided in Chapter 10.

Prior to participating in the workshop, participants completed a demographics questionnaire, the Depression Anxiety Stress Scale-21 (DASS-21; Lovibond & Lovibond, 1995), and the Acceptance and Action Questionnaire-2 (AAQ-2; Bond et al., 2011). Following the workshop, students were asked about their interest in learning more about experiential acceptance/mindfulness and engaging in related practices, how acceptable they found the proposed approach to be, and how effective they thought the approach might be via three items rated on a 7-point Likert scale (1 = not at all; 7 = very much). Students in Study 1 (i.e., the two-session workshop) were asked these questions at the end of the first session and again at the end of the second session. Students in Study 2 only answered these questions at the end of the one-session workshop (Barrasso et al., 2014).

To speak to potential need, Study 1 participants ($N = 36$; 82% White, 77% female, mean age 24 years [SD = 4.46]) reported fairly high levels of anxiety (e.g., 42% reported moderate levels of anxiety and 25% severe or extremely severe levels on the DASS-21) and stress (28% indicated moderate to severe levels). Difficulty with opening up to challenging emotion states was also conveyed, with 27% endorsing clinically-significant levels of psychological inflexibility on the AAQ-2. Study 2 participants ($N = 35$; 85% White, 94% female, mean age 25 years [SD = 5.56]) generally exhibited lower levels of psychological symptoms and less problematic ways of relating to their emotional experiences. Specifically, these students reported experiencing significantly lower levels of anxiety (with 15% indicating moderate levels of anxiety and 6% severe to extremely severe levels) and stress (3% endorsed moderate levels and 9% endorsed severe levels) on the DASS-21. Further, only 6% endorsed clinically-significant levels of psychological inflexibility on the AAQ-2 (Bond et al., 2011). These differences between participants in each sample may be attributable to individual differences, differences in phases of academic training (i.e., Study 1 occurred toward the end of the first year, whereas Study 2 took place prior to students beginning formal training in the OT program), associated stressors, and/or other variables (Barrasso et al., 2014).

Despite differences in symptomatology and psychological inflexibility, students across both samples indicated fairly high levels of interest ($M = 4.71$, $SD = 1.58$) acceptability ($M = 5.58$, $SD = 1.05$), and perceived effectiveness ($M = 5.21$, $SD = 1.24$), with nonsignificant differences between the two groups. Further, comments indicated that students experienced impactful glimpses into relevant processes. For example, when asked to describe the approach presented in the workshop, many spoke to messages to appreciate "the little things" (e.g., "I enjoyed having the reminder to take the time to appreciate the nuances of life that I glaze over at times") and focus on what they care about (e.g., "It was a positive experience in which I was able to learn about mindfulness and contemplate my values and who I am in life"). Other students addressed the climate of the workshop (e.g., "The workshops were very relaxed and informal which allowed everyone to be open and form a common ground"), while others spoke more broadly: "I thought it was a wonderful tool that will be helpful to manage stress levels and put life in perspective" (Barrasso et al., 2014).

In order to preliminarily address predictors of receptivity toward these workshops, bivariate correlations between DASS subscale scores, AAQ-2 scores, and a composite score of receptivity items (i.e., interest, acceptability, and perceived effectiveness) were run; cases from both studies were analyzed together. Results indicate that those participants who reported higher levels of psychological inflexibility and higher levels of depression reported significantly higher levels of receptivity to the workshops (Barrasso et al., 2014).

Overall, the preliminary investigation conducted by Barrasso et al. (2014) suggests that a subset of master's-level OT students experience moderate to severe levels of psychological symptoms and clinically-significant levels of psychological inflexibility, and that these students may be those who are most interested in learning more about acceptance-based behavioral approaches and/or engaging in practices consistent with them.

Challenges and Lessons Learned

The aforementioned programs demonstrate great promise for the utility of ABBT programs for professional students. However, our experience to date suggests that there are a number of challenges that deserve consideration. Moreover, the current state of the research is severely limited. Below we raise some issues for reflection, and we make a number of recommendations to guide future research efforts.

One major issue we grappled with in offering these workshops is whether they should be offered as a required component of orientation to a professional program, integrated into the curriculum, or offered as an adjunctive workshop for interested participants. The schedules of professional students are quite demanding, with many students holding part or full-time jobs in addition to their school responsibilities. For example, many law schools offer the option for students to enroll full-time and take classes during the day, or for students to enroll part-time so that they can maintain full-time jobs during the day and take classes during the evenings. For many students, taking on and finding the time for an additional extracurricular obligation such as an ABBT workshop outside of the school and/or work schedule may prove to be beyond their means. This may help to explain the low enrollment rate (6.4%) and high attrition rate (38%) in the aforementioned voluntary study with law students, despite the fact that there was compensation offered for completing the study (Danitz & Orsillo, 2014).

Unfortunately, it may be that ABBT programs could offer the most potential benefit to those students who would be the least likely to avail themselves of a voluntary, adjunctive program. Students who are struggling academically, are financially disadvantaged, or lacking in family and other social support may be those most at risk in terms of both their psychological well-being and their ability to flourish in graduate school (Chapter 7, this volume, addresses these issues related to undergraduate students). These challenges highlight the benefits of integrating an ABBT program into the curriculum, since it would not require additional time outside of class or work, and it is scheduled during a time that students can attend. The workshops implemented by Barrasso and colleagues (2014) with OT students in class and as part of an orientation program speak to two such possibilities. These findings were particularly promising as they suggest that those who are most in need are the most open to seeking longer-term services or practices after participating in a brief intervention.

However, integrating ABBT programming into orientation or a curriculum is associated with its own set of challenges. Academic programs are under rising pressure to provide an increasingly complex curriculum to students in the most efficient and expedient manner. For example, there is a movement in some states to "squeeze" the academic content of a three-year law school curriculum into two years (e.g., Estreicher, 2012) which would reduce the financial burden of law school and potentially increase the pool of attorneys willing to engage in public service. Thus, continuing to build empirical support for such protocols will likely be quite important in convincing faculty and administrators that the merits of an ABBT program outweigh the cost of losing academic time. Similarly, the time allotted for orientation to a professional program is often quite limited and has competing priorities. We were fortunate that faculty members in the Department of OT valued our work (based on a previously conducted in-class series of workshops) and carved out time for one workshop during orientation.

As we shared our experiences with others within the university, the administrators we worked with in the law program suggested that we provide an online ABBT program that could potentially be more accessible to students with demanding schedules. Certainly there is growing evidence for the efficacy of online learning (Means, Toyama, Murphy, Bakia, & Jones, 2010) and some preliminary evidence for the benefits of online mindfulness-based training (Krusche, Cyhlarova, King, & Williams, 2012; Levin, Pistorello, Seeley, & Hayes, 2014; Reid, 2013). Unfortunately, online courses may be least beneficial for those students who struggle academically (e.g., Wilson & Allen, 2011). This approach to teaching requires students to be self-motivated and disciplined, and it can present some obstacles with regard to the development of strong student-to student and student-to-instructor relationships. Research is clearly needed to determine the potential benefit of online ABBT training for professional students.

We also struggled to determine the number of sessions required for ABBT programs to be most effective. According to published studies, ABBT programs for professional students can range anywhere from one to eleven sessions (Danitz & Orsillo, 2014; Saunders et al., 2007). Brief programs that are cost-effective and time-efficient may be more compatible with the busy schedules of professional students (and may serve to build motivation for longer-term engagement in related practices). However, limiting the number of sessions may reduce the potential impact of the program. A related consideration is the phase of training during which to offer such services. One might make the argument that introducing and offering opportunities for developing such skills should begin as soon as possible and thus workshops during orientation or during the first semester of study are warranted (perhaps with innovative means of following up, such as those implemented by Danitz and Orsillo, 2014). On the other hand, students may be more open to such skills if they have more fully experienced the stresses and challenges of graduate study, and thus it may be more appropriate to offer students such interventions later in their training. Such questions should be explored empirically.

Finally, determining the best composition of participants in an ABBT group program warrants additional reflection. Given the far-reaching benefits of mindfulness- and acceptance-based trainings, all of the programs discussed in this chapter were open to all interested students. However, there may be some benefit to specifically targeting students with the greatest need or those at highest risk of dropout, failure, or burnout, particularly if resources are limited (see Chapter 7, this volume, for relevant discussion related to undergraduates). Further consideration is also required to determine whether students are best served by programs that are profession-specific (e.g., open only to law students, open only to OT students) or interdisciplinary.

Recommendations for Future Research

Although there is considerable interest in offering acceptance- and mindfulness-training to students pursuing various professions, the research into the efficacy of these programs is severely limited.

Sample

Most notably, all of the studies discussed in this chapter have limited external validity. Selection bias is a concern for studies in which participants volunteered to enroll in the mindfulness program (e.g., de Vibe et al., 2013; Reid, 2013). For example, the mind-body skills course discussed by Saunders and colleagues (2007) was available to first-year medical students as an elective that did not offer course credit, so participants were highly self-selected and likely highly motivated. Additionally, most studies used extremely small samples including students who most frequently self-identified as White and were predominately female (e.g., Barrasso et al., 2014; Danitz & Orsillo, 2014), if not entirely female (e.g., Beddoe & Murphy, 2004; Reid, 2013). A recent meta-analysis demonstrated the benefits of mindfulness- and acceptance-based therapy programs with clients from nondominant cultural and/or marginalized backgrounds (Fuchs, Lee, Roemer, & Orsillo, 2013). However, research is needed to determine the acceptability and impact of such programs on a diverse range of graduate students in professional programs.

Outcome Variables

Acceptance- and mindfulness-based programs have been shown to have wide-reaching positive effects, ranging from reducing stress to enhancing client-provider communication (e.g., Beckman et al., 2012; Chiesa & Serretti, 2009). However, the published studies looking at the effect of ABBT programs on professional students, including our own work, have been focused predominately on psychological adjustment as the primary outcome variable (e.g., Danitz & Orsillo, 2014) and have examined outcomes over brief periods of time (e.g., Shapiro et al., 1998). Future studies should also examine the impact of ABBT programming on retention, satisfaction, quality of life, and professional competency over longer periods of time, and they should further attempt to understand predictors and processes of receptivity (as well as follow-through on offers for additional resources and services).

Comparison Groups

Finally, although research on the positive effects of ABBT programs is promising, many studies related to professional programs that have been conducted to date lack control groups (e.g., Hassed et al., 2009; Saunders et al., 2007), and few studies have compared these programs to alternative methods. In a study with medical students and graduate nursing students (as well as undergraduates majoring in pre-health or pre-medical studies), two interventions, a mindfulness meditation intervention and a somatic relaxation intervention, were compared to a control group (Jain et al., 2007). Results demonstrated that both the meditation and relaxation groups had significant reductions in distress and significant increases in positive mood states, although only the meditation group experienced significant decreases in rumination compared to the control group (Jain et al., 2007). Future research should include the comparison of ABBT programs to other established approaches (e.g., traditional CBT workshops, support groups, progressive relaxation programs) in order to further understand the unique benefits of mindfulness- and acceptance-based programs. A comparison intervention would also help control for factors such as group dynamics, support from instructors and fellow students, contact time, and homework.

Interprofessional Practice

Recent changes in health care infrastructure have called for the use of interdisciplinary teams to engage in client- or "patient-centered care" (from here referred to as patient-centered care, since this is the technical term in the literature; US Department of Health & Human Services, 2010). Although graduate student training differs across disciplines, patient-centered care—that is, "respectful of and responsive to individual patient preferences, needs, and values, and ensuring that patient values guide all clinical decisions" (Institute of Medicine, 2001, p. 3)— is valued among them all. In order to achieve successful patient-centered care, practitioners are encouraged to remain emotionally regulated, aware, and attentive

(Shaller, 2007). Moreover, being mindful and empathic has also been emphasized in training to provide patient-centered care (Epstein & Street, 2011). Training in the provision of patient-centered care, however, includes rigorous classes and intensive field work, often resulting in stress and burnout (Birks, McKendree & Watt, 2009). As such, healthcare professionals in training are expected to develop skills in awareness and attention while experiencing high levels of stress.

As evidenced by the latest literature, mindfulness training has predominantly been conducted for and within individual professions. Current professional practice, however, calls for skilled *interprofessional* practice.[4] To date, the notion of interprofessional practice has been primarily addressed through interprofessional education provided by individual training programs (Reeves, Goldman, Burton, & Sawatzky-Girling, 2010). As healthcare reform increasingly emphasizes patient-centered interdisciplinary practice, it is essential that health professional trainees are exposed to a comprehensive method of interprofessional training.

Recently, interprofessional groups have been gathered and provided with mindfulness training. Mindfulness-based groups for working professionals have been conducted in order to promote self-care, decrease likelihood of burnout, and develop awareness (Aggs & Bambling, 2010; Irving, 2011). Similarly, students enrolling in healthcare profession programs have participated in mindfulness-based training, resulting in decreased stress levels (Newsome, Waldo, & Gruszka, 2012). Thus, it appears that interprofessional mindfulness training yields intrapersonal benefits.

As mindfulness training has been associated with improved communication, awareness of others, and empathy, it is possible to conduct mindfulness training sessions in order to foster interprofessional socialization, or the development of competency and confidence in one's field of study, and qualities pertinent to patient-centered care. Mindfulness practice thus may be an appropriate way to introduce students to other professions while providing a rewarding training opportunity and strong sense of common humanity. It is proposed that such mindfulness-based programming offered to students in various healthcare-professionals-in-training programs will have an impact on students intrapersonally, interpersonally, and interprofessionally. Prior to conducting such workshops, however, it is important to consider the logistics and practicality of such an undertaking.

Our developing work in this area (e.g., Lenda, 2014) aims to explore the acceptability and feasibility of such mindfulness-based interprofessional workshops for healthcare professionals in training. Graduate students from multiple programs at a northeastern university (i.e., Counselor Education, Marriage and Family Therapy, Nursing, OT, Speech-Language Pathology, and Social Work) will be invited to participate in a study that involves completing a survey battery and, if feasible, engaging in an interprofessional acceptance-based behavioral workshop. The battery will contain a demographics questionnaire, a researcher-created questionnaire aimed at gauging interest level and scheduling logistics, and measures which speak to intrapersonal (Philadelphia Mindfulness Scale; Cardaciotto et al., 2008; DASS-21 Lovibond & Lovibond, 1995), interpersonal (Interpersonal Reactivity Index; Davis, 1983), and interprofessional (Readiness for Interprofessional Learning Scale, RIPLS; Parsell & Bligh, 1999; adapted by McFayden et al., 2005) functioning.

Participant responses regarding interest and availability may support implementation of a workshop. This workshop would be a modified version of Block-Lerner et al.'s protocol (more details in Chapter 10, this volume). For purposes of fostering interprofessional familiarity and highlighting shared values in alleviating human suffering, a client vignette exercise, similar to one conducted by Simmons et al., 2011 in other forms of interprofessional education, will be added. Data collected from this project are expected to inform the acceptability and feasibility of such interprofessional training.

Concluding Remarks

Graduate education and training in the various professional fields can be an intense and challenging experience that places some students at a heightened risk of developing a range of psychosocial difficulties. Yet it can also be a period of incredible personal and professional growth. Mindfulness and related practices offer great promise for professional students in that they have the potential to alleviate stress, anxiety, and depression, enhance well-being, deepen provider-recipient relationships, and promote strong interprofessional practice. We hope that this chapter offers clinicians, researchers, teachers, and administrators alike a compelling rationale for the potential benefits of offering these types of programs to students engaged in professional training.

Notes

1 Please note that the literature on graduate students in helping professions (e.g., psychology, counseling, social work) is excluded from most parts of this chapter as that work is described in Chapters 4 and 5 of this volume.
2 Although the general results of this workshop on the combined student group (with first year undergraduates and first year law students) are reported elsewhere (Danitz & Orsillo, 2014), here we report on analyses conducted specifically with the law school sample.
3 This practice was introduced to us by Dennis Tirch, Ph.D., who indicated that Christopher Germer, Ph.D. shared an adapted version with him.
4 It is important to note that, while mental healthcare professionals in training are beyond the scope of this chapter in general, since such individuals are part of the interprofessional work that we (Agnes Lenda, Jennifer Block-Lerner) are developing, we have included brief mentions of them in this section.

References

Aggs, C., & Bambling, M. (2010). Teaching mindfulness to psychotherapists in clinical practice: The mindful therapy programme. *Counselling & Psychotherapy Research, 10,* 278–286. doi:10.1080/14733145.2010.485690

Barrasso, C., Kowarz, K., Block-Lerner, J., Cardaciotto, L., Lenda, A., & Shortway, K. (2014, November). A preliminary investigation of curriculum-based acceptance-based behavioral workshops for master's level occupational therapy students. In Z. Moore (Chair), *Innovative mindfulness- and acceptance-based interventions for college student mental health.* Symposium presented at the annual meeting of the Association for Behavioral and Cognitive Therapies, Philadelphia, PA.

Beckman, H. B., Wendland, M., Mooney, C., Krasner, M. S., Quill, T. E., Suchman, A. L., & Epstein, R. M. (2012). The impact of a program in mindful communication on primary care physicians. *Academic Medicine, 87*, 815–819. doi:10.1097/ACM.0b013e318253d3b2

Beddoe, A. E., & Murphy, S. O. (2004). Does mindfulness decrease stress and foster empathy among nursing students? *Journal of Nursing Education, 43*, 305–312.

Birks, Y., McKendree, J., & Watt, I. (2009). Emotional intelligence and perceived stress in healthcare students: A multi-institutional, multi-professional survey. *BMC Medical Education, 9*, 61. doi:10.1186/1472-6920-9-61

Block-Lerner, J., Barrasso, C., & Kowarz, K. (2013). *An acceptance-based behavioral workshop for college students.* Unpublished protocol, Department of Advanced Studies in Psychology, Kean University, Union, NJ.

Bond, F. W., Hayes, S. C., Baer, R. A., Carpenter, K. C., Guenole, N., Orcutt, H. K., . . . Zettle, R. D. (2011). Preliminary psychometric properties of the Acceptance and Action Questionnaire – II: A revised measure of psychological flexibility and acceptance. *Behavior Therapy, 42*(4), 676–688. doi:10.1016/j.beth.2011.03.007

Bridges, D. R., Davidson, R. A., Odegard, P. S., Maki, I. V., & Tomkowiak, J. (2011). Interprofessional collaboration: Three best practice models of interprofessional education. *Medical education online, 16*. doi:10.3402/meo.v16i0.6035

Cardaciotto, L., Herbert, J. D., Forman, E. M., Moitra, E., & Farrow, V. (2008). The assessment of present-moment awareness and acceptance: The Philadelphia Mindfulness Scale. *Assessment, 2*, 204–223. doi:10.1177/1073191107311467

Chiesa, A., & Serretti, A. (2009). Mindfulness-based stress reduction for stress management in healthy people: A review and meta-analysis. *The Journal of Alternative and Complementary Medicine, 15*, 593–600. doi:10.1089/acm.2008.0495

Covey, S. R., Merrill, A. R., & Merrill, R. R. (1994). *First things first: Coping with the ever-increasing demands of the workplace.* New York: Simon & Schuster.

Dammeyer, M. M., & Nunez, N. (1999). Anxiety and depression among law students: Current knowledge and future directions. *Law and Human Behavior, 23*, 55–73. doi:10.1023/A:1022374723371

Danitz, S. B., & Orsillo, S. M. (2014). The mindful way through the semester: An investigation of the effectiveness of an acceptance-based behavioral therapy program on psychological wellness in first year students. *Behavior Modification, 38*, 549–566. doi:10.1177/0145445513520218

Davis, M. H. (1983). Measuring individual differences in empathy: Evidence for a multidimensional approach. *Journal of Personality and Social Psychology, 44*, 113–126. doi:10.1037//0022-3514.44.1.113

de Vibe, M., Solhaug, I., Tyssen, R., Friborg., O., Rosenvinge, J., Sørlie, T., & Bjorndal, A. (2013). Mindfulness training for stress management: a randomised controlled study of Norwegian medical and psychology students. *MBC Medical Education, 13*, 107. doi:10.1186/1472-6920-13-107

Dobkin, P. L., & Hutchinson, T. A. (2013). Teaching mindfulness in medical school: Where are we now and where are we going? *Medical Education, 47*, 768–779. doi:10.1111/medu.12200

Dyrbye, L. N., Harper, W., Durning, S. J., Moutier, C., Thomas, M. R., Massie Jr, F. S., . . . Shanafelt, T. D. (2011). Patterns of distress in US medical students. *Medical Teacher, 33*, 834–839. doi:10.3109/0142159X.2010.531158

Eisenberg, D., Speer, N., & Hunt, J. B. (2012). Attitudes and belief about treatment among college students with untreated mental health problems. *Psychiatric Services, 63*, 711–713. doi:10.1176/appi.ps.201100250

Epstein, R. M., & Street, R. L. (2011). The values and value of patient-centered care. *The Annals of Family Medicine, 9*, 100–103. doi:10.1370/afm.1239

Escuriex, B. F., & Labbé, E. E. (2011). Health care providers' mindfulness and treatment outcomes: A critical review of the research literature. *Mindfulness, 2*, 242–253. doi:10.1007/s12671-011-0068-z

Estreicher, S. (November 30, 2012). The Roosevelt-Cardozo way: The case for bar eligibility after two years of law school. *New York University Journal of Legislation and Public Policy, 15*, 599–617. Retrieved from www.nyujlpp.org/wp-content/uploads/2013/01/Estreicher-The-Roosevelt-Cardozo-Way.pdf

Felton, T. M., Coates, L., & Christopher, J. C. (2013). Impact of mindfulness training on counseling students' perceptions of stress. *Mindfulness, 6*, 159–169. doi:10.1007/s12671-013-0240-8

Finkelstein, C., Brownstein, A., Scott, C., & Lan, Y. U. (2007). Anxiety and stress reduction in medical education: An intervention. *Medical Education, 41*, 258–264. doi:10.1111/j.1365-2929.2007.02685.x

Fuchs, C., Lee, J. K., Roemer, L., & Orsillo, S. M. (2013). Using mindfulness- and acceptance-based treatments with clients from nondominant cultural and/or marginalized backgrounds: Clinical considerations, meta-analysis findings, and introduction to the special series. *Cognitive and Behavioral Practice, 20*, 1–12. doi:10.1016/j.cbpra.2011.12.004

Hassed, C., de Lisle, S., Sullivan, G., & Pier, C. (2009). Enhancing the health of medical students: Outcomes of an integrated mindfulness and lifestyle program. *Advances in Health Sciences Education, 14*, 387–398. doi:10.1007/s10459-008-9125-3

Hayes, S. C., Strosahl, K. D., & Wilson, K. G. (1999). *Acceptance and commitment therapy: An experiential approach to behavior change.* New York, NY: Guilford Press.

Hayes, S. C., Strosahl, K. D., & Wilson, K. G. (2012). *Acceptance and commitment therapy: The process and practice of mindful change* (2nd ed.). New York, NY: Guilford Press.

Institute of Medicine (2001). *Crossing the quality chasm: A new health system for the 21st century.* National Academies Press.

Irving, J. A. (2011). *Mindfulness-based medical practice: A mixed-methods investigation of an adapted mindfulness-based stress reduction program for health care professionals* (Doctoral dissertation). Retrieved from ProQuest, UMI Dissertations Publishing. (AAINR78645)

Jack, K., & Smith, A. (2007). Promoting self-awareness in nurses to improve nursing practice. *Nursing Standard, 21*, 47–52. doi:10.7748/ns2007.04.21.32.47.c4497

Jain, S., Shapiro, S. L., Swanick, S., Roesch, S. C., Mills, P. J., & Schwartz, G. E. R. (2007). A randomized controlled trial of mindfulness meditation versus relaxation training: Effects on distress, positive states of mind, rumination, and distraction. *Annals of Behavioral Medicine, 33*, 11–21. doi:10.1207/s15324796abm3301_2

Kabat-Zinn, J. (2005). *Full catastrophe living: Using the wisdom of your body and mind to face stress, pain, and illness.* New York, NY: Bantam Dell.

Kazdin, A. E., & Blasé, S. L. (2011). Rebooting psychotherapy research and practice to reduce the burden of mental illness. *Perspectives on Psychological Science, 6*(1), 21–37. doi:10.1177/1745691610393527

Khoury, B., Lecomte, T., Fortin, G., Masse, M., Therien, P., Bouchard, V., . . . Hofmann, S. G. (2013). Mindfulness-based therapy: A comprehensive meta-analysis. *Clinical Psychology Review, 33*, 763–771. doi:10.1016/j.cpr.2013.05.005

Krusche, A., Cyhlarova, E., King, S., & Williams, J. M. G. (2012). Mindfulness online: a preliminary evaluation of the feasibility of a web-based mindfulness course and the impact on stress. *BMJ open, 2.* doi:10.1136/bmjopen-2011-000803

Lenda, A. (2014). *The feasibility of interprofessional mindfulness- and acceptance-based workshops for healthcare professionals in training.* Unpublished manuscript, Department of Advanced Studies in Psychology, Kean University, Union, New Jersey.

Levin, M. E., Pistorello, J., Seeley, J. R., & Hayes, S. C. (2014). Feasibility of a prototype web-based acceptance and commitment therapy prevention program for college students. *Journal of American College Health, 62*, 20–30. doi:10.1080/07448481.2013.843533

Lovibond, S. H., & Lovibond, P. F. (1995). *Manual for the Depression Anxiety Stress Scales* (2nd ed.). Sydney, Australia: Psychology Foundation.

Lundgren, T., Luoma, J. B., Dahl, J., Strosahl, K., & Melin, L. (2012). The bull's-eye values survey: A psychometric evaluation. *Cognitive and Behavioral Practice, 19*(4), 518–526. doi:10.1016/j.cbpra.2012.01.004

McFadyen, A. K., Webster, V., Strachan, K., Figgins, E., Brown, H., & McKechnie, J. (2005). The Readiness for Interprofessional Learning Scale: A possible more stable subscale model for the original version of RIPLS. *Journal of Interprofessional Care, 19*(6), 595–603. Retrieved from www.ncbi.nlm.nih.gov/pubmed/16373215

McGarrigle, T., & Walsh, C.A. (2011). Mindfulness, self-care, and wellness in social work: Effects of contemplative training. *Journal of Religion & Spirituality in Social Work: Social Thought, 30*, 212–233. doi:10.1080/15426432.2011.587384

McIntosh, D. N., Keywell, J., Reifman, A., & Ellsworth, P. C. (1994). Stress and health in first-year law students: Women fare worse. *Journal of Applied Social Psychology, 24*, 1474–1499. doi:10.1111/j.1559-1816.1994.tb01559.x

Means, B., Toyama, Y., Murphy, R., Bakia, M., & Jones, K. (2010). *Evaluation of evidence-based practices in online learning: A meta-analysis and review of online learning studies.* Washington, DC: U.S. Department of Education, Office of Planning, Evaluation, and Policy Development. Retrieved from https://www2.ed.gov/rschstat/eval/tech/evidence-based-practices/finalreport.pdf

Newsome, S., Waldo, M., & Gruszka, C. (2012). Mindfulness group work: Preventing stress and increasing self-compassion among helping professionals in training. *Journal for Specialists in Group Work, 37*, 297–311. doi:10.1080/01933922.2012.690832

Orsillo, S. M., & Roemer, L. (2011). *The mindful way through anxiety: Break free from chronic worry and reclaim your life.* New York, NY: Guilford Press.

Parsell, G., & Bligh, J. (1999). The development of a questionnaire to assess the readiness of health care students for interprofessional learning (RIPLS). *Medical Education, 33*, 95–100. doi:10.1046/j.1365-2923.1999.00298.x

Reeves, S., Goldman, J., Burton, A., & Sawatzky-Girling, B. (2010). Synthesis of systematic review of evidence of interprofessional education. *Journal of Allied Health, 39*, 198–203. doi:10.1002/14651858.CD000072.pub2

Reid, D. T. (2013). Teaching mindfulness to occupational therapy students: Pilot evaluation of an online curriculum. *Canadian Journal of Occupational Therapy, 80*, 42–48. doi:10.1177/0008417413475598

Roemer, L., & Orsillo, S. M. (2009). *Mindfulness- and acceptance-based behavioral therapies in practice.* New York, NY: Guilford Press.

Rosenzweig, S., Reibel, D. K., Greeson, J. M., Brainard, G. C., & Hojat, M. (2003). Mindfulness-based stress reduction lowers psychological distress in medical students. *Teaching and Learning in Medicine. 15*, 88–92. doi:10.1207/S15328015TLM1502_03

Saunders, P.A., Tractenberg, R.E., Chaterji, R., Amri, H., Harazduk, N., Gordon, J.S., . . . Haramati, A. (2007). Promoting self-awareness and reflection through an experiential mind-body skills course for first year medical students. *Medical Teacher, 29*, 778–84. doi:10.1080/01421590701509647

Schick, S. R. (1996). Creating lawyers: The law school experience. *The Compleat Lawyer, 13*, 46–49.

Segal, Z. V., Williams, J. M. G., & Teasdale, J. D. (2002). *Mindfulness-based cognitive therapy for depression: A new approach to preventing relapse*. New York, NY: Guilford Press.

Segal, Z. V., Williams, J. M. G., & Teasdale, J. D. (2012). *Mindfulness-based cognitive therapy for depression* (2nd ed.). New York, NY: Guilford Press.

Shaller, D. (2007). *Patient-centered care: What does it take?* Commonwealth Fund. Retrieved from www.commonwealthfund.org/usr_doc/Shaller_patient-centeredcare-whatdoesittake_1067.pdf?section=4039

Shanfield, S. B., & Benjamin, G. A. H. (1985). Psychiatric distress in law students. *Journal of Legal Education, 35*, 65–75.

Shapiro, S. L., Schwartz, G. E., & Bonner, G. (1998). Effects of mindfulness-based stress reduction on medical and premedical students. *Journal of Behavioral Medicine, 21*, 581–599. doi:10.1023/A:1018700829825

Simmons, B., Oandasan, I., Soklaradis, S., Esdaile, M., Barker, K., Kwan, D., . . . Wagner, S. (2011). Evaluating the effectiveness of an interprofessional education faculty development course: The transfer of interprofessional learning to the academic and clinical practice setting. *Journal of Interprofessional Care, 25*(2), 156–157. doi:10.3109/135618 20.2010.515044

Stew, G. (2011). Mindfulness training for occupational therapy students. *The British Journal of Occupational Therapy, 74*(6), 269–276. doi:10.4276/030802211X13074383957869

U.S. Department of Health and Human Services. (2010). *Affordable Care Act and the Health Care and Education Reconciliation Act of 2010*. Retrieved from www.hhs.gov/healthcare/rights/law/reconciliation-law.pdf

Walsh, R., & Shapiro, S. L. (2006). The meeting of meditative disciplines and Western psychology: A mutually enriching dialogue. *American Psychologist, 61*, 227–239. doi:10.1037/0003-066X.61.3.227

Walter, G., Soh, N. L. W., Jaconelli, S. N., Lampe, L., Malhi, G. S., & Hunt, G. (2013). Medical students' subjective ratings of stress levels and awareness of student support services about mental health. *Postgraduate Medical Journal, 89*, 311–315. doi:10.1136/postgradmedj-2012-131343

Warnecke, E., Quinn, S., Ogden, K., Towle, N., & Nelson, M. R. (2011). A randomised controlled trial of the effects of mindfulness practice on medical student stress levels. *Medical Education, 45*, 381–388. doi:10.1111/j.1365-2923.2010.03877.x

Williams, M. K., Teasdale, J., Segal, Z., & Kabat-Zinn, J. (2007). *The mindful way through depression: Freeing yourself from chronic unhappiness*. New York, NY: Guilford Press.

Wilson, D., & Allen, D. (2011). Success rates of online versus traditional college students. *Research in Higher Education Journal, 14*. 1–9. Retrieved from www.aabri.com/manuscripts/11761.pdf

Wilson, K. G., Sandoz, E. K., Kitchens, J., & Roberts, M. (2010). The Valued Living Questionnaire: Defining and measuring valued action within a behavioral frame-work. *Psychological Record, 60*, 249–272. Retrieved from http://opensiuc.lib.siu.edu/cgi/viewcontent.cgi?article=1261&context=tpr

9 Mindfulness- and Acceptance-Based Approaches With College Student-Athletes

Andrew T. Wolanin and Michael B. Gross

Introduction

In ancient times, athletes were depicted as able-bodied, fully functioning, physically gifted individuals. The modern-day athlete is often expected to embody the same way of being: confident, devoid of weakness, mentally tough, and strong. Consistent with this long-standing culture, young athletes are often socialized to conform to a sporting environment that can be emotionally inhibitive and geared toward eliminating supposed barriers to performance deficits, such as "negative" thoughts and emotions, and lack of confidence. This is evident in the dominant approach to performance enhancement, traditional psychological skills training (PST), which rests on the theoretical assumption that optimal performance occurs when athletes learn to control their internal states (Hardy, Jones, & Gould, 1996) and that athletic performance can be disrupted due to "negative" thoughts, emotions, and bodily sensations (Weinberg & Gould, 2003). As such, it may seem on the surface that several of the concepts fundamental to mindfulness- and acceptance-based approaches are foreign to the world of sport. In many ways this is true, as it can be difficult to get athletes to buy into the notion that they do not need to have "positive" thoughts, a certain level of confidence, or eliminate anxiety in order to reach peak performance. Yet athletes often resonate with the benefits of present awareness, as their reported experience of ideal performance states typically involves an acute focus on the moment.

Kabat-Zinn, Beall, and Rippe (1985) are largely credited as being the first to introduce athletes (Olympic rowers) to a mental training program based upon mindfulness meditation. Several decades later, mindfulness- and acceptance-based interventions in sport have expanded, but much remains to be understood about their effectiveness, acceptability, and feasibility with college athletes. As will be described below in our review of mindfulness- and acceptance-based interventions in sport, the evidence base is growing for these interventions, but several questions remain regarding not only outcomes but also the direction of the research. As such, one purpose of this chapter is to briefly review and evaluate the research on mindfulness- and acceptance-based interventions in sport. This chapter also discusses the unique opportunities and challenges that emerge when working with college athletes, coaches, administration, and related professionals when delivering mindfulness- and acceptance-based interventions.

In particular, we will summarize our experiences utilizing the mindfulness-acceptance-commitment (MAC; Gardner & Moore, 2007) approach and other mindfulness- and acceptance-based interventions with student athletes.

Mindfulness- and Acceptance-Based Interventions in Sport

The application of mindfulness- and acceptance-based approaches to the sport domain is in its relative infancy. It was only about a decade ago that Gardner and Moore (2004, 2007) developed the mindfulness-acceptance-commitment (MAC) approach, which is recognized as the first manualized sport psychology intervention to target core processes such as present-moment awareness, acceptance, values, and cognitive fusion. The MAC protocol is theoretically based upon significant advances in the behavioral sciences that were emerging with the rise of third-wave behavioral therapies, such as acceptance-commitment therapy (ACT; Hayes, Strosahl, & Wilson, 1999), dialectical behavior therapy (DBT; Linehan, 1993), and mindfulness-based cognitive therapy (MBCT; Segal, Williams, & Teasdale, 2002). While these treatments gained empirical support in the clinical world, sport psychologists had not yet developed a contemporary model based upon mindfulness and acceptance principles.

MAC consists of seven core modules flexibly completed in seven or more sessions typically lasting 60 minutes. MAC integrates psychoeducation, discussion, and experiential exercises over the course of the following (Gardner & Moore, 2007):

- Module 1: Preparing the client with psychoeducation
- Module 2: Introducing mindfulness and cognitive defusion
- Module 3: Introducing values and values-driven behavior
- Module 4: Introducing acceptance
- Module 5: Enhancing commitment
- Module 6: Skill consolidation and poise—combining mindfulness, acceptance, and commitment
- Module 7: Maintaining and enhancing mindfulness, acceptance, and commitment.

The MAC approach includes a number of forms to be used in conjunction with the program (e.g., in Module 3, athletes complete "performance obituary" and "performance values" forms to help clarify their values). Participants also are strongly encouraged to engage in formal (e.g., Brief Centering Exercise; Mindfulness of the Breath Exercise) and informal (e.g., Washing a Dish Mindfully) mindfulness exercises between sessions (Gardner & Moore, 2007).

Research on the MAC approach has evidenced its effectiveness in a number of domains, including improving concentration (Gardner & Moore, 2004), increasing experiential acceptance (Gardner & Moore, 2004; Hasker, 2010; Schwanhausser, 2009), increasing mindful awareness and attention (Schwanhausser, 2009), and improving performance (Gardner & Moore, 2004; Gross et al.,

2015; Schwanhausser, 2009; Wolanin, 2005). A recent randomized control trial comparing MAC to traditional PST suggests that MAC is effective in reducing psychological, emotional, and behavioral issues among student athletes (Gross et al., 2015). This study also found that participants in the MAC group demonstrated improved performance, reduced experiential avoidance (EA), and when compared to PST participants, improved emotion regulation over time. Taken together, findings from this study suggest that MAC may be able to simultaneously help athletes on and off the field by targeting core mechanisms thought to underlie performance dysfunction and optimal psychological functioning. However, all of the above studies on the MAC approach should be considered within the context of small sample sizes and limited generalizability.

Another mindfulness- and acceptance-based approach that has garnered some empirical support is mindful sport performance enhancement (MSPE; Kaufman, Glass & Arnkoff, 2009; Kaufman & Glass, 2006). Whereas the MAC protocol draws most heavily upon ACT, MSPE is more closely aligned with mindfulness-based stress reduction (MBSR; Kabat-Zinn, 1990) and MBCT. According to Kaufman et al. (2009), both MAC and MSPE emphasize mindfulness and acceptance, but MSPE does not focus as specifically on the development of values-driven behavior. MSPE was originally designed to be a 4-week protocol, but was expanded to the current 6-week program version in which athletes are gradually introduced to mindfulness. Similar to MBSR and MBCT, the 6-week program is comprised of guided meditations (i.e., body scan, sitting meditations), walking meditation, an adapted version of the mindful eating of a raisin exercise (Kabat-Zinn, 1990), and mindful yoga. MSPE also includes a sport-specific meditation that attunes athletes to the motions and sensations they may experience in their particular sport.

In published studies to date, MSPE has only been evaluated among athletes participating in archery, golf, and long-distance running. This is consistent with the contention in Kaufman and Glass (2006) that MSPE may be best suited for athletes participating in sports that require sustained mental focus and fine motor movements. Empirical investigations on MSPE are limited as the evidence base currently only consists of two intervention studies and one follow-up study. Using the 4-week MSPE protocol, Kaufman et al. (2009) found increases in state flow, awareness of experience (decentering), and trait mindfulness among a community sample of archers and golfers. In another study using the 4-week version of MSPE (adapted for runners), De Petrillo, Kaufman, Glass, and Arnkoff (2009) found increases in trait awareness, state mindfulness, and decreased sport-related worry among a sample of recreational long-distance runners. At one-year follow-up of the aforementioned studies, MSPE workshop participants demonstrated a significant increase in trait mindfulness and the ability to act with awareness and significant decreases in task-irrelevant thoughts and task-relevant worries. Further, from pre-test to follow-up, long-distance runners reported significant improvement in their mile times (Thompson, Kaufman, De Petrillo, Glass, & Arnkoff, 2011).

Citing that both MAC and MSPE are "demanding of time and/or resources," Baltzell and Akhtar (2014, p. 162) designed a mindfulness intervention entitled

Mindfulness Meditation Training for Sport (MMTS). This intervention consists of twelve 30-minute sessions delivered over the course of six weeks. The MMTS program recommends that athletes practice meditating on their own for 5–10 minutes per day. According to Baltzell and Akhtar, MMTS sessions are broken down into 20 minutes of psychoeducation on mindfulness and 10 minutes of meditation practice. Further, MMTS consists of the following four main training areas: open awareness capacity, caring thoughts for self and teammates, concentration exercises, and practicing acceptance of negative mind-states. An initial investigation of MMTS examined its effects upon mindfulness, positive and negative affect, satisfaction with life, and psychological well-being (Baltzell & Akhtar, 2014). It was found that MMTS had significant effects on the intervention group's (Division I female soccer players) mindfulness. In addition, levels of negative affect remained stable for the intervention group but significantly increased for the control group (Division I female rowers). In another study, Baltzell, Caraballo, Chipman, and Hayden (2014) used qualitative data via interviews to examine participants' ($N=7$) experiences of MMTS. Thematic analysis supported that participants initially had difficulty understanding the connection between meditation and their sport (soccer), but they perceived an improvement in their ability to accept emotions in both the sport context and other life domains by the end of the intervention. In addition, the data suggested that participants experienced enhanced mindfulness, awareness, and acceptance of emotional experiences.

Although the previously cited models, particularly the MAC approach, are the most well-known mindfulness- and acceptance-based approaches in sport, other models have been used with athletes. Bernier, Thienot, Codron, and Fournier (2009) integrated mindfulness and acceptance components into a traditional PST program for seven young (m age = 15.67) elite golfers. This program consisted of principles and exercises from MBCT and ACT. Along with didactic mindfulness training and in-session exercises, this program also asked the participants to practice a body scan for two minutes one time per day, and use an MP3 player with a "scheduled series of recorded mindfulness and acceptance exercises" (Bernier et al., 2009, p. 326) two times per week. Participants in this study demonstrated improved performance during competition and greater attention to task-relevant information (Bernier et al., 2009). In another study, the effect of mindfulness training on flow, defined in this study as a state of complete concentration on a task that ultimately enhances performance, was investigated using a program designed for student athletes to use on their own (Aherne, Moran, & Lonsdale, 2011). The mindfulness-based program developed for this study included an information sheet describing mindfulness and four exercises (breath, breath and body, standing yoga, and body) from the CD *Guided Meditation Practices for the Mindful Way Through Depression* (Williams, Teasdale, Segal, & Kabat-Zinn, 2007) that athletes were asked to complete based upon a predetermined timetable over the course of six weeks. Findings from this study indicated that participants in the mindfulness-based program demonstrated increases in global flow scores and on the flow dimensions of "Clear Goals" and "Sense of Control."

Mindfulness- and Acceptance-Based Interventions With Injured College Athletes

One of the unique variables that impacts the lives of college student athletes is the occurrence of athletic injury. While college athletics are relatively safe, Hootman, Dick, and Agel (2007) reported a rate of one injury every two games and one injury every five practices for a team of 50 athletes. Although not every college athlete becomes injured during his or her career, many are injured and must cope with the physical and psychological effects of the injury. Recently, there has been some research attention devoted to the use of ACT-based interventions with injured college athletes. Mahoney and Hanrahan (2011) implemented a brief 4-session psychoeducational ACT-based intervention with a small sample of injured athletes during their rehabilitation from ACL injuries. The authors indicated that an analysis of their case study findings provided initial data that athletes have private events such as thoughts, emotions, and sensations during the injury rehabilitation process and that they tend to avoid experiencing the private events and act based on their emotional states.

In addition to the direct ACT intervention studies of injured athletes, there are a number of studies that highlight mechanisms of ACT related to athletic injury. Gallagher and Gardner (2007) investigated the link between schemas, coping strategy, and emotional response to injury in college athletes. They found a relationship between a schema of mistrust, avoidance coping, and a higher level of negative affect after athletic injury, and an inadequacy schema, avoidance coping, and increased negative affect before returning to competition. The relationship between avoidance and negative affect is consistent with targeted mechanisms of ACT interventions.

DeGaetano, Wolanin, and Marks (in press) explored the impact of psychosocial factors and psychological flexibility (PF) on rehabilitation protocol adherence in a sample of injured college athletes. PF (the ability to be mindful of present-moment experiences and to change behavior in the service of one's values; see Chapter 6, this volume), as measured by the Action and Acceptance Questionnaire-II (Bond, et al., 2011), was the only variable to be significantly correlated with athletic training rehabilitation adherence, providing initial evidence that as levels of PF increase, rehabilitation engagement and adherence may increase in injured college athletes.

Furthermore, Mankad, Gordon, and Wallman (2009a) qualitatively examined nine injured athletes' experience of the sport injury rehabilitation process based on the climate of their sporting environment. The primary finding of this study was that the athletes utilized avoidance behaviors and suppressive coping styles due to perceptions that negative emotional displays would be negatively viewed by their peers and coaches. In a case study by Mankad and colleagues (2009b), an Australian gridiron football player recovering from an ACL injury consistently reported using avoidance behaviors and experiencing a high frequency of intrusive thoughts. The authors reported that the athlete would not disclose his emotional symptoms to his teammates and coaches because he viewed them as unacceptable within the athletic environment.

With a focus on reducing the occurrence of injury, Ivarsson, Johnson, Andersen, Fallby, and Altemyr (2015) implemented MAC as an injury prevention program for soccer players. They provided a seven-session MAC intervention to elite soccer players between the ages of 16 and 19, and compared the rate of injury occurrence to a control group of traditional sport psychology presentations. While the results of the intervention were not statistically significant, the authors reported a medium effect size and that 67% of the athletes who received the MAC intervention were injury-free over a 6-month period compared to 40% in of the control group.

Implementing Psychological Services With College Student-Athletes

In 2005, the National Collegiate Athletic Association (NCAA) held a meeting of clinical sport psychologists to review the mental health issues of student athletes, and more recently, the NCAA (2014) published a 112-page booklet entitled, *Mind, Body, and Sport: Understanding and Supporting Student-Athlete Mental Wellness*, which focuses on the mental health of college student athletes. In this booklet, the Chief Medical Officer of the NCAA indicated that the primary concern of student athletes is mental health. Despite this, the majority of NCAA athletic departments do not employ full-time sport psychologists. According to a January 2014 ESPN article by Noren (2014) entitled, "Taking notice of the hidden injury," only 22 NCAA athletic departments employed a full-time licensed mental health professional, and additional research indicates that sport psychologists are employed in some capacity in approximately 23–28% of NCAA Division I athletic departments (Hayden, Kornspan, Bruback, Parent, & Rodgers, 2013; Kornspan & Duve, 2006; Voight & Callaghan, 2001; Wilson, Gilbert, Gilbert, & Sailor, 2009). University counseling centers also tend to employ one staff member familiar with sport psychology services, which suggests that universities recognize a need to provide psychological services to athletes. Zillmer and Gigli (2007) indicate that athletic departments look to sport psychologists to improve student athlete performance on and off the field. This includes providing services to the full range of student athletes including non-clinical, subclinical, and clinical populations. Despite the fact that there are psychological services for college athletes, sport psychologists have not gained "full access" into embedded athletic department positions (Voight and Callaghan, 2001), and gaining access is often the initial challenge of providing mindfulness- and acceptance-based interventions to college athletes. However, it is our contention that as it has become more popular to use sport psychology services to gain a mental edge, and awareness grows regarding the mental health issues faced by college athletes, mindfulness- and acceptance-based interventions serve as an ideal platform to target both performance and overall well-being.

Using Mindfulness- and Acceptance-Based Approaches With College Athletes

We have experience using mindfulness- and acceptance-based interventions with athletes, and have been mentored and trained by the developers of MAC in its theory and application. We have provided a range of services to college athletes (Division I–III levels) for athletic performance enhancement, psychological well-being, clinical concerns, and injury recovery. These services have been provided though a number of contexts, including in our roles in college counseling centers and training clinics and as a consulting sport psychologist and private practitioners.

In almost every case, we both have confronted unique challenges when working with college athletes. Given that the barriers to working with college athletes have been significantly detailed elsewhere (see Ferrante, Etzel, & Lantz, 2002), the remainder of this chapter will focus on the challenges specific to using mindfulness- and acceptance-based interventions with this population by reviewing common ACT processes and logistical issues.

Issues With Implementation: Psychoeducation and ACT Processes

Getting Started and Psychoeducation

In our experience, the initial session with college athletes does not occur without having to first provide psychoeducation to members of an athletic organization. Therefore, it is not uncommon to have to present the psychoeducation piece at least once or twice prior to actually presenting it to the intended population (i.e., college athletes). For example, we recall that on most occasions we have had to first meet one-on-one with the Athletic Director of the Athletic Department or present in group format to college/university administration, then present to the entire coaching staff, and then meet informally with interested coaches one-on-one to discuss the tenets of mindfulness- and acceptance-based interventions and explain program details. This can be challenging, because college athletic departments typically are closed systems composed of many people who can be skeptical of what individuals are essentially "selling" to them. Therefore, we suggest that when presenting the theoretical rationale for mindfulness- and acceptance-based approaches, practitioners might need to be creative (e.g., describing evidence in support of these approaches in clear and compelling language) to gain receptivity for an approach that does not suggest athletes need to think or feel better in order to improve performance. Again, this is quite contrary to the wide held belief that "positive" thoughts and reduced "negative" emotions contribute to more favorable outcomes.

One way of being creative is the use of examples involving popular athletes to convey the message that internal experiences do not need to be controlled, eliminated, or fixed. For example, one story is of Michael Jordan admitting in an interview that he was "most anxious" prior to basketball games at Madison Square Garden against the Knicks. When telling this story, I (Michael Gross) joke that as a huge Knicks fan, I know all too well that anxiety did not hinder Michael Jordan (averaged 31.3ppg) at the famed arena. Another story is how 11-time National Basketball Association (NBA) champion and five-time Most Valuable Player (MVP), Bill Russell, used to vomit prior to basketball games. The following line is a direct quote from Russell's Wikipedia page: "He was so tense before every game that he regularly threw up in the locker rooms; it happened so frequently that his fellow Celtics were more worried when it did *not* happen." It also can be helpful to briefly raise awareness to the fact that mindfulness- and acceptance-based techniques have been used with highly successful teams. For example, under the direction of former head coach Phil Jackson (nicknamed the "Zen Master"), the Chicago Bulls and Los Angeles Lakers won a combined 11 NBA titles. Both of these teams employed a sport psychologist trained in MBSR, and cultivated a culture consistent with the philosophical underpinnings of mindfulness.

In addition to being creative when presenting the theoretical rationale for mindfulness- and acceptance-based interventions, Gardner and Moore (2007) suggest using "simple language" and avoiding jargon. We have found it most effective to use language consistent with the athletic culture to communicate certain points. For example, one purpose of mindfulness- and acceptance-based interventions for athletes, such as MAC, is to enhance regulation of attention so that an athlete's focus remains, as needed, on task-relevant information. To present this concept, it may be helpful to point out that coaches might use lines like "stay focused" or "keep your head in the game," but seldom does anyone actually show an athlete how to do those things. Therefore, common phrases such as "stay focused" might have little effect unless an athlete actually knows how to pay attention. This opens the door to suggest that exercises used in MAC and related interventions can train an athlete's attentional capacity, and therefore help him or her establish a new relationship with phrases such as "stay focused."

It is also possible that this discussion can naturally flow into an introduction to relational frame theory (RFT; see Chapter 2, this volume). It is important to note, for example, that a phrase such as "stay focused" may not serve its intended purpose because it can be verbally associated with countless other phrases. In this case, let's assume "stay focused" triggers an athlete to think, "I can't focus; what's wrong with me?" This could be fine if an athlete is able to gain awareness of this process and allow his or her thoughts to come and go. However, it can be problematic if s/he is now fighting to control or eliminate the verbally associated "I can't focus" while also trying to "stay focused." This ongoing struggle can promote an internal focus and distract from task-relevant cues. It is important to be able to explain RFT in an appropriate manner for coaches who are not trained in psychology and to provide examples that resonate with athletic experience.

In getting started, it is also important to consider time constraints and the often limited availability of student athletes. As will be discussed below, this can become a challenge when attempting to get an entire team together at the same time. We suggest that it is important to be upfront about the time commitment of the program. For example, ideally the MAC approach would be delivered one time per week for 60 minutes over the course of seven weeks. Additionally, consistent with most mindfulness- and acceptance-based interventions, practice is typically necessary outside of program sessions. We like to say that similar to physical exercise, athletes need to train the muscle of the mind, referencing neuroplasticity (i.e., that engaging in an exercise, such as a daily meditation, can provide the mental repetitions necessary to build and sculpt the mind similar to training a muscle in the weight room). That said, it is not uncommon for administrators and coaches to ask for flexibility. For example, we have fielded questions such as, "Can we just do the entire program seven straight days?" and "Can we meet weekly but only for 15 minutes?" Given the nature of the athletic context, we recommend that practitioners demonstrate flexibility when delivering mindfulness- and acceptance-based interventions to college athletes. However, being mindful of maintaining the integrity of the program, we have routinely denied requests such as the above.

Cognitive Defusion and Acceptance

A central premise of ACT is that there are no "wrong" thoughts and emotions, but rather it is the struggle to have the "right" thoughts and emotions that causes a great deal of suffering (Luoma, Hayes, & Walser, 2007). Based on our experiences, athletes are highly prone to using control strategies, and often receive messages that are dissimilar to the central tenets of ACT, as previously mentioned. For example, from an early age athletes hear phrases such as "get your head right," "think positive," and "just relax." Additionally, the term "acceptance" is often misinterpreted to mean giving up or admitting defeat. This may at least partially explain why Gardner and Moore (2007) contend that "clients may struggle with the idea that they do not have to control or eliminate thoughts and feelings" (p. 87). In our experiences, clients *will* struggle with the idea that they do not have to control or eliminate thoughts and feelings. As previously discussed, the athletic culture stresses that a tough-minded and positive mental attitude is key for athletic success, which is ingrained in athletes across sports from an early age. Various control strategies (e.g. positive self-talk, thought stopping, arousal control) are taught to athletes, or they develop illusory correlations between particular internal states and athletic performance.

Athletes tend to struggle most with so-called "negative" thoughts and emotions when they perceive that they are not performing optimally. As the clinician working with college athletes, it is essential to help them understand that the problem is not their thoughts or emotions, but rather how they are relating to their thoughts and emotions. Using real life experiences from athletic participation can be an effective way to convey this point. For example, a baseball player in a slump may believe that negative thoughts and excessive anxiety are hindering his performance. In this case, the player could be asked to gradually practice observing his thoughts and emotions without attempting to change or alter them in any way. This type of gradual practice could include first asking the player to notice his thoughts or emotions in situations such as when putting on his uniform, stretching during warm-ups, taking batting practice, and eating a pre-game meal. We then progress to asking the player to do the same thing in game situations, such as when standing in the deck circle or batter's box.

We often suggest that, much like physical training, attempting to use acceptance and defusion strategies initially in perceived stressful situations will likely be ineffective; thus, there is a need to practice. We may state something like, "You do not just take batting practice prior to Game 1 of the World Series. You take batting practice almost every day." Additionally, in our experiences, when college athletes attempt to employ these strategies in anxiety-provoking situations without practice, they can become quickly discouraged and claim, "This stuff doesn't work." Overall, it is vital to keep in mind that, similar to when implementing mindfulness- and acceptance-based interventions with other individuals, it is necessary to use experiential exercises to convey certain concepts. We contend that these exercises tend to be most effective when they are relatable to a college athlete's specific experience in athletics.

Introducing and Developing Mindfulness

In recent years, there has been an increased amount of attention paid to the application of mindfulness for performance enhancement. This has perhaps been most notably depicted in an ESPN article by Roenigk (2013) describing how the Seattle Seahawks were using "unusual techniques" on their way to becoming Super Bowl champions in 2014. These "unusual techniques" were primarily mindfulness exercises, such as sitting meditations.

As the use of mindfulness rises among athletes, so do potential implementation issues such as helping college athletes and coaches understand what mindfulness is. Certainly, most mindfulness- and acceptance-based practitioners have worked with individuals who have a difficult time grasping that formal mindfulness exercises, such as a breathing meditation or body scan, are not intended to help someone relax, empty the mind, increase positivity, and/or attain a special state of consciousness. Explaining this point to college athletes and coaches can be even more challenging because, as mentioned previously, the athletic culture continues to reinforce the belief that successful performance is directly related to factors such as positive thinking or an optimal emotional state. As such, clinicians need to be careful about how they present mindfulness to college athletes because it is quite easy for the concept to be misunderstood. For example, to foster a football team's "buy-in" to using meditation to develop mindfulness, we grappled with using the following quote from All–Pro football player Russell Okung:

> Meditation is as important as lifting weights and being out here on the field for practice. It's about quieting your mind and getting into certain states where everything outside you doesn't matter in the moment. There are so many things telling you that you can't do something, but you take those thoughts captive, take power over them, and change them. (Roenigk, 2013, paragraph 33)

Although this quote implies that a well-known football player found meditation to be beneficial, it also reinforces the conceptual misunderstanding of mindfulness, particularly the part about taking power over thoughts and changing them.

Consistent with ACT and MBSR, we have found that the most effective way to help college athletes gain a better understanding of mindfulness and ways to develop it is to engage them in experiential exercises during sessions followed by focused dialogue. It is vital to encourage college athletes to discuss their reactions to experiential exercises, because this can help clarify any misunderstandings. For example, during a formal meditation exercise such as the body scan, it is common to hear something like, "I don't think I'm doing it right, I just couldn't relax," or "My mind kept wandering, I'm not good at this." In general, it is important to keep in mind that athletes can be perfectionistic, and this can contribute to a sense that they are not doing something correctly. That said, comments such as the ones above are times to provide feedback, such as "it's natural for the mind to wander—the real practice is being able to notice when the mind has wandered and then being able to non-judgmentally bring it back to whatever the focus of attention is in that particular exercise." This can easily be translated into the athletic context because an athlete's mind may wander to several task-irrelevant stimuli during the course of a practice or game. This is probably impossible to eliminate, so the real key is being able to notice that the mind has strayed from what is relevant and bring it back to the moment.

A final point on developing mindfulness among college athletes relates specifically to them engaging in formal practices. As mentioned above, programs such as MAC and MSPE offer differing doses of meditation practice. In our experiences, many college athletes (and college students in general) experience significant discomfort when doing formal exercises that last approximately 10 minutes or more. Highlighting this point, Wilson et al. (2014) found that several college students (particularly men) preferred to self-administer a mild electrical shock rather than sit with their own thoughts for a period of 15 minutes. Of course, when teaching meditations, we encourage college athletes to sit with discomfort even if they are bored, restless, anxious, etc. However, many athletes remain resistant to what seem like long periods of sitting. As such, it can be beneficial to incorporate formal exercises that involve movement, such as mindful walking, to reduce the risk of dropout or non-compliance.

Teaching Values

Values are a key feature of an ACT intervention and often one of the most difficult to implement when working with college athletes. Teaching values to any college student can be difficult, but athletes have an added history and immersion with a goal- and success-oriented culture that makes teaching values to college athletes even more challenging. For example, when starting to work with a team, we have observed that they will often be very clear about what their team goals are for the season, what their personal statistical goals are, and possibly what their career goals (i.e., professional) are related to athletics. Although many college athletes likely have not formally clarified their values, we like to suggest to them that whether they know it or not, they probably are already engaging in values-driven behavior. For example, we have worked with several athletes who report that balancing academics and athletics can be tremendously stressful, and thoughts arise such as, "I just want to quit." However, despite the discomfort of managing both academics and athletics, they continue to go to class and practice because they value constructs such as commitment, persistence, courage, and learning. In discussing this point, a relevant quote may be added to engage the athletes: Muhammad Ali once said, "I hated every minute of training, but I said, don't quit. Suffer now and live the rest of your life as a champion."

Ultimately, there is a balance that needs to be found between respecting the athlete's goals while teaching the concept of values and the ambiguity that can occur with a values assessment. Clarifying the difference between values and goals is of course necessary, and it can be very beneficial to use experiential exercises. One method that has been employed with college athletes is to ask them to provide a hypothetical article that is written at the end of their playing career (Gardner and Moore, 2007). Another method is to have the college athlete reflect on how they would want an observer (e.g., fan, parent) to describe their athletic performance. This often results in an understanding that people do not view their performance solely in terms of the outcome (scoring), but rather the manner in which the person engages in the performance (consistent and hardworking) that results in the outcome.

We also suggest to college athletes that engaging in values-driven behavior has a lot to do with focusing on the process rather than on outcomes. This can be an important point to make because taking a process-oriented approach has proven to be an aspect of successful teams. For example, Alabama football head coach Nick Saban has built a perennial title contender based upon teaching his players to focus less on results and more on what can be done in the moment. Under Saban's direction, Alabama football players are instructed not to look at the scoreboard, but rather to commit themselves to what needs to be done during the next play (i.e., make a block).

Issues With Implementation: Logistical

Delivery in Non-Traditional Settings

A primary logistical issue when implementing mindfulness- and acceptance-based interventions (and any psychological intervention with college athletes) is the physical space in which the intervention is delivered. Athletic departments have various meeting spaces for athletes and teams of athletes, and we have worked in spaces that are ideal, but unfortunately, also in spaces that are poorly configured and not delineated for private/confidential discussions (e.g., in locker rooms, on the team bus, on the field or court, in weight and athletic training rooms, and in college classrooms). The ethical issues faced in sport psychology have been well documented and discussed (see Etzel & Watson, 2014), but the nature of mindfulness- and acceptance-based interventions sometimes require additional considerations for effective delivery. The experiential nature of mindfulness- and acceptance-based approaches and contact with the athlete's potentially distressing thoughts and emotions requires the clinician to carefully consider confidentiality, potential ethical issues, and ramifications from the college athlete's environment. Unfortunately, there is not a structured way to solve every problem that arises, so clinicians delivering a mindfulness- and acceptance-based intervention in this setting should be fully engaged in the practice themselves and use the challenges as experiential examples. For example, a mindfulness exercise on the side of a busy athletic field is a unique experience for both the athletes and the clinician that can be embraced and explored rather than avoided. Another example is to consider the cognitive fusion that occurs in an athlete's locker room as they are surrounded by sport-specific triggers such as motivational signs, family pictures, previous team photos, and uniforms. The triggers may be used as experiential exercises to notice how one's mind responds to a trigger and becomes fused to particular thoughts and emotions. We believe that the clinician must be able to act flexibly and use logistical difficulties as an opportunity to explore ACT in a personalized manner for the athletes, and spending too much time and effort in creating an ideal environment for the intervention minimizes opportunities to fully model ACT concepts and implement an ACT intervention effectively.

Time Constraints/Team Availability

The life of a college athlete has significant time and logistical factors that influence the implementation of any psychological service or mindfulness- and acceptance-based intervention. One of the primary factors to consider is the challenging schedule of the college athlete due to academic, athletic, social, and personal demands and its potential impact on ACT components. There tend to be small windows of time over the course of a day that are open and unaccounted for by other requirements, leaving minimal time for formal mindfulness practice or between-session experiential exercises. The individual time constraints for each athlete hinder the provision of consistent services, and require a great deal of flexibility from the clinician. Informal mindfulness exercises or unique individualized mindfulness and defusion exercises may be developed for college athletes (see Appendix E for an example). We contend that a key element is to blend the exercises between sessions into life and sport so that college athletes can implement them into their schedules. For example, an athlete can be encouraged to engage in mindful stretching or showering as ways to engage in informal mindfulness practice. Non-traditional times and modalities may be considered due to these time constraints, as early morning or evening meetings may be necessary, or interaction with college athletes may occur through electronic means or by phone. Unfortunately, the time and logistical considerations of implementing a consistent intervention with an individual athlete or a team may reduce the potential success of the intervention.

Missed Sessions

As may be assumed from the time constraints of college athletes, missed individual or group sessions are invariably going to occur, and so the clinician must develop and implement interventions in a flexible manner. There are numerous reasons why college athletes may miss scheduled appointments: An athlete may suffer an injury and have required medical or athletic training appointments, the coach of a team may change the practice schedule that results in a change to the athlete's overall schedule, or weather may cause games to be rescheduled that in turn changes that athlete's entire weekly schedule. Additionally, there can be a stigma associated with receiving services from a mental health professional. In order to meet these challenges, the clinician must design interventions with a repertoire of flexible alternatives aimed at delivering the core features of mindfulness- and acceptance-based interventions. The necessary flexibility often involves shortened interventions, different groups of athletes from session to session, shift of focus of session (i.e., athlete is injured), and shifting of team schedules. We also believe that some college athletes may have a negative reaction to mindfulness exercises, and consequently miss scheduled sessions. Providing active variations of mindfulness and defusion in smaller doses may help athletes have a more positive initial experience with mindfulness, which provides a foundation for future more structured mindfulness sessions.

Future Directions

The above review of the application of mindfulness- and acceptance-based approaches to athletics highlights a number of limitations. First, there are very few studies that have been conducted with college athletes, and even fewer that have compared mindfulness- and acceptance-based interventions to another active intervention. According to a systematic review conducted by Sappington and Longshore (2015), in total there have been 19 mindfulness- and acceptance-based intervention studies conducted with athletes, and at the time of that review, only one (Aherne et al., 2011) has compared a mindfulness- and acceptance-based intervention to another active intervention. Second, small sample sizes limit the generalizability of findings and the interpretability of the data due to low statistical power. Based upon our review, only two studies have sample sizes larger than 20 (Baltzell & Akhtar, 2014; Thompson et al., 2011). Finally, the research has failed to build upon previous findings in a consistent manner, and does not provide clear links between the interventions, mechanisms of change, and outcomes.

An additional area of research that requires more attention is the prevalence and types of psychopathology that occur in the college athlete population. Depression may be prevalent due to multiple risk factors for college athletes (Wolanin, Gross, & Hong, 2015), and other studies have demonstrated that various forms of psychopathology are present (Storch, Storch, Killiany, & Roberti, 2005; Yang et al., 2007). This research will assist practitioners in developing specific evidence-based mindfulness- and acceptance-based interventions for the athlete based on performance enhancement and/or subclinical or clinical issues (Wolanin & Schwanhauser, 2010).

We also believe that more practitioners need to have training in the theory of ACT, evidence-based clinical interventions, and sport psychology interventions to provide mindfulness- and acceptance-based interventions to college athletes. This combination is difficult for prospective graduate students to identify and difficult for graduate training programs to provide due to the unique nature of each piece of the training. Furthermore, training for postdoctoral fellows and early career psychologists may be difficult to obtain and lead to clinicians engaging their services with different populations and intervention modalities.

An additional issue that requires attention is increasing the acceptability of delivery of both general psychological services to college athletes as well as mindfulness- and acceptance-based interventions. The dissemination of ACT interventions to college athletic departments is needed to create a culture that is open and supportive of psychological interventions including ACT. Athletic department administration and coaches need exposure to ACT concepts in order to effectively and consistently engage the student athlete in the context of an ACT intervention. Dissemination of mindfulness and acceptance interventions with college coaches may occur through individual interventions, coaching workshops, or working with the coaching staff of a particular team. While this is often done as part of mindfulness- and acceptance-based interventions delivered directly to college athletes, a more focused effort directed specifically for the performance and/or well-being of the coaches has the potential to create a culture for college athletes that fosters consistent athletic performance and long-term psychological well-being. Athletic training personnel and sport medicine physicians also need to be engaged and introduced to mindfulness and ACT to enhance interdisciplinary care for the college athlete.

Providing mindfulness- and acceptance-based interventions to college student athletes can be difficult, frustrating, and ambiguous due to the multitude of challenges that are unique to the college student athlete experience. Regardless, we contend that this approach is a promising and effective intervention for this population for enhancement of athletic performance and psychological well-being that has the potential to provide benefits beyond the student athlete's athletic career.

References

Aherne, C., Moran, A. P., & Lonsdale, C. (2011). The effects of mindfulness training on athletes' flow: An initial investigation. *The Sport Psychologist, 25,* 177–189. Retrieved from http://journals.humankinetics.com/tsp-back-issues/tsp-volume-25-issue-2-june/the-effect-of-mindfulness-training-on-athletes-flow-an-initial-investigation

Baltzell, A., & Akhtar, V. L. (2014). Mindfulness meditation training for sport (MMTS) intervention: Impact of MMTS with Division I female athletes. *The Journal of Happiness & Well-Being, 2,* 160–173. Retrieved from http://journalofhappiness.net/article.php?volume=2&issue=2&article=143&vid=32

Baltzell, A., Caraballo, N., Chipman, K., & Hayden, L. A. (2014). A qualitative study of the mindfulness meditation training for sport: Division I female soccer players' experience. *Journal of Clinical Sport Psychology, 8,* 221–244. doi:10.1123/jcsp.2014-0030

Bernier, M., Thienot, E., Codron, R., & Fournier, J. F. (2009). Mindfulness and acceptance approaches in sport performance. *Journal of Clinical Sport Psychology, 4,*

320–333. Retrieved from http://journals.humankinetics.com/jcsp-back-issues/JCSP Volume3Issue4December/mindfulness-and-acceptance-approaches-in-sport-performance

Bond, F. W., Hayes, S. C., Baer, R. A., Carpenter, K. M., Guenole, N., Orcutt, H. K., . . . Zettle, R. D. (2011). Preliminary psychometric properties of the Acceptance and Action Questionnaire-II: A revised measure of psychological flexibility and experiential avoidance. *Behavior Therapy, 42*(4), 676–688. doi:10.1016/j.beth.2011.03.007

De Petrillo, L., Kaufman, K., Glass, C., & Arnkoff. D. (2009). Mindfulness for long-distance runners: An open trial using mindful sport performance enhancement (MSPE). *Journal of Clinical Sport Psychology, 4,* 357–376. Retrieved from http://journals.humankinetics.com/jcsp-back-issues/jcspvolume3issue4december/mindfulness-for-long-distance-runners-an-open-trial-using-mindful-sport-performance-enhancement-mspe

DeGaetano, J., Wolanin A. T., & Marks, D. (in press). The role of psychological flexibility in injury rehabilitation. *Journal of Clinical Sport Psychology.*

Etzel, E. F., & Watson, J. C. (Eds.). (2014). *Ethical issues in sport, performance and exercise psychology.* Morgantown, WV: FiT Publishing.

Ferrante, A. P., Etzel, E. F., & Lantz, C. (2002). Counseling college student-athletes: The problem, the need. In E. F. Etzel, A. P. Ferrante, & J. W. Pinkney (Eds.), *Counseling college student athletes: Issues and interventions* (pp. 3–26). Morgantown, WV: FiT Publishing.

Gallagher, B. V., & Gardner, F. L. (2007). An examination of the relationship between early maladaptive schemas, coping, and emotional response to athletic injury. *Journal of Clinical Sport Psychology, 1,* 47–67. Retrieved from http://journals.humankinetics.com/jcsp-back-issues/jcspvolume1issue1march/anexaminationoftherelationshipbetweenearlymaladaptiveschemascopingandemotionalresponsetoathleticinjury

Gardner, F. L., & Moore, Z. E. (2004). A mindfulness-acceptance-commitment (MAC) based approach to athletic performance enhancement: Theoretical considerations. *Behavior Therapy, 35,* 707–723. doi:10.1016/S0005-7894(04)80016-9

Gardner, F. L., & Moore, Z. E. (2007). *The psychology of human performance: The mindfulness-acceptance-commitment approach.* New York, NY: Springer.

Gross, M., Moore, Z. E., Gardner, F. L., Wolanin, A. T., Pess, R. A., & Marks, D. R. (2015). *An empirical examination comparing the mindfulness-acceptance-commitment (MAC) approach and psychological skills training (PST) for the mental health and sport performance of student athletes.* Manuscript submitted for publication.

Hardy, L., Jones, G., & Gould, D. (1996). *Understanding psychological preparation for sport: Theory and practice of elite performers.* New York, NY: Wiley.

Hasker, S. M. (2010). *Evaluation of the mindfulness-acceptance-commitment (MAC) approach for enhancing athletic performance* (Doctoral dissertation). Retrieved from http://dspace.iup.edu/handle/2069/276

Hayden, E. W., Kornspan, A. S., Bruback, Z. T., Parent, M. C., & Rodgers, M. (2013). The existence of sport psychology services among NCAA division I FBS university athletic departments and counseling centers. *The Sport Psychologist, 27,* 296–304. Retrieved from http://journals.humankinetics.com/tsp-back-issues/tsp-volume-27-issue-3-september/the-existence-of-sport-psychology-services-among-ncaa-division-i-fbs-university-athletic-departments-and-counseling-centers

Hayes, S. C., Strosahl, K. D., & Wilson, K. G. (1999). *Acceptance and commitment therapy: An experiential approach to behavior change.* New York, NY: Guilford Press.

Hootman, J. M., Dick, R., & Agel, J. (2007). Epidemiology of collegiate injuries for 15 sports: Summary and recommendations for injury prevention initiatives. *Journal of Athletic Training, 42,* 311–319. Retrieved from www.ncbi.nlm.nih.gov/pmc/articles/PMC1941297/

Ivarsson, A., Johnson, U., Andersen, M. B., Fallby, J., & Altemyr, M. (2015). It pays to pay attention: A mindfulness-based program for injury prevention with soccer players. *Journal of Applied Sport Psychology, 27*, 319–334. doi:10.1080/10413200.2015.1008072

Kabat-Zinn, J. (1990). *Full Catastrophe Living*. New York, NY: Delta.

Kabat-Zinn, J., Beall, B., & Rippe, J. (1985, June). A systematic mental training program based on mindfulness meditation to optimize performance in collegiate and Olympic rowers. Poster presented at the World Congress in Sport Psychology, Copenhagen, Denmark.

Kaufman, K. A., & Glass, C. R. (2006). *Mindful sport performance enhancement: A treatment manual for archers and golfers*. Unpublished manuscript, The Catholic University of America, Washington, DC.

Kaufman, K. A., Glass, C. R., & Arnkoff, D. B. (2009). Evaluation of Mindful Sport Performance Enhancement (MSPE): A new approach to promote flow in athletes. *Journal of Clinical Sport Psychology, 3*, 334–356. Retrieved from http://journals.humankinetics.com/jcsp-supplements-special-issues/jcsp-volume-3-issue-4-december-special-issue/evaluation-of-mindful-sport-performance-enhancement-mspe-a-new-approach-to-promote-flow-in-athletes

Kornspan, A. S., & Duve, M. A. (2006). A niche and a need: A summary of the need for sport psychology consultants in collegiate sports. *Annals of the American Psychotherapy Association, 9*, 19–25.

Linehan, M. M. (1993). *Skills training manual for treating borderline personality disorder*. New York, NY: Guilford Press.

Luoma, J. B., Hayes, S. C., & Walser, R. D. (2007). *Learning ACT: An acceptance & commitment therapy skills-training manual for therapists*. Oakland, CA: New Harbinger.

Mahoney, J., & Hanrahan, S. J. (2011). A brief education intervention using acceptance and commitment therapy: Four injured athletes' experiences. *Journal of Clinical Sport Psychology, 5*, 252–273. Retrieved from http://journals.humankinetics.com/jcsp-back-issues/jcsp-volume-5-issue-3-september-/a-brief-educational-intervention-using-acceptance-and-commitment-therapy-four-injured-athletes-experiences

Mankad, A., Gordon, S., & Wallman, K. (2009a). Perceptions of emotional climate among injured athletes. *Journal of Clinical Sport Psychology, 3*, 1–14. Retrieved from http://journals.humankinetics.com/jcsp-back-issues/JCSPVolume3Issue1March/PerceptionsofEmotionalClimateAmongInjuredAthletes

Mankad, A., Gordon, S., & Wallman, K. (2009b). Psycho-immunological effects of written emotional disclosure during long-term injury rehabilitation. *Journal of Clinical Sport Psychology, 3*, 205–217. Retrieved from http://journals.humankinetics.com/jcsp-back-issues/JCSPVolume3Issue3September/psychoImmunologicalEffectsofWrittenEmotionalDisclosureDuringLongTermInjuryRehabilitation

National Collegiate Athletic Association. (2014). *Mind, body, and sport: Understanding and supporting student-athlete mental wellness*. Indianapolis, IN.

Noren, N. (2014, January 26). Taking notice of the hidden injury: Awareness, better treatment of athletes' mental health begins to take shape. Retrieved from http://espn.go.com/espn/otl/story/_/id/10335925/awareness-better-treatment-college-athletes-mental-health-begins-take-shape

Roenigk, A. (2013, August 23). Seattle Seahawks use unusual techniques in practice. *ESPN The Magazine*. Retrieved from http://espn.go.com/nfl/story/_/id/9581925/seattle-seahawks-use-unusual-techniques-practice-espn-magazine

Sappington, R., & Longshore, K. (2015). Systematically reviewing the efficacy of mindfulness-based interventions for enhanced athletic performance. *Journal of Clinical Sport Psychology, 9*, 232–262.

Schwanhausser, L. (2009). Application of the mindfulness-acceptance-commitment (MAC) protocol with an adolescent springboard diver: The case of Steve. *Journal of Clinical Sport Psychology, 3,* 377–395. Retrieved from http://journals.humankinetics. com/jcsp-back-issues/JCSPVolume3Issue4December/application-of-the-mindfulness-acceptance-commitmentmac-protocol-with-an-adolescent-springboard-diver

Segal, Z. V., Williams, M. G., & Teasdale, J. D. (2002). *Mindfulness-based cognitive therapy for depression.* New York, NY: Guilford Press.

Storch, E. A., Storch, J. B., Killiany, E. M., & Roberti, J. W. (2005). Self-reported psychopathology in athletes: A comparison of intercollegiate student-athletes and non-athletes. *Journal of Sport Behavior, 28,* 86–98.

Thompson, R. W., Kaufman, K. A., De Petrillo, L. A., Glass, C. R., & Arnkoff, D. B. (2011). One year follow-up of mindful sport performance enhancement (MSPE) with archers, golfers, and runners. *Journal of Clinical Sport Psychology, 5,* 99–116. Retrieved from http://journals.humankinetics.com/jcsp-back-issues/jcsp-volume-5-issue-2-june/one-year-follow-up-of-mindful-sport-performance-enhancement-mspe-with-archers-golfers-and-runners

Voight, M., & Callaghan, J. (2001). The use of sport psychology services at NCAA Division I universities from 1998–1999. *The Sport Psychologist, 15,* 91–102. Retrieved from http://journals.humankinetics.com/tsp-back-issues/TSPVolume15Issue1March/TheUseofSportPsychologyServicesatNCAADivisionIUniversitiesFrom19981999

Weinberg, R. S., & Gould, D. (2003). *Foundations of sport & exercise psychology* (3rd ed.). Champagin, IL: Human Kinetics.

Williams, M., Teasdale, J., Segal, Z., & Kabat-Zinn, J. (2007). *Guided meditation practices for the mindful way through depression* [CD Narrated by Jon Kabat-Zinn.] New York, NY: Guilford Press.

Wilson, K. A., Gilbert, J. N., Gilbert, W. D., & Sailor, S. R. (2009). College athletic directors' perceptions of sport psychology consulting. *The Sport Psychologist, 23,* 405–424. Retrieved from http://journals.humankinetics.com/tsp-back-issues/TSPVolume23Issue3September/CollegeAthleticDirectorsPerceptionsofSportPsychologyConsulting

Wilson, T. D., Reinard, D. A., Westgate, E. C., Gilbert, D. T., Ellerbeck, N., Hahn, C., . . . Shaked, A. (2014). Just think: The challenges of the disengaged mind. *Science, 345,* 75–77. doi:10.1126/science.1250830

Wolanin, A. T. (2005). Mindfulness-acceptance-commitment (MAC) based performance enhancement for Division I collegiate athletes: A preliminary investigation. *Dissertation Abstracts International B, 65*(7), 3735–3794.

Wolanin, A. T., & Schwanhauser, L. A. (2010). Psychological functioning as a moderator of the MAC Approach to performance enhancement. *Journal of Clinical Sport Psychology, 4,* 312–322. Retrieved from http://journals.humankinetics.com/jcsp-back-issues/jcsp-volume-4-issue-4-december/psychological-functioning-as-a-moderator-of-the-mac-approach-to-performance-enhancement

Wolanin, A. T., Gross, M., & Hong, E. (2015). Depression in athletes: Prevalence and risk factors. *Current Sport Medicine Reports, 14,* 56–60. doi:10.1249/JSR.0000000000000123

Yang, J., Peek-Asa, C, Corlette, J.D., Cheng, G., Foster, D.T., & Albright, J. (2007). Prevalence of and risk factors associated with symptoms of depression in competitive collegiate student athletes. *Clinical Journal of Sport Medicine, 17,* 481–487. doi:10.1097/JSM.0b013e31815aed6b

Zillmer, E. A., & Gigli, R. W. (2007). Clinical sport psychology in intercollegiate athletics. *Journal of Clinical Sport Psychology, 1,* 210–222. Retrieved from http://journals. humankinetics.com/jcsp-back-issues/jcsp-back-issues/ClinicalSportPsychologyinIntercollegiateAthletics

10 Making Time for Now
Brief and Non-Traditional Mindfulness- and Acceptance-Based Interventions in Undergraduate Education

Donald R. Marks, Jennifer Block-Lerner, Christina Barrasso-Catanzaro, and Karolina M. Kowarz

Introduction

Mindfulness-based interventions have traditionally focused on the 8-week format of mindfulness-based stress reduction (MBSR; Kabat-Zinn, 1990). This MBSR "template program" (McCown, Reibel, & Micozzi, 2010), which requires a time commitment of 25 to 30 hours for course meetings (8 weekly 2.5 hour sessions, plus 1 retreat day of 6–7 hours) in addition to daily practice time, has provided the foundation for many mindfulness-based interventions on which there has been considerable clinical research (Khoury et al., 2013). Examples of these programs, just to name a few, include mindfulness-based cognitive therapy (MBCT; Segal, Williams, & Teasdale, 2013), mindfulness-based relapse prevention (Bowen, Chawla, & Marlatt, 2010), and mindfulness-based relationship enhancement (Carson, Carson, Gil, & Baucom, 2004). Since the start of the 21ˢᵗ century, however, there have been efforts to create "low-dose" formulations of the MBSR program, designed to produce similar effects with reduced time commitments (Klatt, Buckworth, & Malarkey, 2009; Mitchell & Heads, 2015). In some cases, these options have kept the 8-week format but shortened the meeting times; in others, they have reduced both the number of sessions and the meeting duration. Researchers also have begun examining the effects of substantially shorter interventions, including single-session interventions (e.g., Johnson, Gur, David, & Currier, 2015; Shikatani, Antony, Kuo, & Cassin, 2014). In addition, other interventions integrating mindfulness, such as acceptance and commitment therapy (ACT; Hayes, Strosahl, & Wilson, 2012) and other acceptance-based behavioral interventions (Roemer & Orsillo, 2009) have provided alternative frameworks for brief format programs, such as 2-hour workshops (e.g., Blevins, Roca, & Spencer, 2011) and single-day formats (see Noone & Hastings, 2010; Pearson, Follette, & Hayes, 2012).

The university setting offers unique opportunities and constraints for delivery of mindfulness- and acceptance-based interventions. Several researchers have explored programs that integrate these interventions directly into college curricula (e.g., De Bruin, Meppelink, & Bögels, 2014; Ramler, Tennison, Lynch, & Murphy, 2015). One benefit of this approach is that it offers students, whose schedules are often filled with work, school, and social demands, an opportunity to participate that does not involve finding time outside existing class schedules. Another is that the interventions may reach struggling students who could experience the greatest difficulty in finding the time or wherewithal to attend a training program outside their existing course schedules but who could benefit substantially from what these programs have to offer.

Although the study of mindfulness- and acceptance-based curricula in undergraduate settings is in its early days, there is substantial research on mindfulness training for graduate and professional students in human service fields (Bohecker, Wathen, Wells, Salazar, & Vereen, 2014; Cohen & Miller, 2009; Hassed, de Lisle, Sullivan, & Pier, 2009; Reid, 2013; Shapiro, Schwartz, & Bonner, 1998; Stew, 2011). These applications, however, have focused primarily on challenges associated with training in specific disciplines and professions rather than on student experiences in general. Thus, these studies could be seen as more applicable to the professions for which participants are preparing than to the undergraduate experience or life as a student.

Several later studies, however, have reported benefits associated with mindfulness- and acceptance-based programs specifically tailored for undergraduate students. Some of these have examined the integration of brief mindfulness training into existing course curricula, such as a 5-week adaptation of MBSR (Bergen-Cico, Possemato, & Cheon, 2013), while others have employed nearly all of the 8-week MBSR program within a college course (see De Bruin et al., 2014; Lynch, Gander, Kohls, Kudielka, & Walach, 2011; Ramler et al., 2015). Many studies involving undergraduate participants, however, have focused on delivering very brief interventions offered outside the context of an existing course, in ways designed to accommodate students' busy schedules. These brief programs have included short adaptations of MBSR (Canby, Cameron, Calhoun, & Buchanan, 2015; Hindman, Glass, Arnkoff, & Maron, 2015; Jain et al., 2007; Rogers & Maytan, 2012), as well as a range of alternative brief mindfulness- and acceptance-based approaches (Danitz & Orsillo, 2014; Hill, Vernig, Lee, Brown, & Orsillo, 2011; Mermelstein & Garske, 2015; Scent & Boes, 2014). In addition, recent research also has included study of mindfulness- and acceptance-based interventions delivered through online media (Cavanagh et al., 2013; Levin, Pistorello, Hayes, Seeley, & Levin, 2015; Taylor, Strauss, Cavanagh, & Jones, 2014). This chapter will (a) review the brief (6 weeks or shorter) and non-traditional protocols designed for use with undergraduate students and describe the current evidence base for these interventions, (b) discuss work done in our own laboratory on very brief (i.e., 1-session) curriculum-grounded interventions, (c) consider some of the trade-offs involved in designing and delivering brief and online mindfulness- and acceptance-based curricula for undergraduates, and (d) highlight implications for additional research in this area.

Brief Adaptations of MBSR

Several of the brief mindfulness programs developed for use with undergraduates have been adapted from the MBSR template program. Bergen-Cico and colleagues

(2013), for example, used a 5-week program derived from the first half of the MBSR curriculum for a controlled, quasi-experimental study that was integrated into undergraduate health courses. Their "short-term MBSR" program met for 2 hours once per week with no retreat day, resulting in 10 hours of intervention time (compared to 26 hours in the template program). Half the course time was spent in discussion while the other half was devoted to mindfulness practices, including seated meditation, body scan, and mindful movement. Themes for discussion included metacognition, mind-body perspectives, and physical and emotional health. A control group included students enrolled in other undergraduate health courses who received no mindfulness training. Results revealed significant pre-post changes for the short-term MBSR group in mindfulness and self-compassion, with moderate effect sizes, and no significant changes for those in the control condition.

In a study that was not integrated into an existing course, Canby and colleagues (2015) used an adaptation of MBSR shortened to 6 weeks and meeting for 2 hours per week with no retreat day. This abbreviated format featured an introduction to mindfulness skills, including body scan and other practices, as well as key mindfulness concepts, including habitual responses to aversive emotions, strategies for remaining present during stressful situations, the distinction between thoughts and emotions, and interpersonal response styles. Approximately half the meeting time was devoted to experiential exercises, with the remaining half dedicated to discussion or didactic presentation. The study involved undergraduate student volunteers ($n = 19$) and a small number of faculty and staff, as well as a control group ($n = 25$), not randomly assigned, which completed all measures but received no intervention. Those in the treatment condition differed significantly from controls in pre-post change on self-report measures of psychological distress, self-control, mindful awareness, and subjective vitality, with medium to large effect sizes, while those in the control condition showed no significant pre-post change.

Hindman and colleagues (2015) also employed a 6-week mindfulness training program (based on MBSR, MBCT, and ACT) outside the context of an established course. In this case, the program used 1-hour weekly sessions and formal practice requirements were varied across two conditions, with one group expected to engage in up to 30 minutes of formal practice per day and the other having no daily practice requirement. The study of these two formats and a wait-list control condition included 34 undergraduate and graduate student participants. The formal practice program incorporated psychoeducation about stress, automatic pilot, present-moment awareness, compassion, and one's relationship to one's thoughts, as well as several experiential mindfulness practices, including mindful walking, eating, and listening. Participants in the formal practice group were asked to begin with 10 to 15 minutes per day of meditation, which was extended to 30 minutes per day by Week 5. Participants in the informal practice condition received the same psychoeducation materials and covered the same topics as the formal practice group but engaged only in brief mindfulness and acceptance exercises during meetings. Examples of these practices include the "free association task" derived from metacognitive therapy (Wells, 2009) and the "bad cup metaphor" derived from ACT (Hayes et al., 2012), which facilitates distinguishing between evaluations or opinions and descriptions. Homework for those in the informal condition involved only encouragement to incorporate the mindfulness principles learned in the course into their daily lives. Participants in both the formal and informal practice conditions showed significant within-group changes in total mindfulness scores, though effect sizes were larger for those in the formal practice group. No changes in total mindfulness were found for the control condition. Similarly, there were significant and sizable pre-post changes for the formal practice condition in psychological flexibility (PF), self-compassion, and decentering, while the informal practice group showed significant changes only in self-compassion and decentering, with no within-group change for controls. The pre-post increase for self-compassion, it should be noted, was significantly larger for the formal practice than it was for the informal practice group. The study also revealed significant pre-post differences for both the formal and informal practice conditions in depression, stress, and worry. Only those in the formal practice condition, however, reported significant pre-post changes in anxiety, rumination, and life satisfaction. Finally, changes in nonreactivity, worry, and self-compassion were found to mediate the relationship between treatment condition and self-reported stress.

Jain and colleagues (2007) conducted a randomized controlled trial (RCT) of a 4-week adaptation of MBSR, primarily for undergraduate pre-medical and pre-health students along with some medical school and nursing school students ($n = 83$). To accommodate students' exam and holiday schedules, the program consisted of four weekly 1.5-hour sessions and a 6-hour retreat day between Session 3 and Session 4. Practices included the body scan meditation, sitting meditation, hatha yoga (i.e., gentle stretching), walking meditation, and lovingkindness practice. The authors noted that their intervention emphasized cognitive components (e.g., attentional deployment in mindful listening), somatic components (e.g., body scan, mindful movement), and interpersonal components (e.g., lovingkindness practice). Comparison conditions for the RCT included both a somatic relaxation program and a wait-list control group. The somatic relaxation program included progressive muscle relaxation, diaphragmatic breathing, and guided imagery exercises. Both the mindfulness and relaxation programs outstripped the control condition in reduction of self-reported symptom distress. Those in the mindfulness condition also reported significantly greater increases in positive affect than those in either the relaxation or control conditions. In addition, those in the mindfulness group showed significantly larger reductions in rumination than those in the somatic relaxation group, with controls demonstrating an increase in rumination. Moreover, those in the mindfulness condition demonstrated a pre-post reduction in distraction compared to increases in distraction for both the relaxation and control conditions.

Finally, Rogers and Maytan (2013) developed a 4-session adaptation of MBSR specifically for college students and other "emerging adults" (Arnett, 2015). Their approach, *Koru*, consists of four 75-minute small-group sessions and a required daily meditation practice of 10 minutes. During each session, participants are introduced to various mindfulness and mind-body skills, with examples and exercises specifically tailored to this developmental stage. Commitment to attend all four classes is required of participants, and they are also given required readings in Kabat-Zinn's (1994) *Wherever You Go, There You Are.* Greeson, Juberg, Maytan, James, and Rogers (2014) recently compared *Koru* to a wait-list condition in an RCT involving 90 undergraduate and graduate students. Results indicated significant group-by-time interactions for changes in perceived stress, sleep quality, mindfulness, and self-compassion, all in expected directions (with participants in the *Koru* group exhibiting changes in the direction of health/well-being and control participants exhibiting no change) with medium to large effect sizes.

Very Brief Mindfulness- and Acceptance-Based Interventions

In addition to low-dose adaptations of MBSR, researchers have also investigated much briefer mindfulness- and acceptance-based interventions, using presentation formats that differ substantially from the MBSR template program. Although these brief programs have demonstrated significant effects, it must be noted that sample sizes across these studies have typically been quite small.

One example of such a program is Danitz and Orsillo's (2014) single-session 90-minute acceptance-based behavioral therapy (ABBT) workshop for first-year undergraduate students ($n = 28$) and first-year law students ($n = 21$). The intervention, conducted during the first month of the school year, was followed up by three emailed or texted messages that encouraged students to make use of strategies covered in the workshop. Topics addressed in the workshop included the utility of various types of coping strategies (control/avoidance-based vs. those consistent with mindfulness and acceptance) and values (focusing on the type of student that the participant wanted to be and the types of relationships that he or she wanted to have with peers and professors). The researchers evaluated the workshop relative to a wait-list control condition, finding that those who attended ($n = 19$) exhibited significantly lower levels of depression and higher levels of acceptance than those in the control condition ($n = 30$), with moderate effect sizes. Further, increases in acceptance over the course of the semester were associated with decreases in depression during the same timeframe. While these results are promising, as reported in a flowchart of participants through various phases of the study and discussed by the authors, a very small percentage of students who were initially invited to participate actually followed through to the workshop and then completion of follow-up measures. Findings like this lend support to the use of curriculum-grounded interventions; trade-offs of the approaches to be discussed below.

Very brief programs also have been used to focus on delivery of interventions for specific situations or behavioral problems. One example is a 2-session ACT protocol for perfectionism and procrastination that involved 3 hours of intervention time (Scent & Boes, 2014). The intervention incorporated mindful awareness of present-moment experience, including aversive emotional experience and related body sensations, as well as training in techniques for cognitive defusion (i.e., decentering, acknowledging thoughts as thoughts) and cultivation of willingness and action in accordance with one's values. Although their sample size was quite small ($n = 8$) and the study uncontrolled, Scent and Boes found that their 2-week group intervention yielded an increase in PF and an interest in obtaining additional training in mindfulness and acceptance skills.

Hill et al. (2011) developed and implemented a very brief (2-session) mindfulness- and acceptance-based program to prevent retraumatization among college women with histories of child sexual abuse (CSA). The 2-hour sessions in this program featured breathing practices and experiential exercises, including elements of the MBSR curriculum (e.g., mountain meditation), as well as exercises from ACT (e.g., passengers on the bus). Discussions examined typical stressors in college life, as well as coping strategies, the potential utility of aversive emotions, and consideration of the costs and benefits associated with efforts to control one's thoughts, emotions, and sensations. A pilot trial of this intervention included 12 women reporting histories of CSA and 19 without abuse histories; no-treatment controls included 18 with CSA histories and 24 without. An increase in mindful observing skills for the intervention group was the only change by group or time. The researchers did, however, find a protective effect at 2-month follow-up: Women with CSA histories who participated in the intervention were less likely to have been revictimized than those with CSA histories who did not receive the intervention.

Finally, Mermelstein and Garske (2015) tested a very brief mindfulness-based intervention for binge drinking in college students, involving only a single 1-hour session and a program of homework exercises and monitoring. The study randomly assigned participants ($n = 76$), who acknowledged problems with binge drinking (1 or more binge episodes in the past 2 weeks), to either a brief mindfulness condition or no-treatment control group. Participants in the mindfulness group discussed a handout introducing mindfulness and its potential benefits for individuals who engage in binge drinking. They also completed approximately 30 minutes of mindfulness practice, including two brief experiential exercises, a mindfulness of breath practice and an "urge surfing" (Marlatt, 1985) exercise. Additionally, they engaged in a cue exposure exercise in which they applied the mindfulness skills they had just learned while viewing alcohol-related imagery. At the conclusion of the session, participants received a CD including a recording of guided mindfulness practices, and they were asked to commit to 1 hour of formal practice per week over the 4-week intervention. Also, at an assessment session scheduled at the two-week point in the study, participants in the mindfulness condition engaged in a 25-minute exercise involving awareness of thoughts, emotions, and body sensations. Participants in the control condition received no mindfulness intervention or supporting materials, though they did complete the cue exposure exercise and were asked to employ whatever strategies they would normally use in response to any urges to drink. In addition to significant increases in self-reported mindfulness, those in the mindfulness condition reported 2.61 fewer binge drinking episodes than the control group over the 4 weeks of the study (a large effect size), as well as significantly fewer negative consequences of alcohol use than the control group.

Online Delivery Options

The current generation of undergraduate students has been characterized as "digital natives" (Demirbilek, 2014) and "generation C," with the C standing for "connection, communication, and change" (Friedrich, Peterson, & Koster, 2011). For most students born in the 1990s, the Internet and pervasive smart phone technology have always been part of daily life, and steady online delivery of entertainment and information is expected and comforting (Palfrey & Gasser, 2008). Researchers studying mindfulness- and acceptance-based interventions have seen the rise of digital media as an opportunity for providing useful information and experiences. So far, although the number of studies is rather small, these programs have shown effects roughly comparable to those found with brief mindfulness-based interventions delivered in traditional classroom settings.

Taylor and colleagues (2014) based their online intervention on MBCT, which is primarily supported as a relapse prevention intervention for individuals with depression and other psychological difficulties. Eighty undergraduate or postgraduate university students were recruited via posters on campus and randomly assigned to either MBCT-self-help (MBCT-SH) or a wait-list control condition. Students in the MBCT-SH group were asked to read the book *Mindfulness: A Practice Guide to Finding Peace in a Frantic World* (Williams & Penman, 2011) and engage in 20–30 mindfulness practices from an accompanying CD. Significant group-by-time interactions were found for measures of depression, anxiety, and stress; life satisfaction, and self-compassion and mindfulness, with a wide range of effect sizes. Importantly, engagement in the intervention was high. Only four participants (5% of those randomized) did not complete the post-intervention measures. Further, 57.5% reported reading the whole book, with 85% reading at least half. The median number of reported practice sessions per week was between 2 and 3. At 10-week follow-up 57.5% of MBCT-SH participants reported practicing at least once per week.

Cavanagh and colleagues (2013) conducted an RCT of a 2-week self-paced online mindfulness program, entitled 'Learning Mindfulness Online,' for 104 undergraduates. Participants were randomly assigned to the online mindfulness condition or a wait-list control group. The mindfulness program was developed using the Moodle learning management system, and it included both information resources and audio recordings of mindfulness practices. The online learning program was divided into 5 segments, including (a) a video introduction defining mindfulness and its potential benefits, (b) an introduction to mindfulness practices for daily use, (c) frequently asked questions regarding practice, (d) a journal for reflection on daily practice, and (e) additional resources. Daily 10-minute guided practices featured awareness of breathing, bodily sensations, thoughts, and emotions. Although the program was self-guided, participants received four email reminders encouraging them to engage in daily practice and providing suggestions for bringing mindfulness into life activities such as eating or walking. Medium effect sizes for pre-post change in the mindfulness group relative to the wait-list controls were found on mindfulness, perceived stress, and depression and anxiety. One concerning finding, however, was the rate of attrition, 57.4%, in the mindfulness group.

Levin et al. (2015) conducted an open trial of a 4-week online intervention, entitled ACT on college life (ACT-CL), in the context of university counseling centers. The study, which involved 82 students and 30 college counselors, provided online portals for both counselors and their student clients. The counselor portal included training modules with instructional videos introducing both ACT principles and the ACT-CL program. After completing the training, counselors could access a program allowing them to monitor their student clients' progress through the ACT-CL student portal. This portal featured three multimedia self-help instructional sessions approximately 45 minutes each in duration, including training on mindfulness, acceptance, and values. Activities in these sessions were highly interactive, involving students writing and responding to experiential exercises. The program also sent automatic emails to students reminding them of lessons they needed to complete and skills they could practice. Student participants, who included individuals endorsing a range of psychological difficulties, demonstrated significant pre-post change over the 4-week study in several domains, including increases in mindfulness, PF, and engagement with educational values. Students also demonstrated significant reductions in depression, anxiety, and stress with moderate effect sizes. No significant differences were found in life satisfaction. As with the study by Cavanagh and colleagues (2013), student attrition was substantial. While 80% of counselors completed the ACT-CL training and used the client monitoring program, 62% of students failed to complete the training modules. Even so, students did spend an average of 61.7 minutes using the application, and they logged on to the program 3.9 times on average during the 4 weeks of the study. Also, 73% of student participants reported they were satisfied with the program and 90% indicated they would recommend it to others.

Gauging Feasibility and Student Interest

Brief and non-traditional interventions have the potential to expose a wide range of students to mindfulness practices and a stance toward emotional experiences consistent with acceptance. Short-term interventions, like those integrated directly into existing courses, specifically offer opportunities to reach students who do not feel able to commit to much time outside of class. These students may include those who are struggling and require additional time to complete coursework or those who are overloaded with school and other life responsibilities. Additionally, these brief interventions offer unique opportunities to study predictors of engagement and receptivity toward participation in further practice or trainings.

A notable problem, however, for studies of brief mindfulness- and acceptance-based interventions has been identifying interested students and enlisting sufficient student participation, particularly for programs that are not delivered as part of existing courses or treated as part of course requirements. Danitz and Orsillo (2014), for example, invited 1,763 freshmen and first-year law students to participate in a free workshop with a $20 gift card incentive for study completers; only 115 students, 6.5% of those invited, responded. Of 98 enrolling in the study, only 49 students completed, and attrition was higher, 61.2%, among those assigned to the 1-session workshop condition than among wait-list controls, 38.7%. Similarly, in Cavanagh and colleagues' (2013) online intervention, only 42.6% of those in the mindfulness condition completed the study, compared to 70% of wait-list controls, and in Levin and colleagues' (2015) study involving university counseling center therapists and their clients less than 40% of students completed the intervention.

Evolution Toward Curriculum-Based Work

Studies conducted in our own laboratory (Block-Lerner et al., 2012) have yielded mixed results regarding feasibility and student interest. We began with one study which aimed to recruit students from a freshman experience course for 3-session outside-of-class workshops; participation earned students a small amount of credit in the course. Intervention sessions were comprised of didactic and experiential components and addressed topics very similar to Danitz and Orsillo's (2014) acceptance-based behavioral protocol. Of the 165 students we recruited via flyers and in-class announcements from approximately 12 course sections twenty-three of the students, 13.9%, completed the survey in full and indicated some availability to attend the workshops. A total of 10 students, 6.1%, attended one or more workshop meetings; 8 students, 4.8% attended two or three meetings. Of the 10 attending workshops, only 4 participants, 2.4%, agreed to be contacted for a follow-up (third) assessment. Two of the 4 agreed to complete the follow-up survey; the other 2 opted not to after reviewing the informed consent. From those who did make it through all of these steps, the workshop received positive feedback—when asked for general comments on it, one student noted: "Very insightful. I've become aware of the things I am missing out on in life, and things I tend to take for granted." Yet the recruitment and attrition problems seen in other studies were clearly at play here as well and do not allow conclusions about effectiveness to be drawn. In fact, it seemed to us that those few students who made it through all of the hurdles involved in assessment and scheduling were likely not representative of the students most in need of such services.

Informed by that initial study, ongoing work in our laboratory has employed very brief curriculum-grounded interventions to shed light on predictors of receptivity to mindfulness- and acceptance-based approaches in students across multiple programs, disciplines, and developmental levels. One study attempted to address feasibility and receptivity by implementing a single 75-minute workshop into undergraduate psychology courses during scheduled class time (Barrasso-Catanzaro, Block-Lerner, Wolanin, Marks, & Kowarz, 2015). The workshop, led by advanced doctoral students, featured a range of mindfulness- and acceptance-related practices, including values clarification, brief experiential practices, and psychoeducation about mindlessness and mindfulness. Specific exercises included mindful eating; values clarification, using the "Big Rocks" story, speaking to allotting time for the most important things in one's life first (Covey, Merrill, & Merrill, 1994) and the Bull's-Eye Values Survey (Lundgren, Luoma, Dahl, Strosahl, & Melin, 2012); and an exercise involving bringing present-moment awareness and acceptance to a memory of a difficult experience and practicing "holding it" with various gestures and postures that reflect different levels of openness (e.g., clenched fists, open arms, self-embrace).[1] Students ($n = 188$) completed measures just prior to, during, and after the workshop, also during class time.

A small percentage of students attending these classes (less than 5%) elected not to participate in the research and did not complete measures, even though some of these students demonstrated a high level of engagement in the workshop activities themselves (see points below about informed consent). Many students reported positive reactions to the workshop and fairly high levels of interest in continuing to engage in various mindfulness-based practices in the future and likelihood of recommending such practices to others (i.e., the latter two elements comprising our operational definition of receptivity). Specifically, scores on the component items of the investigator-created receptivity measure fell in the 3–4 range on Likert-type scales from 1–5 (with higher scores indicating higher levels of receptivity). To speak to the study's main aim, elucidating predictors of receptivity, students with higher levels of PF and dispositional mindfulness were more receptive to the workshop's practices than students who endorsed lower levels. Further, moderation analyses indicated that those who reported higher levels of psychological distress (as per the Depression Anxiety Stress Scales-21; Henry & Crawford, 2005; Lovibond & Lovibond, 1995) along with higher levels of mindful awareness were more receptive to the workshop (Barrasso-Catanzaro et al., 2015).

In addition to raising important questions about the interaction of symptomatology and aspects of mindfulness in the development of receptivity to mindfulness- and acceptance-based approaches, the results of this project support those of other studies (both our own and those reviewed) which suggest that the implementation of very brief curriculum-based workshops is feasible and acceptable to a wide range of students. Overall, the workshop sought to expose a broad audience of students to brief but substantial glimpses of mindfulness- and acceptance-based practices without burdening them with additional time and scheduling commitments. Because it occurred during regular class time, the workshop also offered students the ability to engage in mental health services with little to none of the stigma related to seeking mental health services.

While brief programs offer the possibility of reaching students who could benefit from mindfulness and related interventions without undue time commitments, additional data are needed about the feasibility of specific mindfulness- and acceptance-based interventions and students' receptivity and response to these interventions. This is especially true given the limited assessment tools available for measurement of receptivity to these practices. Further, especially when available class time is so limited, increased study of the active ingredients of multi-component protocols would serve the field well.

Challenges Faced and Lessons Learned

In addition to using our abysmally low participation rates in the outside-of-class workshops to inform our efforts to ground brief workshops into course curricula, we have continued to learn from the process of bringing these services into the classroom. We offer here discussion of these lessons; we hope it will be useful to others engaged in this work.

Based on feedback from participants, our protocol has evolved to provide additional guidance and time for reflection regarding the program's experiential exercises. A salient example involves the exercise described above that involves "holding" a difficult situation in various ways. One of the authors (Jennifer Block-Lerner) was piloting the exercise in a workshop using it as part of a student's (Karolina Kowarz's) dissertation. This exercise was conducted near the end of the class period and time ran short, leaving little time for debriefing before asking students to work on a post-workshop feedback packet. A student (who previously had been a vocal and seemingly receptive participant) approached the workshop leader, clearly upset, and said, "You have to be really careful with that last exercise," and walked out quickly. The workshop leader experienced this interaction as quite disturbing and at first it led the research team to question the viability of the intervention in this setting. As we reflected on the incident and consulted with our Institutional Review Board, we considered the many contextual factors that led to that student's particular experience. These reflections prompted us to develop a list of important points and potential take-home messages from the exercise (e.g., it's natural to want to close up at times; life can be about a back and forth between different levels of openness). The course instructor shared these with her students via email, and we now always make sure to allow time for at least brief coverage of them after the exercise. Importantly, this was also when we decided to explicitly tell students that their problem or issue of choice could be something small/minor (e.g., hitting the snooze button too many times or trying to find a parking space) or something larger/more substantial. For what it is worth, we have not heard any similar concerns about the exercise since.

We also have given considerable thought to the issue of informed consent in curriculum-based workshops. Students in these workshops typically receive little information about what to expect beforehand; they are essentially a "captive audience," walking into their usual classes, expecting to interact in their usual ways. Mindfulness- and acceptance-based approaches involve a different way of being, and this new tone is set from the moment students enter the room, by things like desks being arranged in a semi-circle instead of the usual rows. Thus, it is important that students have choices, both in terms of how they participate in workshop exercises and, of course, in terms of whether they participate in any research study component. See Appendix F for a script portraying how we have approached this issue.

In conducting curriculum-based work, it is critically important, clearly, to gain support from faculty teaching courses. In our experience, building relationships with colleagues who teach the students one wishes to have access to has numerous mutually beneficial effects. We have tended to develop these connections relatively informally; however, we plan to build a website that will provide information to instructors who might be interested in incorporating such services. However these connections are made, it might also be useful to let instructors know that workshops leaders are willing to fill in if they need to miss a given class session or can even be "on call" to take over class in the event that an emergency situation arises assuming the workshop is a good fit for the course.

Finally, we have also continued to shape the protocol based on particular contexts. For example, we were recently asked to conduct a workshop in an undergraduate course of speech and language pathology students who were in the midst of applying to graduate programs. Really thinking about how to meet this group where they were led us to create a workshop substantially different in form (i.e., more interactive), though seemingly similar in function, protocol. Here we resonate strongly with the sentiments of Hayes, Levin, Plumb-Vilardaga, Villatte, and Pistorello (2013) and Herbert, Gaudiano, and Forman (2013), who emphasize ACT and other acceptance-based behavioral approaches as being principle rather than protocol driven. Taking such a stance allows for flexibility and creativity in designing specific protocols for particular groups of students. Of course, such heterogeneity in form also makes assessing integrity more challenging.

Debates, Trade-Offs, and Questions for Future Research

One significant debate surrounding brief interventions concerns the relative emphasis placed on formal mindfulness practice. While results of the Hindman et al. (2015) study suggested that formal practice is not required to achieve significant decreases in symptom distress, mindfulness, and self-compassion, there are still questions to be answered about programs that lack a formal practice component. Are the gains associated with participation in these programs as substantial and sustainable as those associated with interventions prescribing between-session practice? Hindman and colleagues found that those engaging in formal practice achieved greater changes in mindfulness and greater reductions in stress. Nevertheless, a group engaging in no formal practice, either at home or in sessions, reported significantly reduced symptom distress, including reductions in rumination and worry.

Based on the findings to date it is tempting to conclude that in undergraduate settings interventions involving minimal time commitments and limited formal practice are effective but interventions including formal practice components are *even more* effective. The problem with such a conclusion, however, is that there are exceedingly few head-to-head comparisons of the two approaches. Also, even studies using mindfulness programs with undergraduate participants that adhere closely to the 8-week MBSR template program, such as that used by Ramler and colleagues (2015) or Lynch et al. (2011), have not always yielded expected effect sizes. Before conclusions can be drawn regarding the optimal duration of programs and formal practice requirements, much more information is needed, particularly regarding *how* formal practice influences outcomes and *how* participants in programs without formal practice achieve mindfulness- and acceptance-related benefits.

Trade-offs potentially related to longer formats and formal practice requirements include increased student perception that a program will be too time-consuming, higher rates of non-adherence to program expectations, and participant attrition. Yet the relatively high attrition rates seen with online interventions also suggest that without the structure of a class or group or student-teacher relationship, participation in both didactic instruction and experiential practice is likely to decline. Feasibility studies are needed to ascertain differential responses to course design options. For example, would students who are experiencing significant stress related to workload and academic responsibilities be more likely to enroll in programs involving both limited time commitments and minimal between-session obligations? Similarly, would students less familiar with mindfulness be more receptive to mindfulness-based programs that include brief, focused experiential exercises than to programs including extended formal practices?

Questions concerning optimal program length also require additional investigation. There are numerous studies demonstrating the effectiveness of the 8-week MBSR template program or adaptations of that program with similar time commitments (see Khoury et al., 2013). Yet the university setting often does not lend itself to student involvement in a program requiring that much time. Modifying student schedules and curricula to accommodate a traditional MBSR program might benefit students struggling to juggle work and school commitments. It seems unlikely, however, that the many competing pulls on students' time, including the persistent demands of social media and electronic communication, will abate any time soon. So the question arises, how much time is required to administer an effective mindfulness program in an undergraduate setting? While single-session workshops such as those we have completed in our lab or those described by Danitz and Orsillo (2014) receive favorable reviews from participants, they do not appear to be well-attended when scheduled outside of existing class times and thus the full degree to which they could foster interest in mindfulness- and acceptance-based perspectives or promote mindfulness practice remains unknown. These are empirical questions, and while the studies published to date suggest that programs of widely varying lengths could prove effective for diverse purposes, specific inquiries into program duration and scheduling parameters (e.g., during class time, early or later in the semester) are needed. It would be useful to consider, in this context, existing research regarding the effectiveness of brief therapeutic interventions in general which, as Strosahl, Robinson, and Gustavsson (2012) have suggested, may have far greater potency than typically realized.

Another avenue requiring additional exploration concerns the longitudinal effects of attending brief or non-traditional programs. It would be useful to know, for example, whether exposure to mindfulness and acceptance curricula, even in the context of very brief programs, contributes to long-term changes in behavior (e.g., attending additional training, engaging in formal or informal practice). Likewise, the possibility of identifying particular strategies for follow-up after brief interventions, such as sending text messages with reminders of material covered and suggestions for current practice, as employed by Danitz and Orsillo (2014) in order to facilitate longer-term use of mindfulness and acceptance skills, could be further explored. Once again, long-term effects of short-term interventions have often been underestimated, and study of the lasting power of "sudden gains" related to brief mindfulness- and acceptance-based interventions would be useful (Strosahl et al., 2012).

Finally, in addition to investigating alternate delivery formats, research is also needed regarding possible uses of brief and non-traditional programs. The studies by Hill et al. (2011) and Mermelstein and Garske (2015), for example, offer examples of ways that general interventions and processes involving awareness and acceptance of emotional experience can contribute to brief interventions for specific populations (e.g., victims of abuse, individuals with alcohol use problems). Oman and colleagues (2007) used an adaptation of MBSR to reduce negative spiritual coping (e.g., judging, references to a punitive God) among undergraduates and promote healthy spirituality. Broadly considered, a key function of all mindfulness- and acceptance-based curricula is providing an alternative perspective on human suffering. Specifically, these programs acknowledge the aversive aspects of emotional experience, while also providing a glimpse of alternate ways of responding in the midst of distress. Aversive emotions, such as anxiety and frustration, are recognized as pervasive, and perhaps inevitable, aspects of human experience, which are particularly likely to arise as students encounter both challenging coursework and new environments and social contexts.

Mindfulness- and acceptance-based strategies offer potentially more flexible ways of relating to these challenging aspects of life experience (e.g., by turning toward them, versus avoiding them or letting them dictate one's actions). This flexible perspective, in turn, has the potential to yield benefits that are both widespread and long-term. The extensive empirical literature on PF suggests it is a protective factor relevant to many forms of psychological distress (Hayes, Luoma, Bond, Masuda, & Lillis, 2006). Through the flexible use of mindfulness and acceptance skills, students may learn to spend less time and effort attempting to avoid and control aspects of their inner experience, thereby freeing resources for approaching challenging life tasks and acting in accordance with chosen values (Glaser, n. d.). In addition, through the exploration of mindfulness and acceptance skills in a classroom or group context, students can come in contact with both their own vulnerabilities and the vulnerabilities and emotional experiences described by others.

Indeed, engagement in even the briefest of mindfulness- and acceptance-based trainings has the potential to be profoundly destigmatizing, conveying a sense of one's common humanity (i.e., the challenges inherent in being human). It could also normalize many of the more distressing aspects of life, particularly the inevitable stress response to novel and challenging interpersonal situations and the tendency to use automatic, judgmental labels in response to stress (see Glaser, n. d.). Participants may notice ways that judgmental and stereotypical categorizations of themselves and others have negatively influenced both their perspectives on life and their overall well-being. This more flexible perspective also has the potential to destigmatize participation in other psychological interventions, creating conditions in which students who could benefit from additional services might be willing to pursue them. As Eisenberg, Hunt, and Speer (2012) have noted, many undergraduates do not use counseling services despite endorsing favorable attitudes toward psychological treatment, and it is possible that "merely a nudge of some kind" (p. 229) could facilitate their engagement. Brief mindfulness- and acceptance-based programs could provide this nudge and, in so doing, allow a larger percentage of students who experience psychological distress or behavioral problems (e.g., binge drinking, addiction) to obtain needed services and complete their degree programs.

Note

1 This practice was introduced to us by Dennis Tirch, Ph.D., who indicated that a modified version was introduced to him by Christopher Germer, Ph.D.

References

Arnett, J. J. (2015). *Emerging adulthood: The winding road from the late teens through the twenties* (2nd ed.). New York, NY: Oxford University Press.

Barrasso-Catanzaro, C., Block-Lerner, J., Wolanin, A., Marks, D., & Kowarz, K. (2015). *Integrating mindfulness- and acceptance-based practice into the college curriculum: Examining receptivity in undergraduate students.* Manuscript under review.

Bergen-Cico, D., Possemato, K., & Cheon, S. (2013). Examining the efficacy of a brief mindfulness-based stress reduction (brief MBSR) program on psychological health. *Journal of American College Health, 61,* 348–360. doi:10.1080/07448481.2013.813853

Blevins, D., Roca, J. V., & Spencer, T. (2011). Life guard: Evaluation of an ACT-based workshop to facilitate reintegration of OIF/OEF veterans. *Professional Psychology: Research and Practice, 42,* 32–39. doi:10.1037/a0022321

Block-Lerner, J., Cardaciotto, L., Boone, M., Kowarz, K., Orsillo, S., Pistorello, J., Wilson, K., & Wolanin, A. (2012, November). Building psychological flexibility within and outside of the classroom: ACT-based approaches in higher education. Panel discussion delivered at the annual meeting of the Association for Behavioral and Cognitive Therapies. National Harbor, MD.

Bohecker, L., Wathen, C., Wells, P., Salazar, B. M., & Vereen, L. G. (2014). Mindfully educating our future: The MESG curriculum for training emergent counselors. *Journal for Specialists in Group Work, 39,* 257–273. doi:10.1080/01933922.2014.919046

Bowen, S., Chawla, N., & Marlatt, G. A. (2010). *Mindfulness-based relapse prevention for substance use disorders: A clinician's guide.* New York, NY: Guilford Press.

Canby, N. K., Cameron, I. M., Calhoun, A. T., & Buchanan, G. M. (2015). A brief mindfulness intervention for healthy college students and its effects on psychological distress, self-control, meta-mood, and subjective vitality. *Mindfulness, 6*(5), 1071–1081. Advance online publication. doi:10.1007/s12671-014-0356-5

Carson, J. W., Carson, K. M., Gil, K. M., & Baucom, D. H. (2004). Mindfulness-based relationship enhancement. *Behavior Therapy, 35,* 471–494. doi:10.1016/S0005-7894(04)80028-5

Cavanagh, K., Strauss, C., Cicconi, F., Griffiths, N., Wyper, A., & Jones, F. (2013). A randomised controlled trial of a brief online mindfulness-based intervention. *Behaviour Research and Therapy, 51,* 573–578. doi:10.1016/j.brat.2013.06.00

Cohen, J. S., & Miller, L. J. (2009). Interpersonal mindfulness training for well-being: A pilot study with psychology graduate students. *Teachers College Record, 111,* 2760–2774.

Covey, S. R., Merrill, A. R., & Merrill, R. R. (1994). *First things first.* New York, NY: Fireside.

Danitz, S. B., & Orsillo, S. M. (2014). The mindful way through the semester: An investigation of the effectiveness of an acceptance-based behavioral therapy program on psychological wellness in first-year students. *Behavior Modification, 38,* 549–566. doi:10.1177/0145445513520218

De Bruin, E. I., Meppelink, R., & Bögels, S. M. (2014). Mindfulness in higher education: Awareness and attention in university students increase during and after participation in a mindfulness curriculum course. *Mindfulness, 6*(5), 1137–1142. doi:10.1007/s12671-014-0364-5

Demirbilek, M. (2014). The "digital natives" debate: An investigation of the digital propensities of university students. *Eurasia Journal of Mathematics, Science & Technology Education, 10,* 115–123.

Eisenberg, D., Hunt, J., & Speer, N. (2012). Help seeking for mental health on college campuses: Review of evidence and next steps for research and practice. *Harvard Review of Psychiatry, 20,* 222–232. doi:10.3109/10673229.2012.712839

Friedrich, R., Peterson, M., & Koster, A. (2011). The rise of Generation C. *Strategy + Business, 62,* 1–3.

Glaser, T. (n.d.). Using ACT to teach college students about stigma: An interview with Dr. Jenna LeJeune. Retrieved from https://contextualscience.org/ using_act_to_teach_college_students_about_stigma_a.

Greeson, J. M., Juberg, M. K., Maytan, M., James, K., & Rogers, H. (2014). A randomized controlled trial of Koru: A mindfulness program for college students and other emerging adults. *Journal of American College Health, 62,* 222–233. doi:10.1080/07448481.20 14.887571

Hassed, C., de Lisle, S., Sullivan, G., & Pier, C. (2009). Enhancing the health of medical students: Outcomes of an integrated mindfulness and lifestyle program. *Advances in Health Sciences Education, 14,* 387–398. doi:10.1007/s10459-008-9125-3

Hayes, S. C., Levin, M. E., Plumb-Vilardaga, J., Villatte, J. L., & Pistorello, J. (2013). Acceptance and commitment therapy and contextual behavioral science: Examining the progress of a distinctive model of behavioral and cognitive therapy. *Behavior Therapy, 44,* 180–198. doi:10.1016/j.beth.2009.08.002

Hayes, S. C., Luoma, J. B., Bond, F. W., Masuda, A., & Lillis, J. (2006). Acceptance and commitment therapy: Model, processes and outcomes. *Behaviour Research and Therapy, 44,* 1–25. doi:10.1016/j.brat.2005.06.006

Hayes, S. C., Strosahl, K. D., & Wilson, K. G. (2012). *Acceptance and commitment therapy: The process and practice of mindful change* (2nd ed.). New York, NY: Guilford Press.

Henry, J. D., & Crawford, J. R. (2005). The short-form version of the Depression Anxiety Stress Scales (DASS-21): Construct validity and normative data in a large non-clinical sample. *British Journal of Clinical Psychology, 44,* 227–239. doi:10.1348/014466505X29657

Herbert, J. D., Gaudiano, B. A., & Forman, E. M. (2013). The importance of theory in cognitive behavior therapy: A perspective of contextual behavioral science. *Behavior Therapy, 44,* 580–591. doi:10.1016/j.beth.2013.03.001

Hill, J. M., Vernig, P. M., Lee, J. K., Brown, C., & Orsillo, S. M. (2011). The development of a brief acceptance and mindfulness-based program aimed at reducing sexual revictimization among college women with a history of childhood sexual abuse. *Journal of Clinical Psychology, 67,* 969–980. doi:10.1002/jclp.20813

Hindman, R. K., Glass, C. R., Arnkoff, D. B., & Maron, D. D. (2015). A comparison of formal and informal mindfulness programs for stress reduction in university students. *Mindfulness, 6,* 873–884. doi:10.1007/s12671-014-0331-1

Jain, S., Shapiro, S. L., Swanick, S., Roesch, S. C., Mills, P. J., Bell, I., & Schwartz, G. E. R. (2007). A randomized controlled trial of mindfulness meditation versus relaxation training: Effects on distress, positive states of mind, rumination, and distraction. *Annals of Behavioral Medicine, 33,* 11–21. doi:10.1207/s15324796abm3301_2

Johnson, S., Gur, R. M., David, Z., & Currier, E. (2015). One-session mindfulness meditation: A randomized controlled study of effects on cognition and mood. *Mindfulness, 6,* 88–98. doi:10.1007/s12671-013-0234-6

Kabat-Zinn, J. (1990). *Full catastrophe living: Using the wisdom of your body and mind to face stress, pain and illness.* New York, NY: Delacorte.

Kabat-Zinn, J. (1994). *Wherever you go, there you are: Mindfulness meditation in everyday life.* New York, NY: Hyperion.

Khoury, B., Lecomte, T., Fortin, G., Masse, M., Therien, P., Bouchard, V., . . . Hofmann, S. G. (2013). Mindfulness-based therapy: A comprehensive meta-analysis. *Clinical Psychology Review, 33,* 763–771. doi:10.1016/j.cpr.2013.05.005

Klatt, M. D., Buckworth, J., & Malarkey, W. B. (2009). Effects of low-dose mindfulness-based stress reduction (MBSR-ld) on working adults. *Health Education & Behavior: The Official Publication of the Society for Public Health Education, 36,* 601–614. doi:10.1177/1090198108317627

Levin, M. E., Pistorello, J., Hayes, S. C., Seeley, J. R., & Levin, C. (2015). Feasibility of an acceptance and commitment therapy adjunctive Web-based program for counseling centers. *Journal of Counseling Psychology, 62,* 529–536. doi:10.1037/cou0000083

Lovibond, S. H., & Lovibond, P. F. (1995). *Manual for the Depression Anxiety Stress Scales* (2nd ed.). Sydney, Australia: Psychology Foundation.

Lundgren, T., Luoma, J. B., Dahl, J., Strosahl, K., & Melin, L. (2012). The bull's-eye values survey: A psychometric evaluation. *Cognitive and Behavioral Practice, 19*(4), 518–526. doi:10.1016/j.cbpra.2012.01.004

Lynch, S., Gander, M., Kohls, N., Kudielka, B., & Walach, H. (2011). Mindfulness-based coping with university life: A non-randomized wait-list-controlled pilot evaluation. *Stress and Health, 27,* 365–375. doi:10.1002/smi.138

Marlatt, A. G. (1985). Cognitive assessment and intervention procedures for relapse prevention. In A. G. Marlatt & J. R. Gordon (Eds.), *Relapse prevention: Maintenance strategies in the treatment of addictive behaviors* (pp. 201–279). New York, NY: Guilford Press.

McCown, D., Reibel, D., & Micozzi, M. S. (2010). *Teaching mindfulness: A practical guide for clinicians and educators.* New York, NY: Springer.

Mermelstein, L. C., & Garske, J. P. (2015). A brief mindfulness intervention for college student binge drinkers: A pilot study. *Psychology of Addictive Behaviors, 29,* 259–269. doi:10.1037/adb0000040

Mitchell, M., & Heads, G. (2015). Staying well: A follow up of a 5-week mindfulness-based stress reduction programme for a range of psychological issues. *Community Mental Health Journal,* 1–6. doi:10.1007/s10597-014-9825-5

Noone, S. J., & Hastings, R. P. (2010). Using acceptance and mindfulness-based workshops with support staff caring for adults with intellectual disabilities. *Mindfulness, 1,* 67–73. doi:10.1007/s12671-010-0007-4

Oman, D., Shapiro, S. L., Thoresen, C. E., Flinders, T., Driskill, J. D., & Plante, T. G. (2007). Learning from spiritual models and meditation: A randomized evaluation of a college course. *Pastoral Psychology, 55,* 473–493. doi:10.1007/s11089-006-0062-x

Palfrey, J., & Gasser, U. (2008). *Born digital: Understanding the first generation of digital natives.* New York, NY: Basic Books.

Pearson, A. N., Follette, V. M., & Hayes, S. C. (2012). A pilot study of acceptance and commitment therapy as a workshop intervention for body dissatisfaction and disordered eating attitudes. *Cognitive and Behavioral Practice, 19,* 181–197. doi:10.1016/j.cbpra.2011.03.001

Ramler, T. R., Tennison, L. R., Lynch, J., & Murphy, P. (2015). Mindfulness and the college transition: The efficacy of an adapted mindfulness-based stress reduction intervention in fostering adjustment among first-year students. *Mindfulness.* doi:10.1007/s12671-015-0398-3

Reid, D. T. (2013). Teaching mindfulness to occupational therapy students: Pilot evaluation of an online curriculum. *Canadian Journal of Occupational Therapy, 80,* 42–48. doi:10.1177/0008417413475598

Roemer, L., & Orsillo, S. M. (2009). Mindfulness- and acceptance-based behavioral therapy in practice. New York, NY: Guilford Press.

Rogers, H., & Maytan, M. (2012). *Mindfulness for the next generation: Helping emerging adults manage stress and lead healthier lives.* New York, NY: Oxford University Press.

Scent, C. L., & Boes, S. R. (2014). Acceptance and commitment training: A brief intervention to reduce procrastination among college students. *Journal of College Student Psychotherapy, 28,* 144–156. doi:10.1080/87568225.2014.883887

Segal, Z. V., Williams, J. M. G., & Teasdale, J. D. (2013). *Mindfulness-based cognitive therapy for depression* (2nd ed.). New York, NY: Guilford Press.

Shapiro, S. L., Schwartz, G. E., & Bonner, G. (1998). Effects of mindfulness-based stress reduction on medical and premedical students. *Journal of Behavioral Medicine, 21,* 581–599. doi:10.1023/A:1018700829825

Shikatani, B., Antony, M. M., Kuo, J. R., & Cassin, S. E. (2014). The impact of cognitive restructuring and mindfulness strategies on postevent processing and affect in social anxiety disorder. *Journal of Anxiety Disorders, 28,* 570–579. doi:10.1016/j.janxdis.2014.05.012

Stew, G. (2011). Mindfulness training for occupational therapy students. *The British Journal of Occupational Therapy, 74,* 269–276. doi:10.4276/030802211X13074383957869

Strosahl, K., Robinson, P., & Gustavsson, T. (2012). *Brief interventions for radical change: Principles and practice of focused acceptance and commitment therapy.* Oakland, CA: New Harbinger.

Taylor, B. L., Strauss, C., Cavanagh, K., & Jones, F. (2014). The effectiveness of self-help mindfulness-based cognitive therapy in a student sample: A randomised controlled trial. *Behaviour Research and Therapy, 63,* 63–69. doi:10.1016/j.brat.2014.09.007

Wells, A. (2009). *Metacognitive therapy for anxiety and depression.* New York, NY: Guilford Press.

Williams, M., & Penman, D. (2011). *Mindfulness: An eight-week plan for finding peace in a frantic world.* New York, NY: Rodale.

Part IV

Conclusion

11 Applying Prevention Science to Influence a Cultural Revolution in Higher Education

LeeAnn Cardaciotto, Laura G. Hill, Jennifer Block-Lerner, and Anthony Biglan

Introduction

The landscape of higher education continues to change, and pressures such as those related to achieving enrollment goals, demonstrating the value added of a college degree, and meeting regulatory and accreditor standards, can easily pull the focus of higher education leaders away from the core of colleges and universities: its students. This book has aimed to refocus the attention of administrators, faculty, professional staff that provide student support, and other interested parties on the promotion of student well-being, which is especially important given the relationship between student functioning and key outcomes such as academic performance and persistence/retention (e.g., Arria et al., 2013; Hartley, 2013). Specifically, Chapter 1 described the need to attend to student mental health and well-being, and the compilation of chapters in Part 3 included descriptions and supporting evidence for the application of mindfulness- and acceptance-based interventions for a variety of student populations.

Interestingly, though, a large number of undergraduate students do not self-report significant distress despite the transitions they are undergoing and challenges they face (although this does not imply that they are not at risk or that rates of distress in this population are not increasing; see below for more detail). Although prevalence rates vary by study, in a recent study, less than one-third of students screened positively for a psychological disorder (Eisenberg, Hunt, & Speer, 2013), and results by the American College Health Association (ACHA) indicated stress affected just over one-third of students' academic performance (ACHA, 2009). Further, when asked why they did not receive mental health services (or less than what they might have needed), students most commonly reported that they preferred to cope with issues on their own (54.9%; Eisenberg, Hunt, Speer, & Zivin, 2011). Therefore, in addition to exploring interventions for those students who are at-risk or in need, how can we build on the others' self-directed coping that is promoting healthy functioning and/or resilience? The lens of prevention science may shed some light on this question.

Prevention Science in Higher Education

Mindfulness- and acceptance-based strategies historically have been associated with treatment of individual people or of small groups in clinical contexts. However, the universal nature of their effects—across diagnostic categories, ages, functions, and cultures, and occasionally in non-clinical settings as well—highlights the potential of these strategies as public health interventions. For example, in addition to the work with organizations and with teachers described in Chapter 3, contextual behavioral science has been examined in relation to prejudice toward ethnic minorities (Lillis & Hayes, 2007) and parenting (Whittingham, 2014). For this reason, mindfulness- and acceptance-based approaches are a natural fit for prevention scientists who apply a public health framework to address the social and emotional health and well-being of populations.

Prevention scientists add to the public health framework a particular interest in human development in context and in the design and timing of interventions so that they address risk and protective factors unique to certain developmental phases, certain contexts, or a combination of the two. From the perspective of a prevention scientist, college student populations provide excellent opportunities to implement and evaluate preventive interventions. For one thing, college populations are well defined geographically as well as in terms of who gets included (e.g., all enrolled students or all first-year students); this makes them easier to reach and easier to study than many other populations. For another, all or most students are exposed to specific environmental contingencies: At some colleges, for example, alcohol is sold on campus, and at others, alcohol is not allowed on campus at all. That fact makes some types of preventive environmental interventions easier. But more importantly, the transition to college in early adulthood is a critical developmental stage. Many students will make choices in their daily lives—how much to study, how late to stay out, what to spend money on, whether to do their laundry—and take important decisions about their future without supervision or guidance (or with advice that conflicts with newly emerging values). They need new skills to tackle new academic and social challenges and to learn how to make decisions. And at the same time, as they transition to college, they may lose immediate access to important supports, including the familiarity of context, friends, parents, and adult mentors.

This developmental stage is thus a risky time. First-year college students experience a substantial decrease in social, psychological, and emotional well-being over the course of their first semester (Conley, Kirsch, Dickson, & Bryant, 2014), and at the same time, they experience increased exposure to drugs and opportunities for risky sexual behaviors, decreased structure, short-term loss of high-school opportunities for prosocial behaviors (e.g., relationships with healthy peers and healthy recreational opportunities), and diminished parental monitoring (Schulenberg, Patrick, Maslowsky, & Maggs, 2014). All these factors contribute to an increase in risky behaviors. For that reason, most prevention scientists working with college populations have focused on creating and testing interventions designed to prevent risk behaviors and to reduce the harms associated with them. However, concurrent with overt risk behaviors, the prevalence of stress and stress-related problems among college students has risen in recent years (Higher Education Research Institute, 2015). Universal interventions that focus on reducing stress-related problems and increasing positive mental health have gained in popularity, and a recent meta-analysis showed that skills-training programs can effectively achieve those goals with college students (Conley, Durlak, & Kirsch, 2015). The same meta-analysis noted that training in mindfulness and cognitive-behavioral techniques appears to be especially effective, a conclusion that is echoed by other chapters in this book.

Given their increased independence and the numerous novel situations and decision points that students encounter during this stage, the college context also provides a natural opportunity to train students how to identify and embrace their values and then how to act in accord with those values. At Washington State University, for example, one of the core curriculum classes ("Life Skills and Communication" known as HD205) uses the acceptance and commitment therapy (ACT) hexaflex model to teach students mindfulness and acceptance strategies, defusion and perspective-taking, and values identification and committed action planning. The experiential course provides skills training within the classroom, and homework assignments are designed to help students apply those skills in their daily lives outside of class. Each semester, about 800 students enroll in the class, and at any given time, about 17%–20% of the student population has taken it; that percentage is increasing as the course has grown to accommodate hundreds more students annually than in its first years. Preliminary results of an evaluation with three academic year cohorts (first-year students from 2011, 2012, and 2013), using propensity score matching to account for selection effects, show that students who took HD205 were significantly more likely to have remained enrolled in college than their peers by fall of 2014 (76% vs. 67%; OR = 1.47, $p < 0.001$).

Retention is a tremendously important behavioral outcome. And, we do not yet know how else skills in psychological flexibility (PF) will serve our students. For example, brief curriculum-based workshops (such as those described in Chapter 10, this volume) may expose students to practices that touch them at the time but seem irrelevant soon thereafter. However, as they find themselves struggling with pivotal life events or strong feelings of doubt down the road, they may employ skills from the workshop or choose to seek out resources or support in developing practices that will serve them well (see Chapter 6, this volume, for related discussion).

Often, training in these foundational life skills is relegated to extracurricular workshops, gained by happenstance in leadership roles or community service activities, or not experienced at all by many or perhaps most students. Empirical evidence on acceptance-based behavior therapy (ABBT), though, shows that the pursuit of certain values has particular benefit for well-being (e.g., Ferssizidis et al., 2010). Increasingly, evidence is showing that self-compassion, compassion for others, and prosocial behavior in general is beneficial to both individual people and to those around them (e.g., Welp & Brown, 2013). Thus, to the extent that higher education can more intentionally cultivate this values orientation, it will contribute to a very positive evolution of our culture.

Results emerging from the studies described in this volume and other similar studies are exciting—we have the tools to produce significant, positive changes in the lives of larger populations of college students. An axiom of public health is that small changes in health at the individual level create large changes at the population level (Rose, Khaw, & Marmot, 2008). So, more broadly, by using prevention science techniques to implement, evaluate, and disseminate those tools, a significant component of what Kazdin and Blasé (2011) would refer to as a "portfolio of interventions" (p. 26) in a higher education context, we have the potential not only to improve student health but to change the entire culture of our colleges and universities.

These ideas comport with the work of Biglan and colleagues (e.g., Biglan, 2015; Biglan, Flay, Embry, & Sandler, 2012; Biglan, Hayes, and Pistorello, 2008), who emphasize applying the fruits of behavioral science to inform the creation of "nurturing environments" in contexts such as neighborhoods, workplaces, schools, and families. One way to do this is through the spread of practices that promote PF, described in chapters in this volume and defined as "the ability to contact the present moment more fully as a conscious human being, and to change or persist in behavior when doing so serves valued ends" (Hayes, Luoma, Bond, Masuda, & Lillis, 2006, p. 7), allowing students to confront challenges while maintaining clarity about their values and acting consistently with them (Biglan, 2009).

Considerations and Limitations of the Current Volume

Although this book has examined the application of mindfulness- and acceptance-based approaches for an assortment of student populations within higher education, including first-year students (Chapter 6), at-risk students (Chapter 7), pre-professional students (Chapter 8), student athletes (Chapter 9), and undergraduate students through brief formats (Chapter 10), the demographics of US students are changing. For example, only about 40% of undergraduate students are between the ages of 18 and 24 (US Department of Education, n.d.). Therefore, attention needs to be paid to groups such as adult (non-traditional) learners, online learners, part-time students, and commuters to better understand their unique needs (e.g., attending classes but living and working in contexts that do not encourage education pursuits) and adapt programs to enhance their well-being as "whole people."

To successfully create a "nurturing environment," all key stakeholders need to be involved in planning and program promotion. Chapter 3 explores the potential of applying mindfulness- and acceptance-based approaches with faculty; however, applications with other key stakeholders, such as administrators and professional staff, were not able to be included in this volume. These groups face their own unique challenges, such as meeting demands from superiors and constituents and managing and mediating conflict (Montez, Wolverton, & Gmelch, 2002), for which mindfulness- and acceptance-based approaches could be helpful on a personal level. Applying these approaches to these groups would also increase the likelihood of fostering more widespread, systemic change on campus.

Similarly, in Chapter 9, Wolanin and Gross describe the importance of providing psychoeducation and training to coaching staff to prevent messages that conflict with their work from being given to the student athletes. In short, efforts need to be comprehensive and community-wide to promote optimal well-being. This requires a great deal of buy-in and a shift in mindset by campus decision-makers from a focus on individual problems to a focus on promoting the "nurturing environments" mentioned earlier.

As noted in several chapters in this volume, research on the application of mindfulness- and acceptance-based approaches in higher education is in its infancy, and so it is important that we do not get ahead of the data and draw specific conclusions about how to move forward. However, a holistic, public health approach to promoting well-being within the higher education context appears to be promising. As empirical investigation continues, researchers should follow recommendations to improve the quality of this scholarship. For example, Flay and colleagues (2005) outlined standards that aid in determining whether prevention-oriented programs are efficacious, effective, and/or ready for dissemination, and Valentine and colleagues (2011) advocate for replication that is systematic, thoughtful, and utilizes previous trials.

Further, there are important methodological considerations, such as the informed consent process and choosing ecologically-valid outcome measures (e.g., engagement in extracurricular activities on campus; counseling center usage statistics; DiGiuseppe, 2014). Also, Pistorello et al. in Chapter 6 indicate that although their first-year seminar increased motivation toward intrinsic academic and relational values, it produced modest outcomes in the context of universal prevention. These findings highlight the mountains that remain to be climbed in terms of learning how to maximize efficacy of these interventions for various student populations, including those suffering and those thriving.

In Conclusion

We see this book as providing a guide to one facet of the larger social movement to influence cultural evolution in the direction of greater nurturance. As evidence has accumulated for the value of clinical interventions that emphasize mindfulness, acceptance, and the resilient pursuit of one's values, this approach to living has begun to influence most other facets of society. The present volume attests to the role that higher education is playing in promoting this orientation—both by becoming a place that nurtures a mindful, values-based orientation toward living and by increasing this orientation in all the other facets of society that graduates of our colleges and universities live and work in. It thus stands to play a vital role in the larger transformation of society.

By continuing to develop and test mindfulness- and acceptance-based interventions with the full student body (e.g., in curriculum-grounded interventions as discussed in Chapter 6 and Chapter 10) as well as more intensively with special subpopulations including academically at-risk groups (Chapter 7), college athletes, (Chapter 9), pre-professional students (Chapter 8), and those who serve them, including faculty members (Chapter 3), administrators, and coaches (Chapter 9), cultural change within higher education may indeed be possible. Understanding the processes that underlie mental health (Chapter 2) will help shift to reliance on principles versus protocols. Further, in fostering PF skills in aspiring behavioral health professionals, both within (Chapter 4) and outside (Chapter 5) of the academic classroom, the reach of this cultural change could be even wider. And finally, considering the pivotal role that higher education graduates play in shaping economies, corporate climates, governments, the justice system, schools, other fields/disciplines, and families, the kind of work described in this book, especially if continued in ways that allow the research process itself to shape principles and protocols, has the potential to effect societal change in vast and far-reaching ways—one moment at a time.

References

American College Health Association (2009). American College Health Association – National College Health Assessment Spring 2008 Reference Group Data Report (Abridged). *Journal of American College Health, 57,* 477–488. doi:10.3200/JACH.57. 5.477-488

Arria, A. M., Caldeira, K. M., Vincent, K. B., Winick, E. R., Baron, R. A., & O'Grady, K. E. (2013). Discontinous college enrollment: Associations with substance use and mental health. *Psychiatric Services, 64*(2), 165–172. doi:10.1176/appi.ps.201200106

Biglan, A. (2009). Increasing psychological flexibility to influence cultural evolution. *Behavior and Social Issues, 18,* 15–24. doi:10.5210/bsi.v18i1.2280

Biglan, A. (2015). *The nurture effect: How the science of human behavior can improve our lives and our world.* Oakland, CA: New Harbinger.

Biglan, A., Flay, B. R., Embry, D. D., & Sandler, I. N. (2012). The critical role of nurturing environments for promoting human well-being. *American Psychologist, 67,* 257–271. doi:10.1037/a0026796

Biglan, A., Hayes, S. C., & Pistorello, J. (2008). Acceptance and commitment: Implications for prevention science. *Prevention Science, 9,* 139–152. doi:10.1007/s11121-008-0099-4

Conley, C. S., Durlak, J. A., & Kirsch, A. C. (2015). A meta-analysis of universal mental health prevention programs for higher education students. *Prevention Science, 16,* 487–507. doi:10.1007/s11121-015-0543-1

Conley, C. S., Kirsch, A. C., Dickson, D. A., & Bryant, F. B. (2014). Negotiating the transition to college developmental trajectories and gender differences in psychological functioning, cognitive-affective strategies, and social well-being. *Emerging Adulthood, 3,* 195–210. doi:10.1177/2167696814521808

DiGiuseppe, R. (2014, November). Discussion. In Z. Moore (Chair), *Innovative mindfulness- and acceptance-based interventions for college student mental health.* Symposium conducted at the annual meeting of the Association for Behavioral and Cognitive Therapies, Philadelphia, PA.

Eisenberg, D., Hunt, J., Speer, N. (2013). Mental health in American colleges and universities: Variation across student subgroups and across campuses. *The Journal of Nervous & Mental Disease, 201,* 60–67. doi:10.1097/NMD.0b013e31827ab077

Eisenberg, D., Hunt, J., Speer, N., & Zivin, K. (2011). Mental health service utilization among college students in the United States. *The Journal of Nervous and Mental Disease, 199,* 301–308. doi:10.1097/NMD.0b013e3182175123

Ferssizidis, P., Adams, L. M., Kashdan, T. B., Plummer, C., Mishra, A., & Ciarrochi, J. (2010). Motivation for and commitment to social values: The roles of age and gender. *Motivation and Emotion, 34,* 354–362. doi:10.1007/s11031-010-9187-4

Flay, B. R., Biglan, A., Boruch R. F., Castro, F. G., Gottfredson, D., Kellam, S., . . . Ji, P. (2005). Standards of evidence: Criteria for efficacy, effectiveness, and dissemination. *Prevention Science, 6,* 151–175. doi:10.1007/s11121-005-5553-y

Hartley, M. T. (2013). Investigating the relationship of resilience to academic persistence in college students with mental health issues. *Rehabilitation Counseling Bulletin, 56,* 240–250. doi:10.1177/0034355213480527

Hayes, S. C., Luoma, J. B., Bond, F. W., Masuda, A., & Lillis, J. (2006). Acceptance and commitment therapy: Model, processes, and outcomes. *Behaviour Research and Therapy, 44,* 1–25. doi:10.1016/j.brat.2005.06.006

Higher Education Research Institute (HERI). (2015). *The American freshman: National norms Fall 2014.* Los Angeles, CA: Higher Education Research Institute. Retrieved from http://heri.ucla.edu/pr-display.php?prQry=160

Kazdin, A. E., & Blasé, S. L. (2011). Rebooting psychotherapy research and practice to reduce the burden of mental illness. *Perspectives on Psychological Science, 6*(1), 21–37. doi:10.1177/1745691610393527

Lillis, J., & Hayes, S. C. (2007). Applying acceptance, mindfulness, and values to the reduction of prejudice: A pilot study. *Behavior Modification, 31,* 389–411. doi:10.1177/0145445506298413

Montez, J. M., Wolverton, M., & Gmelch, W. H. (2002). The roles and challenges of deans. *The Review of Higher Education, 26,* 241–266. doi:10.1353/rhe.2002.0034

Rose, G. A., Khaw, K. T., & Marmot, M. G. (2008). *Rose's strategy of preventive medicine: the complete original text.* Oxford University Press.

Schulenberg, J., Patrick, M. E., Maslowsky, J., & Maggs, J. L. (2014). The epidemiology and etiology of adolescent substance use in developmental perspective. In M. Lewis, & K. Rudolph (Eds.), *Handbook of developmental psychopathology* (pp. 601–620). New York, NY: Springer.

U.S. Department of Education (n.d.). Fast Facts. *Institute of Education Sciences, National Center for Education Statistics.* Retrieved from http://nces.ed.gov/fastfacts/display.asp?id=372.

Valentine, J. C., Biglan, A., Boruch, R. F., Castro, F. G., Collins, L. M., Flay, B. R., . . . Schinke, S. P. (2011). Replication prevention science. *Prevention Science, 12,* 103–117. doi:10.1007/s11121-011-0217-6

Welp, L. R., & Brown, C. M. (2013). Self-compassion, empathy, and helping intentions. *The Journal of Positive Psychology, 9,* 54–65. doi:10.1080/17439760.2013.831465

Whittingham, K. (2014). Parenting in context. *Journal of Contextual Behavioral Science, 3,* 212–215. doi:10.1016/j.jcbs.2014.01.001

Appendices

Supplemental Materials (e.g., Scripts, Worksheets, Exercises)

Appendix A
Teaching Resources

See Georgescu & Brock—Chapter 4

Resources for ACT Experiential Exercises

What follows below is a list of resources that could help with the development of a C-CBT course that includes experiential work. We also provide a primer for the class that was taught by the first author and includes both a more didactic skills training component as well as an ACT workshop. Given the flexibility that is available among C-CBTs, we propose these resources without providing an actual template; our hope is that instructors will look to their own training experience, and design the sequence that best suits their style. Many resources include verbatim exercises, and we encourage instructors to rehearse and adapt these to their own style and word use. For example, one year we adapted the exercises for the hard of hearing/deaf by typing them out, having the person read sections of the exercise on cue from co-leader. As such, we encourage making them your own and fitting them to the needs of your specific class.

Suggested Resources for the Instructor:

Dahl, J., Wilson, K. G., Luciano, C, & Hayes, S. C. (2005). *Acceptance and commitment therapy for chronic pain.* Reno, NV: Context Press.

Eifert, G. H., & Forsyth, J. P. (2005). *Acceptance and commitment therapy for anxiety disorders: A practitioner's treatment guide to using mindfulness, acceptance, and values-based behavior change.* Oakland, CA: New Harbinger.

Hayes, S. C, Strosahl, K. D., & Wilson, K. G. (2012). *Acceptance and commitment therapy: The process and practice of mindful change* (2nd ed.). New York, NY: Guilford Press.

Harris, R. (2009). *ACT made simple: An easy-to-read primer on acceptance and commitment therapy.* Oakland, CA: New Harbinger.

Walser, R., & Westrup, D. (2007). *Acceptance and commitment therapy for the treatment of post traumatic stress disorder and trauma-related problems: A practitioner's guide to using mindfulness and acceptance strategies.* Oakland, CA: New Harbinger.

Wilson, K. G., & DuFrene, T. (2009). *Mindfulness for two: An acceptance and commitment therapy approach to mindfulness in psychotherapy.* Oakland, CA: New Harbinger.

Sample of Required Class Readings:

Instructors are encouraged to add readings that they deem useful for student learning.

Chiles, J. A., & Strosahl, K. D. (2004). *Clinical manual for assessment and treatment of the suicidal patient.* Arlington, VA: American Psychiatric Publishing.

Linehan, M. M (2015). *DBT skills training handouts and worksheets* (2nd ed.). New York, NY: Guilford Press.

Luoma, J. B., Hayes, S. C., & Walser, R. D. (2007). *Learning ACT: An acceptance & commitment skills training manual for therapists.* Oakland, CA: New Harbinger.

Possible Assignments to Assess Student Competencies

The sample course presented included a 10-minute summary presentation on the empirical evidence of DBT and ACT for a specific population. Another assignment consisted of having students develop a skills training group and an ACT group tailored specifically for a population of their interest. Students were to take into consideration all necessary steps needed for proposing a group to an identified therapy site. All were engaged in a multiple choice/short answer quiz on the characteristics and management of the multi-problem client in a group setting. Lastly, students were asked to use the vignettes in the Luoma, Hayes, and Walser (2007) book to practice applying what they learned during the ACT training. Last, students can be engaged in mock case conceptualizations from models presented in class as a way to assess competence. Again, instructors are encouraged to consider a variety of assignments for assessment of student competencies.

Appendix B

The BULLI for Academic Life

See Sandoz & Mullen—Chapter 7

Scholar: _____ **Week:** _____

The spot in the center of the targets are Bull's-eyes. They represent full engagement in your academic life (doing things that move you directly toward your values). The outer rings of the dartboard indicate increasingly less engagement. Place **the number of your class** in the area of the target that best represents how you were in that class on that day.

Monday	Tuesday	Wednesday	Thursday	Friday

Class	There	Not	Class	There	Not	Class	There	Not	Class	There	Not	Class	There	Not
1			1			1			1			1		
2			2			2			2			2		
3			3			3			3			3		
4			4			4			4			4		
5			5			5			5			5		
6			6			6			6			6		
7			7			7			7			7		

Notes:

Adapted from Lundgren, T., Luoma, J. B., Dahl, J., Strosahl, K., & Melin, L. (2012). The bull's-eye values survey: A psychometric evaluation. *Cognitive and Behavioral Practice,* 19(4), 518–526. doi:10.1016/j.cbpra.2012.01.004; Murrell, A. R., Coyne, L. W., & Wilson, K. G. (2004). ACT with children, adolescents, and their parents. In S. C. Hayes, K. D. Strosahl, & K. G. Wilson (Eds.), *A practical guide to acceptance and commitment therapy* (pp. 249–273). New York, NY: Springer.

Appendix C
Inviting a Difficulty in

See Danitz, Orsillo, Lenda, Shortway, &
Block-Lerner—Chapter 8

Noticing the way you are sitting in the chair. Noticing where your body is touching the chair. Bringing your attention to your breath for a moment. Noticing the in-breath . . . . and the out-breath . . . Now gently widening your awareness, take in the body as a whole. Noticing any sensations that arise, breathing with your whole body.

When you are ready, bringing to mind a recent stressor. Bringing your attention to the specific emotions that arise and any reactions you have to those emotions. And as you are focusing on this troubling situation and your emotional reaction, allowing yourself to tune in to any *physical sensations* in the body that you notice are arising . . . becoming aware of those physical sensations . . . and then deliberately, but gently, directing your focus of attention to the region of the body where the sensations are the strongest in the gesture of an embrace, a welcoming . . . noticing that this is how it is right now . . . and *breathing into that part of the body* on the in-breath and breathing out from that region on the out-breath, exploring the sensations, watching their intensity shift up and down from one moment to the next.

Now, seeing if you can bring to this attention an even deeper attitude of compassion and openness to whatever sensations, thoughts, or emotions you are experiencing, however unpleasant, by saying to yourself from time to time "It's OK. Whatever it is, it's already here. Let me be open to it."

Staying with the awareness of these internal sensations, breathing with them, accepting them, letting them be, and allowing them to be just as they are. Saying to yourself again, if you find it helpful, "It's here right now. Whatever it is, it's already here. Let me be open to it." Softening and opening to the sensation you become aware of, letting go of any tensing and bracing. If you like, you can also experiment with holding in awareness both the sensations of the body and the feeling of the breath moving in and out as you breathe with the sensations moment by moment.

And when you notice that the bodily sensations are no longer pulling your attention to the same degree, simply return 100% to the breath and continue with that as the primary object of attention. And then gently bringing your awareness to the way you are sitting in the chair, your breath, and, when you are ready, opening your eyes.

Appendix D
Values Assignment

See Danitz, Orsillo, Lenda, Shortway, &
Block-Lerner—Chapter 8

This is a writing assignment we are asking you to do just for yourself. We will not collect this page, it is yours to keep.

Often our attempts to avoid anxiety, worry, and stress cause us to make subtle shifts in our behavior so that we begin doing whatever we are "supposed" to be doing and we lose track of what we *want* to be doing, and what *personally matters* to us as individuals. This assignment is an opportunity for you to look at your academic values and reflect upon ways in which you are living consistently with them.

Briefly write about the academic endeavors that you would like to be engaged in and *why that appeals to you*. Next write about *the kind of student* you would like to be with respect to your work habits and your *relationships* with your teachers and peers. What is your approach to keeping up with work? How much would you like to participate in class? What sort of relationships do you want to have with students and faculty? How would you like to *communicate with others* and *respond to feedback*? What additional *challenges* would you like to take on?

We encourage you to take these next 10 minutes to privately and comfortably do this writing assignment. In your writing, we want you to really let go and explore your very deepest emotions and thoughts about the topics listed above. You will not be asked to share your writing with anyone else.

As you write, try to allow yourself to experience your thoughts and feelings as completely as you are able. This work is based on the evidence that pushing these disturbing thoughts away can actually make them worse; so try to really let yourself go. If you can't think of what to write next, repeat the same thing over and over until something new comes to you. Be sure and write for the entire 10 minutes. Don't be concerned with spelling, punctuation, or grammar; just write whatever comes to mind.

Please keep these instructions and your responses in a safe and private place. We will ask you to read it over again in a few weeks.

Appendix E
Letting Go of Mistakes

See Wolanin & Gross—Chapter 9

As we begin this exercise designed to help you develop the mental toughness and poise to let go of mistakes, establish yourself in a position in which you're sitting upright, with your feet flat on the floor, your arms and legs uncrossed, and hands resting on your laps. Palms up or down. Allow your eyes to close gently or fixing your gaze on a spot out in front of you. Take a moment to get in touch with the sensations in your body as you bring yourself into this moment . . .

It was Michael Jordan who said, "I've missed more than 9,000 shots in my career. I've lost almost 300 games. 26 times, I've been trusted to take the game winning shot and missed. I've failed over and over and over again in my life. And that is why I succeed."

Mistakes are a reality of sports, and for that matter, life. In a football game there will be penalties, turnovers, missed assignments; the list goes on. Therefore, it is not *if* we are going to make mistakes but rather *how* we respond to them. Mental toughness is not built by dwelling on mistakes, but rather by developing the ability to accept them, learn from them, and let them go as you refocus your attention on the present moment.

So to practice this . . . Bring to mind an image of a recent mistake either you or a teammate has made. Perhaps it was from your last game, or during a recent practice. Perhaps it was off the field and occurred in your everyday life. Whatever the case may be, hold that image in your awareness along with the associated thoughts and feelings. Try to picture it vividly and fully. Experiencing whatever comes up for you when you picture this image. Putting out the welcome mat, just taking in whatever arises . . . . Observing, noticing any judgments or emotional discomfort. Making room for any discomfort. Just allowing it to be there . . . Sometimes feelings may grow stronger, sometimes they may grow weaker . . . You are not alone with this feeling. Countless numbers of athletes know this feeling. Just breathe into and out from the sensations of discomfort and notice any thoughts, emotions, and judgments that arise. And now watch those judgments, thoughts, and emotions float away like clouds drifting away in the sky or leaves on a stream floating away into the distance. Watching them fade away, farther and farther, and farther, until

---

they are essentially gone. If they come back, as they often do, simply notice them while they are present and let those experiences too fade or float away.

And as they fall into the background, returning now to the present experience as it is. Not as your mind says it is. Fully experiencing the present moment. Bringing your full awareness to your breath. Right here, right now, in this moment. Feeling the breath flow in and out as you simply are here now in the present moment riding the waves of the breath. It is in this letting go that you become stronger and mentally tough. The fact is, you are not your mistakes. And through repetitions of exercises such as this over and over and over you will learn to quickly let go of mistakes and seize the present moment, day in and day out, on and off the field. And as we come to the conclusion of this exercise, remember mistakes are part of the game of _____ and life. It's how well you recover from them that can be the mark of an effective person and athlete.

Appendix F
Introducing Brief Curriculum-Based Workshops

See Marks, Block-Lerner, Barrasso-Catanzaro, &
Kowarz—Chapter 10

The following scripts are offered to indicate how we introduce the workshop and associated study, just prior to having students read (and have the opportunity to ask questions about) the informed consent form (Part 1) and after navigating informed consent and the pre-workshop questionnaire packet (Part 2). We do not read from the scripts but are sure to cover all of these major points.

Part 1—Introduction to Workshop and Study Prior to Informed Consent

Welcome! (Introduce ourselves) We are very glad to be here today. This workshop is based on an approach that we are passionate about and have found to be helpful—both professionally, in our multiple roles, and personally, in our own lives. This is part of an effort to bring this type of approach to students and other members of the Kean community in various contexts and to look at the ways that it might be valuable. We are grateful to your instructor for allowing us to come in today to share it with you.

As scientist-practitioners/practitioner-scholars, we are interested in studying the value of what we do and how we do it. So, to give us a sense of whether and in what ways it may be helpful to provide such brief introductions, we would like to invite you to fill out a very short set of questionnaires—one before and one after the material we'll cover. You don't have to do this. Everyone is welcome to participate in the workshop, whether or not you complete the measures. And, whether or not you do so will not impact your grades or anything else related to the course. The first part of the packet (before we get started with the workshop) should take 5–10 minutes; the second part should take less than five minutes.

Part 2—After Informed Consent and Prior to Beginning the Workshop

What we hope to do today is to introduce you to a set of practices or tools, ways of thinking about these challenges and stressors and ways of relating to that thinking and those feelings, that may help you/us navigate through these stressors and challenges in ways that move you/us toward what you care most about and the kind of person/people you/we most want to be.

We are going to be sharing a few different practices/exercises in this next hour, and we invite you to participate in whatever ways you would like to. We ask that you practice being open to whatever comes up and maybe be willing to stretch yourself a little/take some risks, even if these are just between you and what is on a piece of paper in front of you. Some of this may feel silly, different, joyful, fun, strange, confusing—it's all part of the process. You are welcome to share reactions to the activities afterward, as time allows, and there will be no pressure to share. You will have a chance to provide feedback at the end of the workshop (further in the packet). Okay, let's get started . . .

Index

Made in the USA
Monee, IL
10 July 2021